Evaluation in Public-Sector Reform

Evaluation in Public-Sector Reform

Concepts and Practice in International Perspective

Edited by

Hellmut Wollmann

Professor Emeritus of Public Administration,
Social Science Institute, Humboldt-Universität, Berlin, Germany

Edward Elgar
Cheltenham, UK • Northampton, MA, USA

Published by
Edward Elgar Publishing Limited
Glensanda House
Montpellier Parade
Cheltenham
Glos GL50 1UA
UK

Edward Elgar Publishing, Inc.
136 West Street
Suite 202
Northampton
Massachusetts 01060
USA

A catalogue record for this book
is available from the British Library

Library of Congress Cataloguing in Publication Data
Evaluation in public-sector reform : concepts and practice in international
    perspective / edited by Hellmut Wollmann.
        p. cm.
    1. Civil service reform. 2. Public administration. I. Wollmann, Hellmut,
    1936–

    JF1525.O73E93 2003
    352.3'67—dc21   2003052827

ISBN 1 84376 160 2

Printed and bound in Great Britain by MPG Books Ltd, Bodmin, Cornwall

Contents

v

Figures and Tables

Figures

Tables

Contributors

Geert Bouckaert is Professor and Director of the Public Management Centre, Katholieke Universiteit Leuven (Geert.Bouckaert@soc.kuleuven.ac.be).

Tom Christensen is Professor at the Department of Political Science, University of Oslo, Norway (tom.christensen@stv.uio.no).

John Halligan is Professor of Public Administration at the University of Canberra, Australia (john.halligan@canberra.edu.au).

Werner Jann is Professor of Political Science, Administration and Organisation at the Economic and Social Science Faculty, University of Potsdam, Germany (jann@rz.uni-potsdam.de).

Per Lægreid is Professor at the Department of Administration and Organization Theory at the University of Bergen, and at the Norwegian Research Centre in Organization and Management (LOS centre) (per.lagreid@aorg.uib.no).

Frans L. Leeuw is Director at the Ministry of Justice´s Department for Policy Research, Analysis and Statistics, Den Haag, Netherlands, and also Professor of Evaluation Studies at the Faculty of Social Sciences, Utrecht University (flleeuw@cuci.nl).

Andrea Lippi is a lecturer in Public management and Policy analysis at the Faculty of Political Science 'Cesare Alfieri' at the University of Florence, Italy (lippi@unifi.it).

Jun Matsunami is Professor of Public Administration at the Faculty of Law, Osaka Gakuin University, Osaka, Japan (matsunam@utc.osaka-gu.ac.jp).

Geraldo Tadeu Moreira Monteiro is Professor at the State University of Rio de Janeiro, Brazil (gtmm@infolink.com.br).

Michio Muramatsu is Professor at the Faculty of Law of Gakushuin University, Tokyo, Japan (michio.muramatsu@gakushuin.ac.jp).

Christopher Pollitt is Professor of Public Management at Erasmus Universiteit Rotterdam (Pollitt@fsw.eur.nl).

Christoph Reichard is Professor of Public Management at the Economic and Social Science Faculty, University of Potsdam, Germany (reichard@rz.uni-potsdam.de).

Jean-Claude Thoenig is Professor of Sociology at INSEAD (Fontainebleau, France) and a senior research fellow at the Centre national de la recherche scientifique (Groupe d'analyse des politiques publiques, Ecole normale supérieure de Cachan, Cachan, France) (thoenig@mailhost.gapp.ens-cachan.fr).

Lois R. Wise is Professor of Public Administration at the School of Public and Environmental Affairs at Indiana University, USA (wise1@indiana.edu).

Hellmut Wollmann is Professor Emeritus of Public Administration at Humboldt-Universität, Berlin (hellmut.wollmann@rz.hu-berlin.de).

Preface

Habent sua fata libelli. [Every book has a life story of its own.]

The guiding idea and leitmotif of this book – that there is a 'Siamese twin' like connection between public-sector reform and evaluation, which has so far been largely ignored in the pertinent debate and calls for being examined – emerged from discussions conducted among members of the Research Committee on Public Policy and Administration ('RC 32') of the International Political Science Association (IPSA), chaired by Lois Wise (Indiana University).

In fall 2000 I was invited to put together a special issue of the Rio de Janeiro based journal Revista Internacional de Estudios Politicos (RIEP) devoted to this theme. In doing so I was fortunate enough to attract internationally renowned scholars and experts in the field as authors. Geraldo Tadeu Moreira Monteiro, who was chief editor of RIEP (and also a member of RC 32), procured the funding for convening and organizing an international conference in September 2001 in Rio de Janeiro at which the special issue of RIEP was presented and discussed. The logical next step was to seek an internationally reputed publisher to turn this special issue into a fully-fledged volume containing thoroughly revised versions of the earlier articles as well as additionally invited ones, thus encompassing a rich set of chapters about the relationship between public-sector reform and evaluation in different national contexts.

Words of thanks need to be said to Dawn Ollila of Indiana University for copy-editing the manuscript in its early stage and to the International Political Science Association (IPSA) for financially supporting this effort. Thanks are also owed to Frank Berg (Berlin) for preparing the camera-ready copy and indexes and, last but not least, to Edward Elgar Publishing for having accepted the book and for having competently guided it towards publication. May the volume find an interested and receptive readership.

Hellmut Wollmann,
Berlin

1. Evaluation in public-sector reform: Towards a 'third wave' of evaluation?

Hellmut Wollmann

1. Introduction: The 'twinned' development of public-sector reforms and evaluation as a 'missing link' in research and debate

The initial premise and thesis of this volume is this: public-sector reform and evaluation have been closely interlinked almost like Siamese twins throughout the past 30 years or so. Yet an inspection of the available literature on public-sector reforms and evaluation reveals a glaring discrepancy: while the fields of public-sector reform and of evaluation have each brought forth a huge body of literature and research, these two realms have been largely treated as separate entities. Their 'twin-like' connection so far has received little attention.

This book aims to contribute to the bridging and filling of this gap. In addition, the volume covers more countries than most of the available publications on public-sector reforms.[1] In addition to addressing the 'usual suspects' in the current international debate (that is, the Anglo-Saxon and Scandinavian countries), the volume contains articles on Continental European countries, Japan, and Latin America – 16 countries in total.

2. The three phases of 'twinning' of public-sector reforms and evaluation

Roughly three phases in the development of public-sector reform and evaluation over the past 30 years can be distinguished: the first wave of evaluation during the 1960s and 1970s; the second wave beginning in the mid-1970s; and a third wave related to the New Public Management (NPM) movement.

During the 1960s and 1970s the advent of the advanced welfare state was accompanied by the concept of enhancing the state's capacity for 'proactive policy making' through a profound modernization of its political and administrative structures, for the pursuit of which the institutionalization and employment of planning and evaluation capacities was seen as strategically important. Conceptually this was premised on a 'policy cycle' revolving around the triad of policy formation and planning, implementation and evaluation, whereby evaluation was deemed instrumental as a 'cybernetic' loop, gathering and feeding back information relevant to policy making. Policy evaluation, ideally conducted as fully-fledged social science-based evaluation research, was primarily directed at the output and outcome of (substantive) policies. Embedded in the reformist mood (and optimism) of the (short-lived) 'planning period', policy evaluation was (in its normative sense) meant to improve policy results and to maximize output effectiveness. This early phase of policy evaluation has been called the 'first wave' of evaluation (for an early conceptualization and interpretation, see Wagner and Wollmann 1986, Derlien 1990). While the US has been the global pacesetter of policy evaluation since the mid-1960s, in Europe, Sweden and Germany were the frontrunners in this 'first wave' of evaluation (for an early perceptive comparative assessment, see Levine 1981).

Since the mid-1970s, in the wake of a world-wide economic and budgetary crisis triggered by the first oil price shock of 1973, policy making has been dominated by the need for budgetary retrenchment and cost efficiency. Consequently, the mandate of policy evaluation has been redefined, in that the implicit task was to reduce policies and maximize input efficiency. From a developmental perspective, this phase was the 'second wave' of policy evaluation. Among the European countries, the Netherlands and Great Britain were exemplars of this wave (see Derlien 1990).

A third wave of evaluation came into being during the late 1980s and 1990s, with ever more pressing budgetary crises in many countries and the New Public Management movement prevalent in international discourse and practice. Drawing on private sector management concepts and tools, NPM is based on a 'management cycle' with a typical sequence of goal setting, implementation and evaluation. While this shows a marked conceptual kinship with the previous 'policy cycle', a profound difference is its constitutive and strategic ties to the ongoing activities of the operational unit concerned. Whereas the cost-efficiency-related evaluation of the 'second wave' was still largely conducted as external evaluation and was mainly meant to check and reduce (expansive and expensive) welfare-state policies, the evaluative activities and tools mandated by and following from the 'management cycle' are, first of all, of an *internal* nature, revolving around agency-based performance management, self-evaluative procedures and reporting, thus forming an integral part of the 'public management package' (see Furubo and Sandahl 2002, pp. 19 ff.). Thus, the 'third wave' is characterized by *internal* evaluative institutions and tools taking centre stage.

3. The many facets of public-sector reforms

The preceding summary of the three phases of public-sector reforms and evaluation during the past 30 years has hinted at great variation in the conceptual and institutional inventory of each phase. The 'planning period' of the 1960s and 1970s engendered a broad spectrum of reform options which addressed the reorganization of governmental and ministerial structures, decentralization and deconcentration of political and administrative functions and territorial reforms, as well as the introduction of policy evaluation as an instrument of policy making. In the 're-trenchment period' of the mid-1970s and 1980s, institutional changes were achieved through deregulation and the privatisation of public assets, while evaluation turned to cost-reducing procedures such as cost-benefit analyses and task scrutinies. Finally, in the current period, NPM-guided institutional reforms, such as downsizing, agencification, contracting, outsourcing and performance management have been on the rise, along with concomitant evaluative procedures (performance monitoring and measurement, controlling, etc.).

From country to country – and even within each country – the mix of reform concepts and components being considered or implemented may vary greatly. On the one hand, NPM is far from being a well-defined and consistent body of concepts. Instead, it is a bundle of different (and sometimes contradictory) concepts (see, for example, Aucoin 1990; Christensen and Lægreid 2001, p. 19). Picking and (eclectically) selecting from what has been somewhat ironically called a 'shopping basket' (Pollitt 1995), the varied concepts and elements of NPM strategies and measures have been portioned and 'packaged' quite differently in different national, regional and local contexts. On the other hand, in many situations reform concepts and components which stem from previous reform periods may have persisted and may lend themselves to amalgamation with NPM-specific elements. Furthermore, the current modernization thrust may open a window of opportunity for implementing or reviving previous reform concepts (such as decentralization of political and administrative responsibilities). For the sake of analytical differentiation it seems advisable to make a distinction between traditional reform concepts and elements (particularly those of the 'planning period') and NPM concepts (in the narrow sense).

4. The many faces and variants of evaluation

Departing from a broad understanding of the evaluation function
In order to capture the broad scope of pertinent analytical tools which have been put in place since the early 1960s for an evaluative purpose, on the one hand, a broad definition seems advisable. On the other hand, lest such a definition become a catch-all (and thus 'catch nothing') concept, some delineation is, of course, needed.

At this point we depart from a broad understanding of evaluation as an analytical procedure and tool meant to obtain all information pertinent to the assessment of the performance, both process and result, of a policy program or measure. To be sure, a bewildering array of concepts and terms has made its appearance in this field, especially given the recent 'third wave' development of new vocabulary (such as management audit, policy audit and performance monitoring). In light of a definition which focuses on the function of evaluation and, thus, looks beneath the 'surface' of varied terminology, it becomes apparent that the different terms 'cover more or less the same grounds' (Bemelmans-Videc 2002, p. 94). Thus, analytical procedures which have come to be called 'performance audit' will be included in our definition, except, however, for 'financial audit', which checks the compliance of public spending with budgetary provisions and would not be included in evaluation (see Sandahl 1992, p. 115, Barzelay 1997: 235 ff. for a detailed discussion and references). In the next sections further definitional distinctions and differentiations of 'evaluation' will be submitted.

Evaluation of public-sector reform policies and measures versus evaluation of 'substantive' policies
Substantive policies have been called, as it were, the 'normal' policies (such as social policy, employment policy or housing policy) which essentially target the socio-economic situation and development in the

policy environment. By contrast, public-sector reform policies are, by definition, directed at remoulding the political and administrative structures. Thus, one may speak, in institutionalist parlance, of institution policy[2] or, in policy science terminology, of polity policy[3] or of meta-policy making.[4]

Whereas 'substantive policies' can, simply stated, be seen as aiming directly at attaining their 'substantive' goal and policy 'output' (say, the reduction of unemployment or the improvement of the environment), public-sector reform policies have a more complicated 'architecture'. As a first step they aim at effecting changes in political and administrative institutions as the immediate and 'closest' target of their intervention. In the further sequence of goals, the institutional changes, once effected, are, in turn, intended to bring about further (and 'ultimate') results, whether it be that the operational process ('performance') of public administration or that the (final) 'output' and 'product' of the administrative operation is improved.

This sequence of goals can be translated into a corresponding set of evaluation questions. The evaluation questions can address whether and how the intended institutional changes (such as the creation of agencies, the intra-administrative decentralization of responsibilities and resources or the installation of benchmarking) have been achieved (or implemented). As a result of this implementation focus, one might speak of implementation evaluation[5] (in fact, this evaluation variant conceptually has much in common with implementation research in political science, of which Pressman and Wildavsky's 1974 study was a pacesetter).

The evaluation questions may then target the operational performance and 'process improvement' (Pollitt and Bouckaert 2000, p. 115) resulting from a reform measure (such as the 'speeding up' of administrative activities or their accessibility to citizens). One might speak of performance evaluation. Finally, evaluation may be mandated to find out whether the output and outcomes of administrative activities have been affected by the reform. This may be termed 'output evaluation', 'impact evaluation' or 'result evaluation' (see Bemelmans-Videc 2002, p. 93). But the reach of the evaluation may go still further, including more 'remote' effects such as 'systemic' effects (Pollitt and Bouckaert 2000, pp. 120 ff.) or impacts on the 'broader political-democratic context' (Christensen and Lægreid 2001, p. 32).

Monitoring versus evaluation research

Under methodological auspices *monitoring* can be seen as an evaluative procedure which aims at (descriptively) identifying and/or measuring the effects of an ongoing activity without raising the question of causality. In fact, in the 'third wave' of evaluation monitoring has come to play a pivotal role as an internal indicator-based and result-oriented procedure and tool of information gathering and reporting.

By contrast, *evaluation research* can be understood as an analytical exercise which typically employs social-scientific methodology. It is usually commissioned to tackle evaluation questions and projects of a higher complexity, typically posed by the 'causal question', that is, as to whether the observed result or output can be causally related to the policy 'intervention' (programme component, activity) concerned.

When dealing with the evaluation of public-sector reform policies and measures evaluation research confronts methodological problems that are even thornier than in policy evaluation in general (see Pollitt 1995 and Pollitt and Bouckaert, Chapter 2 in this volume).[6] A few potential methodological problems are these:

1. goals and objectives that serve as a measuring rod are hard to identify, particularly because modernization measures mostly come in bundles;
2. goals are hard to translate into operationalizable and measurable indicators;
3. good empirical data to 'fill in' the indicators are hard to get, and the more meaningful an indicator is, the more difficult it is to obtain viable data;
4. the more 'remote' (and, often, the more relevant) the goal dimension is, the harder it becomes to operationalize and to empirically substantiate it (for example, outcomes, 'systemic' effects [see Pollitt and Bouckaert 2000, pp.120 ff], or effects on the 'broader political-democratic context' [see Christensen and Lægreid 2001, p. 32]);
5. side effects and unintended consequences[7] are hard to trace; and
6. methodologically robust research designs (quasi-experimental, 'controlled' time-series, etc.) are rarely applicable (ceteris paribus conditions difficult, if not impossible, to establish; number of cases [N] too small; 'before'-data not available for a 'before/after' design; etc.).

'Normal' ('primary') evaluation versus meta-evaluation ('secondary' evaluation)

Meta-evaluation is meant to analyse an already completed ('primary') evaluation using a kind of 'secondary' analysis. Two variants can be discerned. First, the meta-evaluation may review the already completed ('primary') evaluation in terms of whether it was done using an appropriate methodological approach. One might speak of a 'methodology-related' meta-evaluation. Second, the meta-evaluation may have to accumulate the substantive findings of the already completed ('primary') evaluation and synthesize the results. This could be called a 'synthesizing' meta-evaluation.

Internal versus external evaluation

An *internal* ('in house' or agency-based) evaluation is one conducted by the operating unit itself in an exercise of 'self-evaluation'. In fact, the internal self-evaluation operation is a key procedure and component of the entire monitoring and feedback system which is pivotal to NPM's (internal) management and accounting system.

External evaluation is initiated, and either conducted or funded and 'contracted out', by an agency or actor outside of and different from the operating unit. This external unit may exist within the core executive government (for instance, by the Finance Minister or the Prime Minister's Office); it may be another political/constitutional actor (particularly parliament or a court of audit); or it may be an organization expressly created for that external evaluation function (such as an ad hoc commission or task forces).

In-house evaluation versus 'contractual research'

In order to cope with a (methodologically or otherwise) complex piece of evaluation in light of limited analytical resources and competence, the agency and institution that initiates an external evaluation (or the operating unit itself, in the case of a methodologically demanding internal evaluation) may prefer to 'contract out' the evaluation to a self-standing (ideally independent) semi-public non-profit or university-based research institute or commercial research unit (such as a consultancy firm). In such a case, the evaluation is carried out by the (commissioned) research unit as *contractual research* (see Wollmann 2002a); the (commissioning) agency finances and monitors the 'contractual' evaluation and 'owns' the results thereof.

In contrast with evaluation research as 'commissioned' (contractual) research on public-sector reforms, mention should be made, at this point, of *academic research* which, following the 'intra-scientific' selection of topics, concepts and methods and funded by (independent) foundations or university resources, studies public-sector reform in an implementation or evaluative perspective with what may be called an 'applied basic research' approach.

Ex-ante, ongoing and ex-post evaluation

Reference should briefly be also made to the 'classical' distinction between ex-ante, ongoing/interim and ex-post evaluation. Ex-ante evaluation is meant to anticipate and pre-assess the (alternative) courses of policy implementation ('implementation pre-assessment') and policy results and consequences (for instance, environmental impact assessments).

Ongoing evaluation has the task of monitoring and checking the processes and (interim) results of policy programmes and measures while the implementation and realization thereof is still going on. As 'formative' evaluation, it is designed to monitor and feed process data and (interim) result data back to the policy makers and project managers while the measure and project still is in its developmental and 'formative' stage, that is, in a stage that still allows the correcting and re-orienting the policy measures. As NPM hinges conceptually and instrumentally on the strategic idea of institutionalizing permanent internal processes of data monitoring and (feedback) reporting, ongoing evaluation forms a central component of the 'new public management package'.

Ex-post evaluation constitutes the classical variant of (substantive) policy and programme evaluation, particularly in the fully-fledged evaluation *research* type.

(Rigorous) evaluation versus 'best practice' accounts

While (rigorous) evaluation aims at giving a comprehensive picture of 'what has happened' in the policy field and project under scrutiny, encompassing successful as well as unsuccessful courses of events, the best practice approach tends to pick 'success stories' of reform policies and projects, with the analytical intention of identifying the factors that explain the 'success', and with the 'applied' (learning and 'pedagogic') purpose of fostering 'lesson drawing' from such experience in the intranational as well as in the inter- and transnational contexts. On the one hand, such 'good practice' stories are fraught with the (conceptual and methodological) threat of 'ecological fallacy', that is, of a rash and misleading translation and transfer of (seemingly positive) strategies from one locality and one country to another. On the other hand, if done in a way which carefully heeds the specific contextuality and conditionality of such 'good practice' examples, analysing, 'telling' and diffusing such cases can be a useful 'fast track' to evaluative knowledge and intra-national as well as trans-national learning (see Jann and Reichard, Chapter 3 in this volume).

Quasi-evaluation: Evaluation as an interactive learning process
Vis-à-vis these manifold conceptual and methodological hurdles 'fully-fledged' evaluation of public-sector reforms is bound to face (and also in light of the reluctance which policy makers and top administrators often exhibit towards getting researchers from outside intimately involved in 'in-depth' evaluations), Thoenig proposes (in Chapter 11 of this volume) a type of 'quasi-evaluation' which would be less fraught with conceptual and methodological predicaments than a 'fully-fledged' evaluation and more disposed towards focusing on, and restricting itself to, the information- and data-gathering and descriptive functions of evaluation rather than an explanatory one. Thoenig perceives more than one advantage to the 'quasi-evaluation' approach. First, such conceptually and methodologically 'lean' evaluation designs may find easier access and wider application in an evaluation territory otherwise fraught with hurdles (he causticly remarks that 'there is no surer way of stifling evaluation at the outset than to confine it to the ghetto of methodology' [see Chapter 11 in this volume]). Second, a conceptually and methodologically pared-down variant of 'quasi-evaluation' may be conducive to more 'trustful' communication between the policy maker and the evaluator and to promoting a 'gradual learning process that fosters an information culture' (Chapter 11 in this volume).

References

Aucoin, Peter (1990), 'Administrative reform in public management. Paradigms, principles, paradoxes and pendulums', *Governance*, 3[2], 115–37.
Barzelay, M. (1997), 'Central audit institutions and performance auditing: A comparative analysis of organizational strategies in the OECD'. in *Governance*. vol. 10, no. 3, pp. 235–60
Bemelmans-Videc, M.L. (2002), 'Evaluation in the Netherlands 1990–2000. Consolidation and expansion', in Jan-Eric Furubo, Ray C. Rist and Rolf

Sandahl (eds), *International Atlas of Evaluation*, New Brunswick and London: Transaction, pp. 115–28.

Christensen,Tom and Per Lægreid (2001), 'A transformative perspective on administrative reforms', in Tom Christensen and Per Lægreid (eds), *New Public Management*, Aldershot: Ashgate, pp. 13–39.

Derlien, Hans-Ulrich (1990), 'Genesis and structure of evaluation efforts in comparative perspective', in Ray C. Rist (ed.), *Program Evaluation and the Management of Government*, New Brunswick and London: Transaction, pp. 147–77.

Furubo, Jan-Eric, Ray C. Rist and Rolf Sandahl (eds) (2002), *International Atlas of Evaluation*, New Brunswick and London: Transaction.

Furubo, Jan-Eric and Rolf Sandahl (2002), 'A diffusion-perspective on global developments in evaluation', in Jan-Eric Furubo, Ray C. Rist and Rolf Sandahl (eds), *International Atlas of Evaluation*, New Brunswick and London: Transaction, pp. 1–26.

Hood, Christopher (1991), 'A public management for all seasons?', *Public Administration*, 69[Spring], 3–19.

Knoepfel, Peter and Werner Bussmann (1997), 'Die öffentliche Politik als Evaluationsobjekt', in Werner Bussmann, Ulrich Klöti and Peter Knöpfel (eds), *Einführung in die Politikevaluation*, Basel: Helbing & Lichterhan, pp. 58–77.

Levine, Robert A. (1981), 'Program evaluation and policy analysis in western nations: An overview', in Robert A. Levine, Marian A. Solomon, Gerd-Michael Hellstern, and Hellmut Wollmann (eds), *Evaluation Research and Practice: Comparative and International Perspectives*, Beverly Hills and London: Sage, pp. 12–27.

Pawson, Ray and Nick Tilley (1997), *Realistic Evaluation*, London: Sage.

Pollitt, Christopher (1995), 'Justification by works or by faith? Evaluating the New Public Management', *Evaluation*, 1[2 (October)], 133–54.

Pollitt, Christopher and Geert Bouckaert (2000), *Public Management Reform*, Oxford: Oxford University Press.

Pressman, Jeffrey and Aaron Wildavsky (1974), *Implementation* (1984 3rd ed.), Berkeley: University of California Press.

Rist, Ray C. (ed.) (1990), *Program Evaluation and the Management of Government*, New Brunswick and London: Transaction.

Ritz, Adrian (1999), *Die Evaluation von New Public Management*, Bern: IOP-Verlag.

Sandahl, Rolf (1992), 'Evaluation at the Swedish national audit bureau', in J. Mayne et al. (eds), *Advancing Public Policy Evaluation*, Amsterdam: Elsevier, pp. 115–21.

Sanderson, Ian (2000), 'Evaluation in complex policy systems', *Evaluation*, 6[4], 433–54.

Vedung, Evert (1997), *Public Policy and Program Evaluation*, New Brunswick: Transaction.

Wagner, Peter and Hellmut Wollmann (1986), 'Fluctuations in the development of evaluation research: Do regime shifts matter?', *International Social Science Journal*, 108, 205–18.

Wollmann. Hellmut (ed.) (2001). 'Evaluating public-sector reforms', special issue of *Revista Internacional de Estudios Politicos*,127–43.

Wollmann, Hellmut (2002a), 'Contractual research and policy knowledge', *International Encyclopedia of the Social and Behavioral Sciences*, 5, 11574–11578.

Wollmann, Hellmut (2002b), 'Verwaltungspolitik und Evaluierung: Ansätze, Phasen und Beispiele im Ausland und in Deutschland, Evaluation und New Public Management', *Zeitschrift für Evaluation*, 1, 75–101.

Notes

1. Important exceptions are Pollitt and Bouckaert 2000 (which covers public-sector reform in 10 OECD countries, including the Netherlands, France, and Germany) and Furubo, Rist, and Sandahl's 2002 'atlas' of evaluation, which contains as many as 21 country reports.
2. On the distinction between substantive policy (*substanzielle Politik*) and institution policy (*Institutionenpolitik*) see Knoepfel and Bussmann 1997, p. 59, and Ritz 1999, p. 28.
3. This refers to the distinction made in policy science and policy studies between policy (as the contents of policy making), politics (as the process of policy making) and polity (as the institutional setting thereof).
4. This term was coined by Yezekel Dror.
5. See Christensen et al. in Chapter 4 of this volume: 'Process evaluation tracks the extent to which programme or practices were put in place as intended and monitor how implementation has progressed'.
6. For a penetrating discussion of the methodological issues of evaluation (research) at large, see Pawson and Tilley 1997.
7. See Jann and Reichard in Chapter 3 of this volume: 'No organizational change of even modest complexity will happen without the most common of all social phenomena: unintended and even counterintuitive processes and results'.

2. Evaluating public management reforms: An international perspective

Christopher Pollitt and Geert Bouckaert

1. Introduction

It is an honour to be asked to lead off this volume on evaluating public-sector modernization. However, the editor's invitation was also something of a poisoned chalice. Evaluating management reforms across the globe is, for many reasons, an almost impossible task. Understandably, it rarely has been attempted, and then usually by those – such as politicians, management consultants and gurus – who are free from the scientific inhibitions of the scholar (see, for example, Dorrell 1993).

We see our task, therefore, as twofold. Naturally, we will do our best to fulfil the mission given to us by the volume editor – to produce 'an internationally comparative assessment'. Before we do that, however, we consider it vital to explain why such comparisons are so difficult, and to identify some of the cautionary considerations that need to accompany the reading of any evaluative text such as this. We therefore begin with five sets of interacting problems which make life difficult for the comparative evaluator.

The first problem: units of analysis
The very phrase 'international comparisons' seems to presuppose that nation-states are the most appropriate unit of analysis for assessments of public management reforms. In many ways, perhaps they are. Certainly nation-states remain distinctive entities in the world of public management. They tend to have their own politico-administrative systems, administrative cultures and so on, and it seems very common for such factors significantly to influence the trajectory of administrative reform. In our own study of ten countries we found strong evidence for national distinctiveness (Pollitt and Bouckaert 2000) and we are far

from alone in arriving at this conclusion (see, for example, Christensen and Lægreid 1998; Flynn and Strehl 1996; Hood 1996; Olsen and Peters 1996; Premfors 1998, Wollmann 1997). New Public Management (NPM) may have affected many countries, but some much more than others. Furthermore, even those that are heavily under its spell tend to adapt NPM 'ingredients' in quite individual ways, to produce distinctive national cuisines.

These differences are problematic because, to put it colloquially, we are constantly in danger of comparing apples and pears. Different countries start from different places, have different histories and pursue different trajectories. Common and general rhetoric about 'good governance', 'efficiency', 'quality' and 'trust' may in fact conceal heavily path-dependent developments, in which the particular mix of priorities in, say, Finland is quite different from that in Australia. (For an excellent general treatment of path dependency, see Pierson 2000; for an account of Finnish priorities in a comparative context, see Bouckaert, Ormond and Peters 2000).

To reduce the danger of comparing apples and pears (fruitlessly, if readers will permit the pun), there may be a case for becoming more specific and detailed – for coming down from the level of national comparisons either to sectoral analysis or to more particular comparisons of individual instruments or processes. To generic managerialists, sectoral analysis may seem slightly conservative and narrow, but for many public service professionals comparative studies of the practice in their field (such as health care, schools or the probation service) seem to hold more promise than the highly generalized nostrums of management gurus. As a recent example, a major reorganization of UK probation services has followed a review and synthesis of international research on re-offending rates, and evidence of effective practice from local probation services across the country (Her Majesty's Inspectorate of Probation, 1998; see also Furniss and Nutley 2000). Unfortunately, however, we are not able to provide a reliable overview of sectoral evaluations. Our own knowledge is limited to one or two sectors. Thus, although our impression is that international evaluations of management reform conducted on a sectoral basis are still infrequent, we cannot be sure of how much work of this kind has been undertaken. Perhaps there is more useful material here than we have been able to find.

Turning to evaluations of specific instruments and processes, one might, for example, compare the introduction of Total Quality Management (TQM) in the public-sectors of Sweden, the UK and the USA, or one might investigate the consequences of attempts to introduce accruals accounting in Finland, New Zealand and the Netherlands. Even here, though, there can be methodological problems. Many – perhaps most – reforms are extensively 'edited' or 'translated' when they are transferred from one jurisdiction to another (Sahlin-Andersson 1996). For example, TQM turns out to possess a variable, somewhat chameleon-like identity (Joss and Kogan 1995; Zbaracki 1998). Similarly, re-engineering has become a term used to cover a wide variety of change activities, by no means all of them as radical as the original architects of 'BPR' had wanted (Packwood, Pollitt and Roberts 1998; Thompson 2000). However, one would at least be comparing different kinds of apples. Unfortunately, as far as we are aware, there are few international comparisons of this 'instrument and process' type. It is a wide-open field for future scholarship. For the moment, therefore, we cannot base our comparisons on such work. We must stay with nation-states as our unit of comparison, despite the limitations that choice imposes.

The second problem: units of meaning
The problem is more than one of comparing dissimilar entities. Public management reform is not simply a matter of shuffling different shaped pieces, as if one were solving a jigsaw puzzle. The pieces have their own meanings, and these may vary from country to country (or even from sector to sector). For example, in the early 1990s, executive agencies in the UK were commonly seen as being at the cutting edge of new developments. They represented efficiency, specialization and a performance management approach. At the same time, in Finland, agencies (national boards) tended to be seen as the outdated remnants of legalistic, procedurally-oriented bureaucracy. So while the UK central government was rapidly multiplying the number of its agencies, the Finnish central government was merging, downsizing and generally reducing its agency population (Pollitt et al. 2001).

As seen in the example of agencies in Finland and the UK, public management reform often has a strongly symbolic dimension. This poses problems for evaluation. The mainstream development of the field of evaluation has tended to be strongly rationalist – what are the goals, and what evidence is there that they have been achieved. (See, for example, Shadish, Cook and Leviton 1991.) Most of the conventional tools for evaluation–cost-benefit analysis, quasi-experimentation, econometric modelling, functional benchmarking and so on – fail to capture the symbolic and rhetorical significance of reform. For politicians – often the initiators, or at least the facilitators of reform – the short-term rhetorical and symbolic effects of reform are highly important. For example, Tony Blair has already reaped political gains over his opponents by stressing 'evidence-based policymaking' and the attractions of a supposedly non-ideological philosophy of 'what works', long before the actual impacts of many of his policies could be assessed (Cabinet Office 2000; Davies, Nutley and Smith 2000; Harrison 1998). More generally, cultural and rhetorical aspects appear to play an important part in many public-sector reforms, and in so far as conventional approaches to evaluation overlook or ignore them, our understanding of the what and why of reform is thereby impoverished (Hood 1998; Pollitt 2001).

The third problem: scarcity of key data

Let us begin with a traditional definition of what types of data – and produced by which methods – would be required to confirm scientifically the effectiveness of NPM-type reforms. Full analytic rigour would require something akin to a randomized clinical trial, with a control group, placebos, double-blind refereeing and so on (for early American and British classics, see Campbell and Stanley 1963 and Cochrane 1972, respectively). In real life, however, this kind of experimentalism can only very rarely be attained in the field of management reform. The 'treatment' cannot be kept secret, placebos cannot be devised and, for a mixture of ethical and practical reasons, credible control groups cannot be established. It is almost unknown for management reforms to be subjected to true experimental procedures.

If we become more realistic, and relax our methodological demands somewhat, we might think in terms of a before-and-after study. First, we would need an accurate picture of the status quo ante. This would include quantitative data relating to the key criteria by which we intended to judge the reform, for example, cost, technical efficiency or service quality (the issue of criteria is discussed further later). Second, we would need an equally accurate description of the state of the world after the reform had been implemented. Third, we would need to be able to predict what the state of the world would have been if no reform had taken place, and the pre-existing system had continued (that is, a 'counterfactual' situation [see Elster 1978]). Within this framework we would then compare our second description with both the counterfactual and the status quo ante. The differences between the reform situation and the counterfactual would yield some measure of the impact of the reform (Pawson and Tilley 1997).

Unfortunately, even this somewhat less demanding approach is far beyond any analysis that governments have actually conducted. NPM

remains quite innocent of these kinds of traditional 'scientific' evaluations. However, there have been some less rigorous investigations. In
1995 Pollitt reviewed broad-scope evaluations of public-sector management reform and found them fairly limited. Since then the situation
has improved slightly, but has certainly not been transformed. It is still
the case that many – probably most – major reform programmes have
been announced and implemented without any plans for systematic and
independent evaluation in place. (Some, like the New Zealanders in
1991 and the European Commission with respect to its MAP 2000
reforms, tack on an evaluation after the reform is well underway – an
action which is much better than nothing, but which usually precludes
the establishment of reliable baselines for before and after comparisons.) One of the most radical reformers, the UK, performed little serious analysis during the heady days of reform between 1987 and 1997,
although the Labour government has since launched many evaluations.
The Australians and the New Zealanders both attempted major evaluations, and the Americans put in place a number of evaluations around
the 1993 National Performance Review (NPR) and the 1992 Government Performance and Results Act (GPRA). The Finns also conducted
a series of evaluations of their reforms in the late 1980s and early 1990s
(Holkeri and Summa 1996). However, despite many reforms during the
1980s and early 1990s, there appear to have been no independent
broad-scope evaluations in (for example) Canada, France, the Netherlands, Sweden or the UK.

Even where serious evaluations have taken place, the kind of data
required for a reliable judgement about some of the big issues frequently turn out to be inaccessible. For example, neither the extensive
Australian evaluation of 1992 nor the New Zealand review of 1991
were able to give estimates for the total costs of the reform programmes
or the savings which had resulted from them (Task Force 1992; Steering Group 1991). The New Zealand study also noted that 'there is no
reliable data which enables a comparison of productivity in the Public
Service over the period from the introduction of the reforms' (Steering
Group 1991, p. 26). Essentially final impacts (or outcomes) frequently
are difficult both to measure and to attribute to particular causes. When
citizen ratings of governments rise, is it because of reform or because
the economy is doing better? When complaints go up, is it because of
poorer service or an improved complaints system? When the employment service fails to reach its target for placing the long-term unem-
ployed, is that because it is an ineffective service or because the econ-

omy is in a downturn, and employers are simply not hiring? Constructing convincing counterfactuals is a difficult and rarely-practised art.

The fourth problem: multiple criteria

If a judgement as to the effects of NPM-style reforms is to be reached, the available data must be subjected to a set of criteria. But what criteria should these be? Official documents are often vague, failing either to define key terms such as 'productivity' or 'quality', or mentioning a whole series of criteria without explaining how these are to be reconciled with one another or, where necessary, traded off against each other (see Pollitt and Bouckaert 2000, Chapter 7). Here we can do no more than briefly indicate what are the most common criteria in use, and say something about how they may be defined and measured.

A first criterion is that of savings, understood as a reduction in inputs. Governments like this idea, as it helps them show that they are not wasting the taxpayers' money and that they have the public administration 'under control'. Furthermore, 'savings' appears to be a simple notion, readily understood by the average citizen. However, 'savings' is not such a straightforward matter. It can have many different technical meanings (such as an absolute reduction in spending compared with the previous period, a reduction below the previously forecast level of spending, or a reduction in unit costs [see Pollitt and Bouckaert 2000, pp. 100–01]). What is more, one always has to be on guard in case savings within one jurisdiction has been achieved partly or wholly by transferring expenditure to another jurisdiction (as is the case in many decentralization programmes in which the central government shifts responsibility for programmes to subnational levels of government). Finally, of course, savings may be perfectly genuine, but may cause negative effects on other criteria such as outputs (lower efficiency) or outcomes (lower effectiveness).

A second criterion could be better processes: faster services, one-stop shops that make access more convenient for the public, or better 'customer care' in the shape of more friendly and more highly trained staff (Bouckaert 2001). Some of the provisions of the citizens' charters that have been introduced in Belgium, Finland, France, Italy, Portugal and the UK are of this type (see, for example, Bouckaert 1995; Pollitt 1994 and Schiavo 2000). There are also a number of national and international service quality competitions which assess improvements of this type (see, for example, Loeffler 1995 and Borins 1998). Specific measures of process improvement may be reasonably clear, but their broader significance is not necessarily straightforward. For example, claims for benefits may be processed more quickly, but with a higher level of inaccuracies. Hospital treatment for a given condition may be quicker and more flexibly provided, but without any effect on the health status outcomes (that is, processes improve, but outcomes stay the same).

Third, one could look for greater efficiency in reforms (where efficiency is defined as the input/output ratio). Certainly 'efficiency' has been a term much used in the Anglophone world (Pollitt 1993). Furthermore, many attempts have been made to measure changes in efficiency (for example, by the Budget Department or the Chancellor of the Duchy of Lancaster in 1997). While this is certainly a useful measure, especially if part of a time series, it does have some limitations. Like process improvements, efficiency benefits may not lead to better outcomes – in fact efficiency may sometimes be improved to the detriment of effectiveness. For example, if staff-student ratios are increased in educational establishments, so that teachers teach more students and generally work more intensively, overall learning may decline, because the amount and quality of attention given to the individual child is reduced and teachers become more overworked and narrowly instrumental in approach.

Fourth, there is what many would regard as the 'gold standard' test: whether the effectiveness of public programmes is improved. Effectiveness is defined here as the impacts of the programme on the outside world in relation to its original objectives (objectives/outcomes). Does a new treatment improve the health status of patients? Does a new system of schools produce better-educated students? Does a new policing strategy actually reduce crime? Does a new family benefit reduce poverty? Effectiveness is a very powerful criterion, but often a difficult one to apply to management reforms. Part of the problem is long time lags – a large-scale administrative reform may take three years or more, and it may be several years after that before one can compare programme outcomes with the status quo ante. Another part of the problem is complexity – even when an outcome can be measured, to what extent can it be attributed to the particular programme rather than to other factors?

Fifth, some reform advocates stress the importance of improving the capacity of the administrative system. The world is becoming more complex and events are moving more quickly, runs the argument, so the system of public administration needs to adapt to these new conditions. This may be perfectly true, but it is a difficult criterion to operationalize. How can the capacity of such a system be measured? How can the capacity of a system in two or more states be compared? Governments have as yet contributed little to our understanding of how to do these things.

Finally, the rhetoric of reform often seems to use ideal types as a criterion for reform success. For example, particular measures will be justified because they are intended to make government smaller, or more decentralized, or more closely partnered with business and voluntary sectors. Behind such rhetoric lie visions of ideal types of systems: 'lean', 'close to the citizen', 'partnerships' and so on. The 'success' of a reform is then defined in terms of how far it moves the existing system towards one or more of these ideal states. This type of ideological or doctrinal criterion is frequently difficult to operationalize or apply. Even when this *is* possible, the relation between the 'ideal system' and the other criteria of success may be quite ambiguous. Is a more decentralized system always more effective? Is a smaller government always a better government? Are projects undertaken in partnership with private sector firms always cheaper and more successful? Clearly the answers to each of these questions is 'it depends'. However, this complication does not restrain reform leaders from deploying the rhetoric of decentralization, partnership and so on, which clearly has payoffs of its own (Pollitt 2001).

Thus, even if we had more and better data, the business of assessing reforms would still be complex. There are multiple, interconnected criteria, and a high score on one may sometimes be purchased with a reduced performance on another. Different groups will maintain perfectly legitimate differences of opinion as to which criteria in a given time and place should have priority. Indeed, the complexity arises within the NPM paradigm itself. The above-mentioned criteria are all taken from the reformers' own rhetoric. If one goes outside the paradigm – for example, to look at criteria such as equality or gender or trust or loyalty or law-abidingness – then the challenge of evaluating NPM becomes still more formidable. Examples of interesting attempts to do this include a UK study of how compulsory competitive tendering – although it enhanced efficiency – degraded equal opportunities employment policies (Escott and Whitfield 1995), and an analysis which indicates that solidaristic values in Swedish society are in decline, and that the increasing availability of exit options from public services may be helping to increase social inequalities (Micheletti 2000).

The fifth problem: the elusiveness of change
The sheer fact of intensive activity does not necessarily imply a major impact. Neither does a lot of talk necessarily imply a lot of activity.

When evaluating management reforms it is important to separate talk about reform from actual decisions to reform, and then carefully to check whether the decisions have really been implemented as new practices. Finally, there is the question of whether new practices have actually changed outcomes (Pollitt 2001). Reforms can slither to a standstill, or get pushed off course, at any point along the sequence of talk-decision-practice-impact. There can be advantages to saying one thing and doing another (Brunsson 1989).

Furthermore, even when they reach the stage of actual practice, just looking at one particular element may be misleading. Coherence among reforms is by no means guaranteed. One new practice may contradict another, or vital components may be missing. Performance contracts may be introduced without an adequate performance measurement system to support them. External audits may be reformed while internal audit remains traditional or even non-existent. Three-year budgeting may be introduced, but without the underlying stability of resources that would permit it to function as intended.

Looking at the different stages through which most reforms pass, one can say that the rhetoric of change is usually fairly accessible. 'Talk is cheap', as the saying goes. Frequently information about reform decisions is also easy to acquire. Governments like to give their decisions some prominence. Information about changes in practice – the implementation of reforms – is often more difficult to acquire. Of course there are many of case studies that indicate improved processes. In many (but not all!) countries such basic items as driving licences, identity cards, passports and tax forms are much easier to obtain than they were ten or fifteen years ago. We also have volumes of data about improved response times while waiting in hospital emergency rooms, having benefit claims processed or moving through customs barriers (see, for example, Chancellor of the Duchy of Lancaster 1997). Even the accuracy of weather forecasts is improving (National Audit Office 1995). There are, however, at least two important qualifications that need to be made. First, there is almost certainly a built-in bias in reporting: successes are feted and failures concealed or just not talked about. Politicians and public servants do not generally go to conferences to tell the story of how their reform failed. Second, what process information frequently does not show is whether (hidden) parts of the system have paid the price for improvements in other parts of the system (for example, when a target for processing a certain percentage of benefit claims within a limited time has been achieved by making a minority of the most complex cases wait longer than before [see National Audit Office 1998]).

Last but not least, information about results – especially final outcomes – is often non-existent or hard to find.

2. The big picture

We are now almost at the point where we can begin to consider the 'results' of reform. However, before launching into the specifics of the matter, it is necessary to do some scene-setting. Without some indications of the problems the reforms were to address, it is difficult to assess them. In this section, therefore, we identify some of the main motives for reform, and very briefly describe the types of reform activities that have taken place (for a more detailed description, see Pollitt and Bouckaert 2000, especially the appendix).

In broad terms, the motives for reform have been fairly international, even if their relative priorities have varied over time and according to the particular starting points and circumstances of the jurisdictions concerned. One strong motive – particularly during the economically troubled periods of the early 1980s and early 1990s – has been simply to save money. The story is well known. Many governments have faced a 'scissors movement' of growing welfare costs and declining possibilities for new taxation. Cutting public expenditure, or at least reducing its rate of growth, has been high on the agenda.

Second, there has been a widespread desire to remedy the perceived poor performance of significant parts of the public-sector. As standards of education improve, and increasingly affluent populations become accustomed to higher standards of service from the private sector, they become less and less willing to accept inflexible, bureaucratic responses from public services. So both service quality and improved productivity have been the goals of many jurisdictions. Some politicians and some civil servants believe that such improvements will also help governments to redress the falling levels of citizen trust (and therefore legitimacy) which many surveys seem to show across Western Europe and North America.

Third, as reforms to save money and improve performance have got underway, it has become apparent that some of these changes may alter the pattern of responsibilities across different administrative and political actors. Many countries have begun to search for new mechanisms for public accountability (see, for example, Sharman 2001) and some have felt obliged to reconsider how to protect and enhance standards in public life (see, for example, SIGMA 1999).

We now move to a very brief overview of the changes themselves. Overall, there has been a truly large volume and wide variety of management reform. It seems very probable that the reform process has intensified in the period since 1985, and that international contacts have played an important part in the global 'trade' in particular types of reform (Pollitt and Bouckaert 2000).

The intensity of reform has varied considerably from country to country. Certain countries (Australia, New Zealand, the UK and the USA) have been extremely active (on Australia and New Zealand, see also Halligan, Chapter 5 in this volume). One reform has followed another in an almost dizzying sequence (see, for example, Boston et al. 1996; Pollitt and Bouckaert, 2000; Savoie 1994). These are countries that have championed NPM and 'reinvention' (Kettl, 2000). A second group of countries has also been busy with administrative reform, but less radically (and, in a way, less boastfully) than the first group. These 'modernizers' have been less iconoclastic, less doctrinaire and less carried away with privatization, contractualization and the wonders of market mechanisms than the first group. They include France, the Nordic countries, the Netherlands and Canada (see, for example, Guyomarch 1999; Kickert 2001; on Sweden and Norway see also Christensen et al., Chapter 4 in this volume). A third group has been – for a variety of reasons – much more cautious (or inhibited). Prominent members of this group have been Germany and Japan, although it should be noted that there has been a good deal of reform in Germany at the local level (Derlien 1998; Wollmann 1997 and in this volume), and that, since the late 1990s, Japan has begun to develop programmes of quite NPM-ish administrative change (see Muramatsu and Matsunami, Chapter 9 in this volume). Fourth, one should mention the developing world and the transitional states of central and eastern Europe (Bouckaert and Timsit 2000). Many of these countries have attempted to implement various elements of NPM, with varying success. In quite a few of these cases such reforms were urged by international organizations such as the World Bank, SIGMA or the European Commission, or by ex-colonial mentors such as the UK Department for International Development. One is reminded of programmes of agencification in such widely separated places as Tanzania, Jamaica and Latvia. At the present time there are signs that some of these countries (and even some of the international bodies) are beginning to regret certain features of this process. In Latvia, for example, steps are now being taken to rein in the

150-plus agencies which were created during the 1990s. It has become clear that steering and accountability mechanisms are inadequate, and that a large proportion of the national budget is now earmarked for agencies that are largely beyond the control of their parent ministries.

One way of classifying reform efforts is to think in terms of four main strategies that any given jurisdiction might use. The first of these is to *maintain*: to keep the administrative machine much as it is, but to tighten up and streamline wherever possible. The second is to *modernize*: to make more fundamental changes in structures and processes, for example, by changing the budget process to an output rather than an input orientation; to create new types of public-sector organization, such as autonomous agencies; or to change the employment contract for civil servants. The third is to *marketize*: to introduce Market-Type Mechanisms (MTMs) to the public-sector, in the belief that this will generate greater efficiency and better performance (OECD 1993). For example, in the UK the Conservative governments of the 1990s introduced an 'internal market' to the National Health Service, requiring hospitals to compete for patients based on the price and quality of their services. In this way activities remain within the state sector, but state organizations are obliged to behave more and more like private-sector companies. The fourth strategy is to *minimize*: to shrink the state sector as much as possible, by making the maximum use of privatization and contracting. Public assets are sold, and activities previously performed by public servants are contracted by the commercial and voluntary sectors. This strategy reflects a pessimistic attitude towards the potential of the public-sector for good management and towards the legitimacy of state ownership.

In general terms the 'Anglo-Saxon' countries (Australia, New Zealand, the UK and the USA) have gone further and faster down the roads of marketizing and minimizing than have most continental European countries. For obvious reasons, these latter two strategies also tend to create the greatest resistance from public-sector organizations and unions themselves. Therefore marketizing and minimizing are not only more radical but also more conflictual than modernizing or maintaining. The possible gains are said – by their proponents – to be greater, but the risks of failure and significant recalcitrance are also higher. Continental European states have preferred a central thrust towards modernization, seasoned with the occasional pinch of marketization and privatization.

It will not have escaped the reader's notice that our global map has some huge gaps in it. The Mediterranean countries, South America, most of Asia and many other territories have not even been mentioned. The reason for this is simple: we do not know enough to say anything. Hopefully, one major achievement of this special issue will be to lessen the extensive ignorance among the NPM countries concerning what has been going on in these parts of the world.

'Results' at last

After setting out all the difficulties we at last arrive back at the original question: what have been the results of public management reforms, from a comparative perspective? Given the aforementioned problems, we hope readers will understand why what we say here will be both incomplete and festooned with qualifications. Nevertheless, we hope it will set the scene for the more detailed papers later in this special edition, and, perhaps, that it may encourage other scholars either to draw attention to useful evaluations that we have missed or to launch new evaluations themselves.

First, let us consider the evidence with respect to saving money and reducing the size of governments – probably the two most prominent goals for many countries when the international reform movement took off during the 1980s. At first glance the results here seem to be straightforward: 'many of the nations with the most aggressive reform efforts saw reductions in government spending as a share of the economy during the 1990's and the pay of government employees 'fell most in the nations that engaged in the most aggressive reforms' (Kettl, 2000, pp. 52–3; see original for detailed tables and graphics, based mainly on the OECD databank). Furthermore, the most vigorous reformers were able to record substantial reductions in the numbers of 'bureaucrats'. Mrs Thatcher downsized the non-industrial civil service by more than 20 per cent. Vice President Al Gore's NPR reduced the US federal workforce by 299,600 FTEs (13.9 per cent) by the end of fiscal year 1998 (Maas and van Nispen 1999). An insider review of the financial management reforms in New Zealand came to the conclusion that the (post reform) 'apparatus was an effective instrument for controlling and reducing central government expenditure' – although it also pointed out that the effects of the new instruments and the priorities of the new government could not be differentiated from one another (Brumby et al. 1996). In Canada, reforms in the mid-1990s permitted the achievement of the first balanced budget in three decades (see Aucoin and Savoie 1998).

Closer inspection of these 'results' does not entirely demolish the correlation between reform and savings/downsizing, but it does introduce considerable doubt and ambiguity. Most obviously, it needs to be acknowledged that ratio measurements such as government spending or GDP are determined as much by economic growth rates as by changes in government spending. Overall, the period 1990–2000 was one of strong economic growth, so the proportion taken by government spending would fall even if the absolute amount of such spending remained the same or grew slowly. This may explain why Ireland, a state that was hardly a leader in NPM-type reforms, comes ahead of New Zealand and the UK in terms of reductions of government outlays as a percentage of GDP. If one focused on a different time period – say, the early 1980s or the early 1990s, when growth was slow or negative – then a very different conclusion could be drawn.

An even more serious interpretive issue is the direction of causation. It would be quite unwarranted simply to assume that if the percentage of government outlays to GDP fell, this was necessarily due to NPM-type reforms. On the contrary, the fall could be the result of the most traditional kind of crude expenditure cuts. One Swedish study found exactly that – that expenditure reductions tended to stimulate management reforms, rather than the other way around (Murray 1998).

Furthermore, we are entitled to be cautious about bald claims that the number of civil servants has been reduced by such-and-such. Quite often such statements conceal a more complex situation, in which duties have been relegated to other public-sector organizations (such as local authorities or quangos) whose staff has consequently increased (on Sweden, see, for example, Micheletti, 2000). Alternatively, more work may have been contracted out, so that even core welfare-state services are being run by for-profit companies, as is increasingly the case in Australia, the UK and the USA (on the USA, see Peterson 2000). Thus, government is smaller in terms of people but not in terms of responsibilities.

Finally, we should note that the correlation between 'aggressive' reform and savings/downsizings, though substantial, is far from complete. The OECD figures contain some apparent anomalies. Consider the change in the ratio between government outlays and GDP. In this measure Greece comes well 'ahead' of the UK, and Belgium considerably 'ahead' of Australia. One can only conclude that, of course, there must be other things going on apart from NPM. One leading scholar, although generally quite optimistic about the impact of public management reforms, concedes that, despite the OECD databank, 'no good reliable data are available in any country regarding the savings that the reforms produced' (Kettl, 2000, p. 51).

Our second evaluative criterion was that of improved processes. Here it is easy to find examples of success, but hard to give an overall picture. The literature relaying cases and anecdotes of process improvement is extensive (for example, Borins 1998; Chancellor of the Duchy of Lancaster 1997; Gore 1996; and Osborne and Gaebler 1992). Part of the problem, as noted earlier, is that we are probably being presented with a biased selection. There is a smaller and less obtrusive literature which tells a different story. For example, Packwood et al. (1998) show how a large and expensive re-engineering effort at a major UK teaching hospital fell far short of its original expectations. Thompson (2000) describes an even bigger re-engineering project at the US Social Security Administration. After five years of effort it failed to meet most of its targets; the SSA no longer classifies it as 'classic re-engineering'. Similarly, the UK Department of Social Security spent much of the 1980s and early 1990s implementing a grandiose new 'Operational Strategy', but both the estimated savings and the projected service improvements failed to materialize (National Audit Office 1999, p. 25). There are definitely some successes and some failures. The relative incidence of these contrasting outcomes for any country is not known, nor do we have a clear and reliable model of what may be the crucial contextual differences between success and failure (see Pawson and Tilley 1997).

Many of the comments about improved processes also apply to the assessment of efficiency. Here, too, there are plenty of examples of productivity gains (for example, Chancellor of the Duchy of Lancaster 1997) but it is quite difficult to interpret the validity and reliability of much of the quantitative evidence. National audit offices in a number of countries (among others, Sweden, the UK and the USA) have sought a new role in validating the wave of performance indicator data which is now flowing out of executive government. Again, to generalize, it is clear that the application of NPM techniques sometimes yields considerable increases in efficiency, but on other occasions there are disappointments or even perversions (Pollitt, 2000; Smith 1996). We are beginning to have some idea of what the main risk factors may be, but identifying and weighing these in specific contexts is still far more craft than science.

Effectiveness was our fourth criterion. Conceptualizing the final outcomes of management reform is less straightforward than for other programmes, such as poverty reduction or health care. Measuring them is also difficult. In an ideal world the reformer might hope for a cultural shift in the public service that would embed the values of responsiveness, quality and efficiency. But how can an independent observer ascertain to what extent these things have happened, and to what extent they were due to a particular reform rather than to other contemporary influences? A rather small number of studies tackle these issues with any sophistication. One good example is Thompson's assessment of the US NPR. He arrives at the conclusion that, while much has been achieved, 'many of the NPR's higher order objectives have not been met on a systematic basis' (Thompson, 2000, p. 508).

Our fifth and sixth criteria were both systemic. One was to produce a more flexible system, more capable of adapting to change. The other was to move towards an ideal, lean, decentralized, entrepreneurial NPM state. As mentioned earlier, it is almost impossible to operationalize either of these criteria in the form of one or two simple measures. Perhaps, therefore, the best we can do is to take note of the impressions conveyed in works of broad synthesis by national experts. Beginning with New Zealand, the 1991 evaluation came to the conclusion that there were 'substantial' benefits in terms of system capability (Steering Group 1991, p. 11). In 1996, Boston et al. acknowledged the remarkable scale and thoroughness of the changes in that small country, but also pointed to unfinished business and continuing tensions between divergent objectives. The UK was another reform leader. What is clear from the British experience is that reform is endless. After a full 15 years of intensive management reform, Tony Blair's New Labour government published a white paper outlining more measurement, more targetry, more evaluation, more IT, and more cultural change for civil servants (this time so that they would become comfortable with 'joined up' and 'networked' ways of working [Davies, Nutley and Smith, 2000; Prime Minister and Minister for the Cabinet Office 1999]). Evidently, despite a whole generation of NPM, the ideal is still some way off. In the Netherlands change was less hectic, and probably ran less deep. Kickert concludes that 'All political attempts at a more fundamental renewal of state and administration have failed. The Dutch consensus democracy with its endless deliberation and eternal search for compromise and consensus ensures that revolutionary changes will never occur' (Kickert 2001).

In France, successive waves of administrative reform have certainly brought changes, but the elements of continuity (such as the centrality of the *grands corps* and their particular type of technocratic professionalization, or the political strength of the public service unions) are at least as noticeable as those of change (Guyomarch 1999; Rouban 1995). In Canada, eight years of change under Prime Minister Brian

Mulroney produced no consistent direction or model, and the much-vaunted Public Service 2000 programme of 1989 seems to have fizzled out (Auditor General of Canada 1993; Savoie 1994). Reform since 1993 appears to have been more successful, but also in some ways more traditional (Aucoin and Savoie 1998). Not surprisingly, the Norwegian system seems to have proved even more resilient – the NPM messages coming from the international community have been heavily 'edited' to conform more closely with some traditional Nordic virtues (Christensen and Lægreid 1998).

One could continue to list such references, but they probably would not take us very much closer to a final judgement about systemic transformations (Bouckaert, 2000). It would take a profound scepticism not to accept that there has been both structural change and a cultural shift in those countries which have pushed NPM ideas hardest – Australia, New Zealand and the UK. Even in these countries, however, strong elements of continuity can be discerned and – perhaps more interestingly – 15 or more years of reform have brought little in the way of stability or satisfaction. If there is a new culture now in place, it is not quite clear what it is, or who fully subscribes to it and who merely mouths the rhetoric and waits for the next change of fashion. These countries almost seem addicted to administrative reform. So too, in a less structural, more process-oriented way, is the USA. Elsewhere it is doubtful whether the term 'transformation' can really be justified. Incremental, or at least gradual, negotiated change has been the norm in Germany, the Netherlands and the Nordic states. Larger changes have taken place in France, but certainly the French themselves would resist the suggestion that these have been pursuant of the NPM model.

Reflections

What is perhaps most remarkable about the NPM in practice has been the amateurishness of its proponents on their own chosen ground of performance. Rhetorically, the NPM has been all about improving performance – making governments more cost-conscious, efficient, effective, responsive, customer-oriented, flexible, and transparent. In practice, however, the steps taken to check whether these performance improvements have actually been realized have often been 'too little, too late', and very light on independence.

There is a lack of reflexivity here – the reformers have preached a performance orientation, but have only occasionally applied that requirement to themselves. Of course, to have done so would have been difficult. As this paper has made clear, the methodological and practical problems confronting would-be evaluators are considerable. At the same time it seems clear that it would have been perfectly possible to do much more analysis than has actually been attempted. The UK government could have set up an evaluation of the attempt to introduce an internal market in the largest organization in the UK – the National Health Service – but it did not. The New Zealand governments of the mid- and late 1980s could have put in place systematic evaluations of their radical organizational reforms, but they did not. The Canadian Prime Minister from 1984 until 1993, Brian Mulroney, could have asked for an independent analysis of his many management initiatives, but did not choose to. The Dutch government launched an agencification programme in 1991, but the official assessment of it contains precious little quantitative data, and completely misses an obvious opportunity to check whether promises of greater efficiency and higher quality services were actually fulfilled (Ministerie van Financien 1998). Where independent assessments have been undertaken, as often as not, they reveal ambiguities and significant gaps in the evidence (Auditor General of Canada 1993; General Accounting Office 1998; National Audit Office 1998; Pollitt 1995; Thompson, 2000).

How can this paradox – a performance-oriented set of reforms that lacks a proper check on its own performance – be explained? There are several possibilities. One is that there has been a cynical plot to conceal the real – and unpleasant – nature of these changes from the public. We find it an unlikely explanation – too many different kinds of regimes in too many different countries have toyed with NPM ideas for organized deception to be very credible. Another is that what we are dealing with here is best described as a kind of religion – the NPM is a system of belief founded on faith, and therefore should not be analysed as though it were some kind of body of scientific knowledge subject to objective tests. This is perhaps a more persuasive interpretation. It would lead us to look for the mechanisms by which the faith is spread – to identify the missionaries and to look for the nature of their appeal, the symbols they use and the proverbs and stories they tell, and how these are translated or edited to fit the perceptions of dominant groups in local jurisdictions (see, for example, Hood and Jackson 1991; Hood 1998; Premfors 1998; Williams, 2000; Wright 1997).

One particularly interesting aspect of the faith in NPM is its relationship with the older set of beliefs about the nature of liberal democracy. At first, in the pioneering Anglo-Saxon countries during the 1980s, there seemed little connection. 'Managerialism' and its values seemed to be a separate enterprise (Hood 1991; Pollitt 1993). During the last decade, however, the proponents of NPM have come to terms with the traditional vocabulary of democracy. Nowadays we hear a great deal about citizens' charters, 'empowerment', 'inclusion', 'partnership', 'networked solutions' and 'accountability' (Clarke, Gewirtz and McLaughlin, 2000). Governments present management reforms as being at one with a more guiding, less authoritarian, more cooperative, less exclusive role for themselves. In the USA, especially, explicit rhetorical connections have been made between management reform and the legitimacy of the government in the eyes of its citizens. Some of these alleged links are highly questionable (Bok 1997; Norris 1999; Pollitt and Bouckaert, 2000, pp. 142–6). However, it is clear that NPM believers have felt a need to acknowledge and ally themselves with the continuing power of the 'old religion'.

Finally, such an anthropological perspective reopens the question of how reform should be evaluated. If we are dealing with a set of pre-scientific beliefs (NPM), then perhaps an appropriate angle to take would be to ask how this particular set of doctrines helps its priests and followers to protect their interests, reinforce their reputations and maintain social order? But academics should not expect such an investigation to be easy, since its very nature would challenge the paradigm of instrumental rationality upon which NPM (and many successful careers) are so explicitly founded. Within NPM's own terms, such an improved understanding of how its doctrines are propagated would have no 'added value' – it would be 'merely academic'.

References

Aucoin, P. and D. Savoie (1998), *Program Review: Lessons for Strategic Change in Government*, Ottawa, Canadian Centre for Management Development.

Auditor General of Canada (1993), 'Canada's public service reform, and lessons learned from selective jurisdictions', *Report, 1993*, Chapter 6, Ottawa, Auditor General of Canada.

Bok, D. (1997), 'Measuring the performance of government', in J. Nye, P. Zelikow and D. King (eds), *Why People Don't Trust Government*, Cambridge, US: Harvard University Press, pp. 55–76.

Borins, S. (1998), *Innovating with Integrity: How Local Heroes are Transforming American Government*, Washington DC: Georgetown University Press.

Boston, J., J. Martin, J. Pallot and P. Walsh (1996), *Public Management: The New Zealand Model*, Auckland: Oxford University Press.

Bouckaert, G. (1995), 'Charters as frameworks for awarding quality: the Belgian, British and French experience', in H. Hill and H. Klages (eds), *Trends in Public Sector Renewal: Recent Developments and Concepts in Awarding Excellence*, Europaischer Verlag der Wissenschaften, Beitrage zur Politikwissenschaft, Band 58, Frankfurt am Main: Peter Lang, pp. 185–200.

Bouckaert, G. (2000), 'Techniques de modernisation et modernisation des techniques: évaluer la modernisation de la gestion publique', in L. Rouban (ed.), *Le service publique en devenir*, Paris, L'Harmattan, pp. 107–28.

Bouckaert, G. (2001). 'Pride and performance in public service: some patterns of analysis', *International Review of Administrative Sciences*, 67, 9–20.

Bouckaert, G., D. Ormond and G. Peters (2000), *A Potential Governance Agenda for Finland*, Helsinki: Ministry of Finance, Research Report No. 8.

Bouckaert, G. and G. Timsit (2000), *Administrations and Globalisations*, Brussels: International Institute of Administrative Sciences.

Bourgon, J. (1998), *Fifth Annual Report to the Prime Minister on the Public Service of Canada*, Ottawa: Privy Council Office.

Boyne, G. (1998), 'Bureaucratic theory meets reality: public choice and contracting in local government', *Public Administration Review*, 58 [6 (November/December)], 474–84.

Brumby, J., P. Edmonds and K. Honeyfield (1996), 'Effects of public sector financial reform (FMR) in New Zealand', paper presented to the Australasian Evaluation Society Conference, 30 August.

Brunsson, N. (1989), *The Organisation of Hypocrisy: Talk, Decisions and Actions in Organisations*, Chichester: John Wiley.

Budget Department (1997), *Public Sector Productivity in Sweden*, vol. 3, Stockholm: Budget Department, Swedish Ministry of Finance.

Cabinet Office (2000), *Adding It Up: Improving Analysis and Modelling in Central Government*, London: Performance and Innovation Unit, Cabinet Office.

Campbell, D. and J. Stanley (1963), *Experimental and Quasi-Experimental Evaluations in Social Research*, Chicago: Rand McNally.

Chancellor of the Duchy of Lancaster (1997), *Next Steps: Agencies in Government: Review 1996*, Cm3579, London: The Stationary Office.

Christensen, T. and P. Lægreid (1998), 'Administrative reform policy: the case of Norway', *International Review of Administrative Sciences*, 64, 457–75.

Clarke, J., S. Gewirtz and E. McLaughlin (eds) (2000), *New Managerialism, New Welfare?*, London: Sage.

Cochrane, A. (1972), *Effectiveness and Efficiency in Health Care*, London: Provincial Hospitals Trust.

Davies, H., S. Nutley and C. Smith (eds) (2000). *What Works? Evidence-Based Policy and Practice in Public Services*, Bristol: The Policy Press.

Derlien, H.-U. (1998), *From Administrative Reform to Administrative Modernization*, Bamberg: Verwaltungswissenschaftlichte Beitrage 33.

Dorrell, S. (1993), 'Public sector change is a world-wide movement', speech by the Financial Secretary to the Treasury. Stephen Dorrell, to the Chartered Institute of Public Finance and Accountancy, London, 23 September.

Elster, J. (1978), *Logic and Society: Contradictions and Possible Worlds*, New York: Wiley.

Escott, K. and D. Whitfield (1995), *The Gender Impact of CCT in Local Government*, Manchester: Equal Opportunities Commission.

Flynn, N. and Strehl. F. (eds.) (1996), *Public Sector Management in Europe*, London: Prentice Hall/Harvester Wheatsheaf.

Furniss, J. and S. Nutley (2000), 'Implementing what works with offenders – the Effective Practice Initiative', *Public Money and Management*, 20 [4 (October/December)], 23–8.

General Accounting Office (1997), *Performance Budgeting: Past Initiatives Offer Insights for GPRA Implementation*, GAO/AIMD–97–46, Washington DC: GAO, March.

General Accounting Office (1998), *The Results Act: Observations on the Department of State's Fiscal Year 1999 Annual Performance Plan*, Washington DC: GAO/NSIAD–98–210R.

Gore, A. (1996). *The Best-Kept Secrets in Government: A Report to President Bill Clinton*, Washington DC: US Government Printing Office. National Performance Review.

Guyomarch, A. (1999), '"Public service", "public management" and the modernization of French public administration', *Public Administration*, 77[1], 171–93.

Harrison, S. (1998), 'The politics of evidence-based medicine in the UK', *Policy and Politics*, 26[1], 15–31.

Her Majesty's Inspectorate of Probation (1998), *Strategies for Effective Offender Supervision: Report of the HMIP What Works Project*, London: Home Office.

Holkeri, K. and H. Summa (1996), 'Contemporary developments in performance management: evaluation of public management reforms in Finland: from ad hoc studies to a programmatic approach', paper presented to PUMA/OECD, Paris, 4–5 November.

Hood, C. (1991), 'A public management for all seasons', *Public Administration*, 69[1 (Spring)], 3–19.

Hood, C. (1996), 'Exploring variations in public management reform of the 1980s', pp. 268–317, in H. Bekke, J. Perry and T. Toonen (eds.), *Civil Service Systems in Comparative perspective*, Bloomington and Indianapolis, Indiana University Press.

Hood. C. (1998). *The Art of the State: Culture, Rhetoric and Public Management*, Oxford: Oxford University Press.

Hood, C. and M. Jackson (1991), *Administrative Argument*, Aldershot: Dartmouth.

Hupe, P. and L. Meijs (2000), *Hybrid Governance*, The Hague: Social and Cultural Planning Office.

Joss, R. and M. Kogan (1995), *Advancing Quality: Total Quality Management in the National Health Service*, Buckingham: Open University Press.

Kettl, D. (2000), *The Global Public Management Revolution: A Report on the Transformation of Governance*, Washington DC: Brookings Institution.

Kickert, W. (2001), *Public Management Reforms in the Netherlands: Social Reconstruction of Reform Ideas and Underlying Frames of Reference*, Delft: Eburon.

Lægreid, P. and P. Roness (1999), 'Administrative reform as organized attention' in M. Egeberg and P. Lægreid (eds), *Organizing Political Institutions: Essays for Johan P. Olsen*, Oslo: Scandinavian University Press.

Lane, J.-E. (2000), *New Public Management*, London: Routledge.

Loeffler, E. (1995), *The Modernization of the Public Sector in an International Perspective: Concepts and Methods of Awarding and Assessing Quality in the Public Sector in OECD Countries*, Speyer Forschungsberichte 151, Speyer: Forschungsinstitut fur Öffenliche Verwaltung.

Lowndes, V. and C. Skelcher (1998), 'The dynamics of multi-organizational partnerships: an analysis of changing modes of governance', *Public Administration*, 76[2 (Summer)], 313–34.

Maas, G. and F. Van Nispen (1999), 'The quest for a leaner, not a meaner government', *Research in Public Administration*, 5, 63–86.

Meyer, M. W. and V. Gupta (1994), 'The performance paradox', *Research in Organizational Behavior*, 16, 309–69.

Micheletti, M. (2000), 'End of big government: is it happening in the Nordic countries?', *Governance*, 13[2 (April)], 265–78.

Ministerie van Financien (1998), *Verder met resultaat: het agentscapsmodel 1991–1997*, Den Haag: Ministry of Finance.

Murray, R. (1998), 'Productivity as a tool for evaluation of public management reform', paper presented to the European Evaluation Society Conference, Rome, 29–31 October.

National Audit Office (1995), *The Meteorological Office: Evaluation of Performance*, HC693, 25 August, London: HMSO.

National Audit Office (1998), *Benefits Agency: Performance Measurement*, HC952, 25 July, London: The Stationary Office.

National Audit Office (1999), *Government on the Web*, HC87, 15 December, London: The Stationary Office.

Norris, P. (ed.) (1999), *Critical Citizens: Global Support for Democratic Governance*, Oxford: Oxford University Press.

OECD (1993), *Managing with Market-Type Mechanisms*, Paris: PUMA/OECD.

OECD (1997), *In Search of Results: Performance Management Practices*, Paris: PUMA/OECD.

Olsen, J. and G. Peters (eds) (1996), *Lessons from Experience: Experiential Learning in Administrative Reform in Eight Democracies*, Oslo: Scandinavian University Press.

Osborne, D. and T. Gaebler (1992), *Reinventing Government: How the Entrepreneurial Spirit is Transforming the Public Sector*, Reading, US: Addison Wesley.

Packwood, T., C. Pollitt and S. Roberts (1998), 'Good medicine? A case study of business process re-engineering in a hospital', *Policy and Politics*, 26[4 (October)], 401–15.

Pawson, R. and N. Tilley (1997), *Realistic Evaluation*, London: Sage.

Peterson, M. (2000), 'The fate of "big government" in the United States: Not over but undermined?', *Governance*, 13[2 (April)], 251–64.

Pierson, P. (2000), 'Increasing returns, path dependence and the study of politics', *American Political Science Review*, 94[2], 251–67.

Pollitt, C. (1993). *Managerialism and the Public Services: Cuts or Cultural Change?*, 2nd edition, Oxford: Blackwell.

Pollitt, C. (1994), 'The Citizen's Charter: A preliminary analysis', *Public Money and Management*, 14[2], 1–5.

Pollitt, C. (1995), 'Justification by works or by faith? Evaluating the New Public Management', *Evaluation*, 1[2 (October)], 133–54.

Pollitt, C. (2000), 'How do we know how good public services are?' in G. Peters and D. Savoie (eds), *Governance in the 21st Century: Revitalising the Public Service*, Montreal and Kingston: Canadian Centre for Management Development and McGill-Queen's University Press, pp. 119–52.

Pollitt, C. (2001), 'Convergence: The useful myth?', *Public Administration*, 79[4], 933–47.

Pollitt, C. and G. Bouckaert (2000), *Public Management Reform: A Comparative Analysis*, Oxford: Oxford University Press.

Pollitt, C., K. Bathgate, K. A. Smullen and C. Talbot (2001), 'Agency fever? Analysis of an international policy fashion', *Journal of Comparative Policy Analysis*, 3, 271–90.

Premfors, R. (1998), 'Re-shaping the democratic state: Swedish experiences in a comparative perspective', *Public Administration*, 76[1 (Spring)], 141–59.

Prime Minister and Minister for the Cabinet Office (1999), *Modernising Government*, Cm413, London: The Stationary Office.

Rouban, L. (1995), 'The civil service culture and administrative reform', in B. G. Peters and D. Savoie (eds), *Governance in a Changing Environment*, Montreal and Kingston: Canadian Centre for Management Development and McGill-Queen's University Press, pp. 23–54.

Sahlin-Andersson, K. (1996), 'Imitating by editing success: the construction of organizational fields', in B. Czarniawska and G. Sevon (eds), *Translating Organizational Change*, Berlin: de Gruyter, pp. 69–92.

Savoie, D. (1994), *Thatcher, Reagan and Mulroney: In Search of a New Bureaucracy*, Toronto: University of Toronto Press.

Schiavo, L. (2000), 'Quality standards in the public sector: Differences between Italy and the UK in the Citizen's Charter initiatives', *Public Administration*, 78[3], 679–98.

Shadish, W., T. Cook and L. Leviton (1991), *Foundations of Program Evaluation*, London: Sage.

Sharman, Lord (2001), *Holding to Account: The Review of Audit and Accountability for Central Government*, Report by Lord Sharman of Redlynch, London: H. M.Treasury, February.

Shortell, S., J. O'Brien, J. Carman, R. Foster, E. Hughes, H. Boerstler and E. O'Connor (1995), 'Assessing the impact of continuous quality improvement/total quality management: concept versus implementation', *Health Services Research*, 30[2], 377–401.

SIGMA (1999), *European Principles for Public Administration*, SIGMA papers 27, CCNM/SIGMA/PUMA(99)44/REV1, Paris: OECD/SIGMA/PUMA.

Smith, P. (1996), 'On the unintended consequences of publishing performance data in the public sector', *International Journal of Public Administration*, 18[2/3], 277–305.

Steering Group (1991), *Review of State Sector Reforms*, Auckland, 29 November.

Talbot, C. (1996), *Ministers and Agencies: Control, Performance and Accountability*, London: CIPFA.

Task Force on Management Improvement (1992), *The Australian Public Service reformed: an evaluation of a decade of management reform*, Canberra: Management Advisory Board, AGPS.

Thompson, J. (2000), 'Reinvention as reform: Assessing the National Performance Review', *Public Administration Review*, 60[6 (November/December)], 508–21.

Williams, D. (2000), 'Reinventing the proverbs of government', *Public Administration Review*, 60[6 (November/December)], pp. 522–34.

Wollmann, H. (1997), 'Modernization of the public sector and public administration in the Federal Republic of Germany: (Mostly) a story of fragmented incrementalism', in M. Muramatsu and F. Naschold (eds), *State and Administration in Japan and Germany: A Comparative Perspective on Continuity and Change*, Berlin: de Gruyter, pp. 79–103.

Wright, V. (1997), 'The paradoxes of administrative reform', in W. Kickert (ed.), *Public Management and Administrative Reform in Western Europe*, Cheltenham: Edward Elgar, pp. 7–13.

Zbaracki, M. (1998), 'The rhetoric and reality of total quality management', *Administrative Science Quarterly*, 43, pp. 602–36.

3. Evaluating best practice in central government modernization[1]

Werner Jann and Christoph Reichard

In memoriam Frieder Naschold 1940–1999[2]

1. Introduction

This paper summarizes some of the results of a comparative evaluation study dealing with major achievements of central state modernization in different western 'reform-countries'. Unlike other evaluation efforts described in this volume and elsewhere, this project attempts neither to identify modernization trajectories of different countries and their effects, nor to categorize or typologize countries (see Pollitt and Bouckaert [Chapter 2] and Christensen, Lægreid and Wise [Chapter 4] in this volume). Nor does it try to reconstruct the policy process of modernization, to trace and justify agenda setting, to identify the 'drivers of change', to discuss varying concepts and their rational or ideological background, nor to analyse implementation strategies or effects on administrative performance and ultimate outcomes. Finally, its primary interest is not to compare the results of different countries, the reform concepts and/or modernization strategies, nor to rank them by picking winners and losers. Instead, this project aims to identify changes that have already been implemented and that have proven their worth. We are looking at and trying to identify new practices, which have evolved in similar ways in different countries, despite noticeably different administrative traditions, cultures and reform paths. We are attempting to understand and explain these changes. We are well aware that contexts differ widely, that there is a great difference between 'talk' and 'action', and that there are additional defining and independent variables that are not covered by this analysis. We are still convinced that it is possible – and necessary – to learn from the experiences of other countries (see also Christensen and Lægreid 2001, Kettl 2000, Kickert 1997, Loeffler 1995, Pollitt and Bouckaert 2000, Peters and Savoie 1998, Ridley 1996).

We present partial results of the evaluation study that was originally proposed by Frieder Naschold. The basic idea was to establish a team of international experts on public administration and management who would identify key innovations in the field of central government reforms, and to contribute these innovative ideas to the ongoing and recently revived debate in Germany. A team of experts from seven countries, whose experiences were of particular interest to Germany, was selected: Carsten Greve and Lotte Jensen (Denmark), Walter Kickert (Netherlands), June Pallot (New Zealand), Stig Montin (Sweden), Kuno Schedler (Switzerland), Fred Ridley and Morton Davies (United Kingdom), and Don Kettl (United States). Each expert had the task of selecting, describing and analysing the most successful innovations in his or her country, based on a common research framework. The reports from the selected countries were thoroughly discussed at two conferences in Berlin, and a short summary of the most important findings was published in German (Naschold, Jann and Reichard 1999). The following is a brief overview of some of the most interesting findings.[3]

The political and professional debates about public-sector modernization in Germany in the late 1990s initiated the evaluation study. There is a basic consensus among experts that the Federal Republic of Germany is not at the 'forefront' of public-sector modernization (see, for example, the comparative study of Pollitt and Bouckaert 2000, pp. 235 ff.). Administrative reforms inspired by the dominating Anglo-Saxon model of New Public Management (NPM) were not begun until the early 1990s in Germany, and they were undertaken mostly at the local level. Since then there have been significant developments in many municipalities, although the long-term impact is rather mixed and still uncertain (see Jann 1997, 2002; Reichard 1997, 2001; Wollmann 2000). Some federal states (*Länder*) followed suit and began to introduce a number of managerial reforms, though on a much smaller scale; at the federal level, managerial and reformist challenges were ignored for quite some time. Some argue that this was perfectly reasonable, since the federal government was preoccupied with German unification and the transfer of the capital from Bonn to Berlin. Others disagree, claiming that the government should have used these unique 'windows of opportunity' to promote a more radical governmental reform: not only to introduce some managerial spirit into the federal government, but also to implement reforms that have been on the agenda as far back as the 1970s, such as the modernization of personnel and financial management systems and of the traditional structures of federal ministries. It was not until the mid-1990s – towards the end of the conservative-liberal Kohl era – that a somewhat blurred vision of a 'lean state' (*schlanker Staat*) was developed by a blue-ribbon expert commission. However, implementation of the numerous reform proposals was unsystematic and half-hearted, to say the least (Jann and Wewer 1998, König and Füchtner 1998; see also Wollmann, Chapter 7 in this volume).

In September 1998, when the federal government changed from the Kohl regime to the 'red-green' coalition government headed by Gerhard Schröder, there were widespread assumptions – and overly optimistic expectations – about a possible new reform mood and a boost for the German public-sector. Modernists, mostly leftists in favour of a strong, democratic government, saw a chance to strengthen and ultimately rebuild public services through reforms. The conservative-liberal vision of a 'lean state' was replaced by the new vision of the 'activating state'. The political changes seemed to provide a unique opportunity to introduce approaches of 'new' governance and management structures on the central state (*Bund*) and also to some extent at the state (*Länder*) level. This in turn stimulated the idea to undertake a comparative evaluation study in order to gather and analyse innovative developments in different reform-minded countries. To identify 'best practices' and inject these findings into the German discussion could thus provide timely and relevant inputs into the ongoing policy processes and 'advocacy coalitions'.

The study was designed as an evaluation report dealing with the assessment of *implemented* governmental reforms at the central-state level. The selected country reports, which provide the foundation of this study, were to be based, whenever possible, on existing evaluations – performed either by government and auditing agencies, or by scientists and other independent institutions. As much as possible, country studies were to refer to clearly defined policy areas and specific projects, not to general modernization strategies and programmes. The study's focus on evaluation made the major difference. The country reports were to deal with existing innovative practices, and not with concept development and analysis – which still seems to be quite common for 'state of the art' reports on public-sector modernization, especially of the NPM type.

The findings of the country reports have been based on available evaluation studies, official documents, government statements, and other information – including the experience and the informed, critical judgements of the rapporteurs. Team members sought to identify common traits and experiences among the selected countries. Obviously experiences, strategies, successes and failures differed widely, even within the relatively homogeneous sample of 'reform countries'. However, we identified some important common tendencies. We will concentrate on three of the main findings: a new logic of steering at central government level (agencification and contract steering), innovations in the field of personnel (normalization of personnel systems) and public financial management (budgeting and accounting). We will conclude with some observations about implementation strategies (administrative policy) and some general lessons learned from this international cooperative research effort.

2. Agencies and contracts

Nearly all of the seven governments have adopted and implemented some of the well-known concepts and instruments of NPM for the inter- and intra-organizational modernization of ministries and other government authorities. This follows, more or less, the logic of decentralization, performance-oriented contract management and the monitoring of results. These elements, implemented at the level of central government, seem to have successfully altered the relationship between ministries and their subordinated authorities, thus establishing a 'new logic of steering': trying to overcome classical political and bureaucratic control and oversight and moving in the direction of new forms of agencification and contract steering.

In each country surveyed we observe the same general trend: a growing devolution of tasks from ministries and central departments towards – at least in some cases – more independent public, private or hybrid agencies and organizations. In nearly all countries this also entails some form of vertical decentralization towards local governments, regions or other subnational units. Local government systems and federalism differ more widely than do other administrative contexts; we will concentrate on the horizontal devolution of tasks (see Figure 3.1; for a brief overview about new forms of vertical coordination and multi-level management, see Naschold in Naschold, Jann and Reichard 1999). In every country surveyed there is, of course, outsourcing and contracting out of specific services and tasks, privatization – that is, conferring responsibilities and tasks to the private sector – and corporatization (creating hybrid organizations, at least partially owned by the public).

The well-known concepts of contracting out, corporatization and privatization do not really change prevailing organizational arrangements – even though they certainly have an effect on the size of the public-sector. Instead, processes of agencification seem to introduce new elements of steering and control, in particular via the widespread use of contracts and published reports, combined with new forms and more freedom in budgeting and personnel systems at the lower level. It is thus this new relationship between certain 'contract agencies' and their parent departments that is remarkable, not the establishment of new agencies as such. Many countries, like Sweden, have had independent agencies for a long time and are not under pressure to devolve ministerial tasks to agencies, as is the case in the United Kingdom.

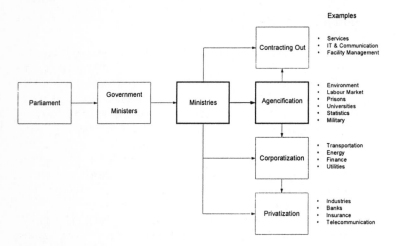

Figure 3.1 Variants of institutional arrangements

Most of the tasks conferred to agencies in Britain have never been in the domain of ministries in Germany (Döhler and Jann 2001). The significant new concept is how these agencies are controlled and steered. The reports demonstrate a broad variety of new contractual relationships in all countries surveyed. There are approximately 150–300 cases on average per country. They can be found not only in the most prominent reform states – Great Britain and the Scandinavian countries – but also in the Netherlands, Switzerland and the United States, and in all kinds of ministries and policy sectors: from education and the labour market to prisons and the military.

The stated objectives of these new institutional arrangements are in many ways the well-known tenets of NPM, that is, more flexibility, transparency of costs and performance, enhanced quality, productivity, efficiency and effectiveness – at the central-government level, between ministries and the rest of public administration. Other more demanding objectives are the limiting of existing independence or even autonomy of government organizations and facilitating the formulation and implementation of new and changing priorities.

Most of the reform countries follow these general strategies:

1. moving from strict, detailed line-item budgeting towards more globalized, result-oriented budgets;
2. changing civil service from classical, unified systems of pay, career and promotion towards more specialized and individualized arrangements for different sectors, agencies and types of personnel; and
3. transferring classical, rule-oriented bureaucratic and hierarchical arrangements in the direction of goal-oriented, flexible, inter-organizational relationships and networks.

The most important and most innovative instrument with which to achieve these elusive goals is the use of contracts between ministries and their subordinated agencies, which are found in nearly all countries surveyed. The form and function of these contracts are relatively similar (see also Fortin and Hassel 2000). The typical contract is a written document, usually signed by the minister and the head of the agency. It is not a formal contract – that is, it is not legally binding – but it contains specific information and agreements about goals and results to be achieved: the quality of services, the time and resources necessary to produce certain outputs, the increase and measurement of productivity, the assessment of customer 'satisfaction' and the evaluation of the output or overall outcome of agencies. Contracts may include agreements about future priorities and posteriorities, the conditions under which these results are to be achieved (that is, laws or other legal frameworks) and especially the resources available (finance, personnel and other assets). Finally, contracts deal with mutual responsibilities and the conditions under which they may be terminated or changed. Usually contracts cover three- to four-year terms and try to define clear results and achievements. They give agencies considerable latitude in their use of resources. Agencies are thus freed from typical restrictions on their use of financial resources and personnel, and also on organizational arrangements and the use of management instruments.

Another important instrument used in conjunction with contractual steering is new forms of reporting. Nearly all countries introduced specific requirements for agencies to deliver yearly reports in a format similar to that of private sector 'business reports'. The aim of the new reporting requirements is to provide internal stakeholders (chief executives, ministries) and external stakeholders (parliament, audit offices, and also citizens and the general public) with a more transparent, comprehensive and reliable picture of the public agencies. The form and content of these agency reports are sometimes stipulated in government regulations. Usually reports must provide information about last year's activities, finances, results (outputs and sometimes outcomes), personnel and organizational changes; some countries also require information about environmental matters, gender streamlining, and so on. In the Scandinavian countries, reports are integrated into the yearly budgeting process. Deviations of expenditures and results from targets have to be explained carefully. Sometimes performance-indicator-based comparisons with other organizations are mandatory. The documents are publicly accessible via the Internet. In some countries, such as Sweden, reports are even evaluated and rated by the national auditing offices.

The main question, of course, remains: What, if any, is the overall effect and outcome of these new contractual arrangements? Again, evaluations and critical summaries in the national surveys show a surprisingly similar picture. Despite conceptual problems and implementation difficulties (see below), the overall picture is encouraging. The available evaluation studies show that contractual steering strengthens efficiency and supports adequate levels of service and quality of government agencies. Furthermore, these studies, which compare 'new' contract agencies with 'old-fashioned' hierarchically-controlled authorities, provide evidence that contract agencies have a clearer goal orientation and have improved productivity. Contract agencies also support other elements of New Public Management, such as cost accounting or personnel management. They also help to create a comprehensive and structured dialogue between departments and agencies. All in all, evaluation shows that contracting strengthens transparency and makes it easier to assess performance and failure.

In nearly all of the countries surveyed, a significant 'cultural change' is one of the most important results observed. Employee attitudes and behaviour became more performance-oriented and efficiency-minded – certainly a more managerial but also a more self-confident pattern.

Contract agencies are becoming more and more attractive to young, ambitious and well-educated employees from traditional ministries, even finance departments – which surely indicates a good measure of success.

It is remarkable that most countries – with the obvious exceptions of New Zealand and the United Kingdom – did not base the introduction of contract agencies on the well-known NPM doctrines of 'principal/agent-theory' and 'purchaser-provider split'. When this was explicitly – and somewhat critically – noted in a OECD-PUMA report, the response of the Danish finance ministry was quite interesting. The Danes argued that contracts were, in their view, an instrument to enable new, more efficient dialogues and consultations between agencies and their parent departments. They were not introduced to enforce more rigid control mechanisms. Contracts are a flexible instrument to promote organizational adjustment and learning, and not to control the subordinated organizations. The overall aim is a better informed and structured dialogue to establish political and financial priorities and posteriorities. As the Danish case study put it, contracts are used in a rather 'soft' version, as a means of communication, signalling governance by *contact* rather than governance by *contract* (see also Jensen 1998).

The same can be said of the Swedish case. Here, overly rationalistic concepts of steering and control are also viewed with some scepticism, in no small part because of the systematically evaluated – and rather sobering – experiences with the Swedish version of PPBS in the 1960s and 1970s. Instead, Swedish reformers stress the flexibility of contract management, which has been found to balance the contradicting demands and interests of politicians and bureaucrats. A rather ad hoc, flexible approach is therefore adequate. Contracts are used to overcome some of the well-known pathologies of bureaucratic control by establishing continuing reports, debates and consultations on the aims, instruments, performance and results of government policies. Relationships between ministries and agencies are built on more than 200 years of Swedish experience with freestanding agencies, and are therefore characterized more by trust than by command and control. Top-down supervision and directing is much less important than the coordination of goals, activities and resources. Again, in the words of the Swedish case study, 'trust bounding' – rather than 'rule bounding' or 'contract bounding' – might be a more appropriate way to characterize the development of the relationships between different institutions in the Swedish welfare state.

Despite these generally positive evaluations there are, of course, severe problems and conflicts hidden in the new steering logic of contract agencies (see also Pollitt et al. 2001). The available independent evaluations, as well as some official reports from audit offices and finance ministries, mention a number of recurring problems:

1. existing contracts are too easy, objectives are not ambitious enough and undemanding;
2. not all stated objectives are achieved (and quite often this has not even been realized by responsible ministries);
3. important activities of agencies are not covered by contracts;
4. objectives are often too specific (with too much details, leading to goal displacement and other traditional bureaucratic responses);
5. objectives are too vaguely formulated which makes it difficult or even impossible to measure their achievement; and
6. quite often there are no penalties for unmet goals and promises.

Beyond these general, well-known shortcomings of contractual management, other specific problems are recognized. In most countries it is obvious that contracts are influenced more by agencies than by their parent departments. Politicians, who are also ministers, are very rarely involved in the actual negotiating of contracts, and in general the interest of political actors (such as parliaments and political parties) and the general public in these arrangements is exceedingly small, to say the least.

On a more technical level, reports are criticized for being too long, too extensive, too descriptive and insufficiently analytical. There is a tendency to bureaucratize the process, to concentrate on pseudo-exact figures, models, and formal requirements, but not on their practical relevance. In many cases, the available data is not the essential or required data. Problems of asymmetrical information might have become more obvious and even more transparent through contractual arrangements, but did not disappear.

Finally, it is obvious that not all organizations are satisfied with contracts. Different participants follow different objectives and agendas when promoting and introducing contracts. Some agencies experienced a loss of autonomy and felt that ministerial control had intensified since the introduction of contracts. Some ministries exercised less control over agencies after the introduction of contracts. Not surprisingly, contractual arrangements deal with differing perceptions of interests and power – who will benefit as a result, and who will lose.

In the end, one might ask whether or not contract management is a new form of public governance. The rather detailed Scandinavian evaluation studies seem to suggest that contract management is probably very seldom found in the pure, technocratic form described in managerial textbooks, but nevertheless in an exceedingly valid and practical form. There is little of the 'hard contracting', with specific, quantifiable objectives and tangible negative or positive sanctions, advocated in the textbook approach. However, a variety of open and systematic processes of negotiating and adjusting objectives, processes, performance, and of shared learning have been observed. Contract management is seen less as a zero-sum game of autonomy and control than as a shared process of learning and adjusting.

3. Normalization of personnel systems

The second overall result of the evaluation study concerns the important and significant changes in the field of personnel management. Most countries have undertaken remarkable efforts in the field of human resource management, and to a large extent, they have renewed and reshaped their civil service systems. At long last, governments seem to have recognized that reform efforts require the active participation and effective motivation of their staff. In nearly all of the reform countries we can observe the following innovations (see also Bossaert et al. 2001):

1. an overall 'normalization' of the civil service, that is, the convergence of public- and private-sector labour regimes and conditions towards a similar and unified system;
2. the decentralization of personnel competencies from central cadre agencies to single ministries and agencies;
3. a more pluralistic recruitment of different professions into civil service positions, such as the recurrent enrolment of economists, political scientists and (public) managers;
4. introduction of performance-based pay concepts and of fixed-term contracts for top bureaucrats;
5. establishment of a specific 'Senior Executive Service' for developing and remunerating top managers in adequate and innovative ways; and
6. new forms of effective downsizing of government personnel.

The most interesting and radical innovation that is particularly evident in Sweden, Switzerland and the Netherlands is the harmonization of the civil-service systems with the general private sector-oriented labour regime of a country ('normalization', as the Dutch call it; see Kickert 2000, pp. 83–7). This is also true for classic European administrative states like France, Italy, Spain and Germany (see Farnham and Horton 2000). The advantage of this paradigmatic change is seen in the opening up of the civil service, and its 'untangling' of an isolated and detached state cadre system. At its core is the reduction of traditional privileges, which are no longer seen as being functional. Normalization is supposed to increase the opportunities for rotation and interchange of personnel between the public and the private sector. It can also contribute to more performance-oriented labour and pay conditions in the public sector, thus promoting equalization, learning and competition between the two sectors.

Among other things, normalization means that most government employees – excepting a small core group of civil servants who may still enjoy specific rights (such as judges, police officers, and special core members of government) – have a 'normal' labour contract. This means that their labour relations are regulated by the common labour laws of their respective states. Employees no longer enjoy lifelong tenure, special pension schemes or other traditional privileges. They are, more or less, treated like the rest of the workforce.

Another consequence of normalization is a more 'normal' way of recruiting and educating personnel for positions in public-sector organizations. Most of the reformist states in our study are recruiting more or less the same professions and qualifications as the private sector. In contrast, classic administrative systems are recruiting and educating their employees in specific, exclusive ways, isolated from the private sector, and making rotation between private and public sectors difficult, if not impossible. This broad mix of professions and the regular exchange of personnel between public and private sectors seem to be an important precondition for a 'cultural change' from bureaucratic to more professional and performance-oriented, managerial values.

Enhancing performance orientation in human resource management is another important topic in leading reform states. Many countries have restructured the incentive system for their public personnel towards more fair assessments and rewards of 'performance'. On the one hand, a broad spectrum of non-monetary incentives is offered, among them clear decision competencies and responsibilities, more challenging tasks, satisfying team contacts and a motivating leadership behaviour.

On the other hand, all states are experimenting with new performance-related pay schemes for leadership personnel.

Several of the reform countries have had positive experiences with a specific Senior Executive Service (SES), which regulates the recruitment, training, compensation, promotion and dismissal of senior executives. Such a system promotes performance orientation at the executive level and makes recruitment of managers – even from the private sector – more competitive. However, existing salary differences between the public and private sectors are still an obstacle to recruiting high potentials into a SES position.

Of course, evaluations and assessments are not always positive. Most of the countries do report positive effects of performance-related pay, but there are also problems, primarily with measuring performance and with the withholding of previously paid bonuses. If criteria are unclear and if bonuses are too small or are available to only a small number of employees, performance-related pay systems generate by far more de-motivation than motivation (OECD 1997). Also, the decentralization of competencies for personal management, recruiting and remuneration is not without its shortcomings. Some evaluation results suggest abuse by managers, especially when they did not have clear competencies or when managers were ill prepared for the new tasks.

A potential pitfall of all these reform strategies is the substitution of job attitudes common in private business for the specific values and ethical attitudes of the traditional civil cervice. The disappearance of traditional civil-service ethics may, in the end, increase the dangers of corruption and opportunistic behaviour. There are some indications that this possibility is not at all unrealistic.

4. Accrual accounting and output budgeting

Finally, financial management systems, particularly accounting, budgeting and financial reporting were identified as useful and necessary instruments for administrative modernization, especially providing governments with an adequate transparency of the financial situation, the consumed resources and existing assets and liabilities. All countries in our study have undertaken serious efforts to renew their financial management systems and practices, and all seem to be on the road to converge their concepts with private-sector and commercial approaches. Two forms of innovation are particularly relevant: the move towards accrual and resource-based accounting concepts, and recent developments in the field of output budgeting.

The majority of 'reform states' have recently, mostly in the last decade, introduced concepts of accrual accounting, that is, an accounting system in which financial transactions are recorded as they are 'accruing' (Olson et al. 1998). In practice this means that the use and consumption of resources, such as investments or human capital, are recorded during their entire time span within the accounting system: such as by depreciation, by calculating capital charges or by recording pension provisions. Such a resource-based accounting system is widely recognized in the private sector, and the main essentials of this system have been transferred – often via common national accounting standards like GAAP (Generally Accepted Accounting Principles) – to the public sector. This system normally contains at least three major components: a cash-flow statement (cash receipts and expenditures), an income statement (comparable to a statement of profits and losses in private business, recording revenues and expenses), and finally a balance sheet (recording all assets and liabilities, including public infrastructure and heritage assets, pension provisions and in most cases also equity).

It is argued that this type of accounting system provides much more information on all kinds of financially relevant transactions and assets than does a traditional cash-based public accounting system. It apprises heads of divisions or sections of the total costs and products of their units, thus providing relevant data for more efficiency-oriented decisions. It furthermore promotes intergenerative justice, because it records the consumption of resources in the period in which the consumption occurred ('accrued'). This seems especially relevant for long-term debts or for future pensions to be paid to civil servants. In fact, this accounting system draws a more realistic picture of the economic and financial situation of a specific public-sector organization or of the government as a whole.

Some of the countries in our study rely entirely on an accrual accounting system, while others employ both accrual and cash systems: accrual accounting for single government departments and agencies, and cash accounting for whole-of-government accounting. Some countries even apply both concepts at the aggregated government level. All in all, there seems to be a clear trend: the international, professional community has more or less agreed on common public-sector accounting principles which coincide with existing private sector principles, with some particularities in evaluating assets or calculating costs. The 'International Public Sector Accounting Standards' (IPSAS) of the International Federation of Accountants are recognized as an almost complete, detailed example. Another interesting trend is the convergence of the accounting and budgeting systems to a common accrual-based standard. In a number of countries (such as New Zealand, Sweden and the United Kingdom), both systems are based on accrual data, that is, on the present and future consumption and creation of resources.

Nearly all of the countries studied have also experimented with flexibility in budget formulation and execution, with output-oriented budget structures. This is definitely not a new trend. For decades, nations have undertaken continuous efforts to change their budgeting concepts from pure input budgeting to output-oriented budgeting variants. The most well-known activities focused on PPBS in the 1960s and 1970s. For several reasons, mostly due to technocratic and rationalistic 'overkill', these early efforts have not been very successful or sustainable. However, within the general NPM movement and its rationalistic underpinnings, governments have rediscovered the challenge of output budgeting and have established new concepts and applications of this kind of budgeting. The budgets of all countries are gradually becoming more globalized, containing comparatively few items and allowing the transfer of funds between items. The central budgets of Sweden and the United States consist of only 500 and 1500 different items, respectively, compared with more than 8000 items in the German federal budget. The trend towards a 'single-line budget' gives financial managers and heads of departments or smaller units more flexibility in decision-making during the budget year.

Another new budgeting concept is multi-year budgeting, specifically introduced in Sweden. From a financial management point of view, it seems highly recommendable not to rely solely on one-year budgets, but to make mid-term financial commitments and developments more transparent. However, this type of budgeting requires a high level of discipline on the part of political decision-makers to stay within the agreed-upon multi-year items. The secret of the Swedish case seems to lie in a generally accepted procedure: the parliament first decides on the total volume and maximum expenditure levels ('landmarks') of each ministerial budget before detailing the appropriations.

In every country studied we find remarkable opportunities for making budget execution more flexible. For the most part, the transfer of appropriations between different items within the same product group is no longer restricted. Furthermore, carrying over of financial resources to the following budget year is, with some limitations, generally possible and acceptable. Some systematic evaluation studies (mostly from the Scandinavian countries) prove that flexibility of budget execution can lead to remarkable efficiency gains.

Product- or program-oriented structures of the central state budget can be found in certain countries (OECD 2000). Political decision-makers are provided with output and impact target data, related budget appropriations, and information about how these targets have been met. Basically, parliament is to decide upon a global amount of money to be allocated to a certain agency or product group. The governmental department (ministry or agency) can then distribute these resources in a flexible manner within the margins of the budget and the framework of set targets.

More flexibility in budget execution is accompanied by strict regulations concerning financial reporting. Politicians and top executives who are ultimately responsible for the budget want to have sufficient knowledge of the financial status and the intended results to be achieved. Thus, several countries – such as New Zealand, Sweden or Denmark – have established comprehensive 'whole-of-government' and agency reports that include all relevant data concerning programmes, activities, costs, cash flows, assets and liabilities (see above, the section on 'reporting').

The available evidence also suggests some problems and shortcomings. On the one hand, several crucial factors – such as naïve technocratic and rationalistic assumptions concerning political decision-making – that plagued the first budgeting experiment three decades ago, are still applicable today. The more flexible and output-oriented budgeting is, the more the classic instruments of political control and influence become obsolete. 'Innovative' instruments of controlling are not yet fully developed. Furthermore, decentralized and globalized budgeting exacerbates the problems of fragmentation and coordination. On the other hand, the actual output budgeting – compared with preceding systems – is integrated into a more comprehensive concept of public management, and is more streamlined because of its lump-sum characteristic. Therefore, output budgeting seems to be more realistic and viable than it was thirty years ago. Obviously globalized budgeting is only feasible if it is coupled with an informative monitoring and reporting system.

The same holds true for the new system of accrual accounting. It offers additional and more realistic information about the short- and long-term use of public resources, but it reduces the opportunities for control by finance ministries, by parent ministries of agencies and by parliament. Because it offers viable choices in evaluating assets, liabilities and future resource consumption, this concept allows more and better opportunities to manipulate accounts. It is therefore not as clear-cut and definitive as a cash-based accounting system, and it is obviously much more ambitious in its demands on accountants and on daily operations.

5. Lessons learned?

What, if anything, can be learned from these examples of 'best practice'? First of all, we can see that certain innovations at the central-state level are working – at least in certain respects, and under certain conditions. Reforms never work exactly as intended. There are always problems of assessment, of causal relationships and of unintended consequences. But reforms do have effects, and some of these effects are positive. It is obvious that success stories about reform concepts, initiatives and evaluations ought to be viewed with the utmost scepticism. No organizational change of even modest complexity will happen without the most common of all social phenomena: unintended and even counterintuitive processes and results. Still, this does not imply that change is impossible or that outputs and results are random.

'Best practice' is hard to identify and can never be understood and explained without a thorough understanding of its context. Some countries, such as Denmark, are drawing their own conclusions, sometimes even identifying quasi-official 'best practice'. It is evident that other countries can learn from these experiences and from beneficial practices. By trying to identify, understand and learn from 'success stories', even though the success may be modest or debatable, we can gain 'usable' knowledge concerning institutional policies, their conceptual framework and probable effects (Lindblom and Cohen 1979). Underlying evidence and causal assumptions about their success may be somewhat shaky, but they allow us to draw lessons in our own context.

The second apparent lesson is that contexts differ. Our administrations probably are much more diverse than our private companies, especially in a 'globalized' world. In particular, political and administrative systems of different states differ so much that all simple lessons are false because all simple causal relationships are 'over-determined'. We should be rather suspicious of all comprehensive models with deceptively simple, cookie-cutter approaches to good government and governance. However, if we realize that contexts differ and that outcomes depend on many variables and influences, we certainly can still draw valid lessons from the experiences of others. This is particularly true if lessons from good practice are perceived as being useful to policy-makers, if they provide information based on empirical data and if they are adopted in an incremental approach (see Thoenig, Chapter 11 in this volume).

Some conclusions drawn from the different implementation strategies and administrative policies of the reform countries may be used as a final example. In nearly all of our cases, reforms appear to be more successful if they are coordinated and implemented by important central actors, usually either by the finance ministry or, even better, by the centre of government. A clear reform and communication strategy seems to help demonstrate to participants and observers that administrative modernization is high on the political agenda and that important political actors care. The Netherlands case is an exception (Kickert 2000). It is, for obvious reasons, not an easy strategy to transfer to Germany, owing to its highly fragmented, consensus-oriented, legalistic political and administrative system. Still, it benefits us to look at these other experiences as we design a viable implementation strategy.

Another lesson concerns the availability of evaluation studies. One of the findings of our comparative study is the unequal distribution of available evaluations of the ongoing modernization projects. Put rather crudely, there is a clear north-south divide. In Scandinavia there is quite a remarkable number of systematic evaluations of governmental reforms available, although they are not always sufficient and 'state-of-the-art'. Some of these evaluations have been done by government agencies – usually by finance ministries or auditing offices – but there are also more independent evaluations by scientists and research organizations. For instance, between 1994 and 1998, Denmark's ministry of finance performed no less than six evaluations of contract agencies: one very comprehensive study from the National Audit Office and six empirical evaluation studies from independent academic institutions (for evaluative activities in New Zealand, see John Halligan, Chapter 5 in this volume). Some of these studies, also from official sources, apply a comparative research design (trying to compare, for example, contract agencies with traditional ones) or attempt systematic before-and-after assessments of performance and productivity. Obviously, the observed degrees of openness of bureaucrats towards (at times disappointing) evaluation data can also be seen as an indicator of different 'evaluation cultures', of a more empirical/incremental culture in Scandinavia and a more prescriptive/rationalistic culture in the Anglo-Saxon countries.

We conclude with a word about the design of this research project. National experts gave their own subjective assessment of concepts, strategies and results, based on a common framework and questionnaire, and then thoroughly discussed the results with each other. If we agree that contexts are of utmost importance, that effects are difficult to measure, and that causal assumptions are unreliable, this seems to be an appropriate and reliable way of conducting a comparative research project. In the end, we cannot deliver tested and quantified research results. Both the assessment of national experiences and successes and the overall appraisal of comparative findings rely heavily on the knowledge, experience and informed judgement of individual researchers. Although it is dependent on the individual assessments of these researchers, such comparative research seems to be more informative – at least for policy advice – than other forms of pseudo-exact investigations. If Frieder Naschold would have been with us to complete this research project, we are sure our conclusions would have been somewhat different and, probably, more courageous.

References

Bossaert, D. et al. (2001), *Civil Services in the Europe of Fifteen: Trends and New Developments*, Maastricht: Europ. Inst. of Public Administration.

Christensen, T. and P. Lægreid (eds) (2001), *New Public Management*, Aldershot: Ashgate.

Döhler, Marian and Werner Jann (2002), Germany, in *Distributed Public Governance: Agencies, Authorities and other Government Bodies*, Paris: OECD, pp. 97–112.

Farnham, David and Sylvia Horton (2000), The flexibility debate, in: Farnham, David and Sylvia Horton (eds), *Human Resources Flexibilities in the Public Services*, Houndsmills, London, pp. 3–22.

Fortin, Y. and H. van Hassel (eds) (2000), *Contracting in the New Public Management*, Amsterdam: IOS Press.

Jann, Werner (1997), 'Public management reform in Germany: A revolution without a theory?', in W. J. M. Kickert (ed.), *Public Management and Administrative Reform in Western Europe*, Cheltenham: Edward Elgar, pp. 59–80.

Jann, Werner (2003), 'State, administration and governance in Germany – Competing traditions and dominant narratives', in *Public Administration*, pp. 95–118.

Jann, Werner and Göttrik Wewer (1998), 'Helmut Kohl und der "schlanke Staat": Eine verwaltungspolitische Bilanz', in Göttrik Wewer (ed.), *Bilanz der Ära Kohl: Christlich-liberale Politik in Deutschland 1982–1998*, Opladen: Leske und Budrich, pp. 229–66.

Jensen, L. (1998), 'Interpreting new public management: The case of Denmark', *Australian Journal of Public Administration*, pp. 54–65.

Kettl, D. (2000), *The Global Public Management Revolution: A Report on the Transformation of Governance*, Washington: Brookings Institution Press.

Kickert, W.J.M. (ed.) (1997), *Public Management and Administrative Reform in Western Europe*, Cheltenham: Edward Elgar.

Kickert, W.J.M. (2000), *Public Management Reforms in The Netherlands*, Delft: Eburon.

König, Klaus and Natascha Füchtner (2000), *'Schlanker Staat' – eine Agenda der Verwaltungsmodernisierung im Bund*, Baden-Baden: Nomos.

Lindblom, Charles E. and David K. Cohen (1979), *Usable Knowledge: Social Sciences and Social Problem Solving*, New York and New Haven: Yale Univ. Press.

Löffler, E. (1995), *The Modernization of the Public Sector in an International Perspective: Concepts and Methods of Awarding and Assessing Quality in the Public Sector in OECD Countries*, Forschungsbericht No 151, Speyer: Hochschule für Verwaltungswissenschaften.

Naschold, Frieder, Werner Jann and Christoph Reichard (1999), *Innovation, Effektivität, Nachhaltigkeit: Internationale Erfahrungen zentralstaatlicher Verwaltungsreform*, Berlin: Sigma.

OECD (1997), *Performance Pay Schemes for Public Sector Managers: An Evaluation of the Impacts*, Paris: OECD.

OECD (2000), *Accrual Accounting and Budgeting Practices in Member Countries: Overview*, PUMA/SBO (2000)11 – Paper, Paris: OECD.

Olson, O. et al. (eds) (1998), *Global Warning: Debating International Developments in New Public Financial Management*, Oslo: Cappelen Akad. Forlag.

Peters, B. G. and D. J. Savoie (eds) (1998), *Taking Stock: Assessing Public Sector Reforms*, Montreal: McGill-Queen's Univ. Press.

Pollitt, Christopher and Geert Bouckaert (2000), *Public Management Reform. A Comparative Analysis*, Oxford: University Press.

Pollitt, C. et al. (2001), 'Agency fever? Analysis of an international policy fashion', *Journal of Comparative Policy Analysis: Research and Practice*, pp. 271–90.

Reichard, C. (1997), 'Neues Steuerungsmodell: Local reform in Germany', in W. Kickert (ed.), *Public Management and Administrative Reform in Western Europe*, Cheltenham: Edward Elgar, pp. 59–79.

Reichard, C. (2001), 'New approaches to public management', in K. König and H. Siedentopf (eds), *Public Administration in Germany*, Baden-Baden: Nomos, pp. 541–56.

Ridley, F. (1996), 'The new public management in Europe: Comparative perspectives', *Public Policy and Administration*, pp. 16–29.

Wollmann, Hellmut (2000), Local government modernization in Germany: Between incrementalism and reform waves, in: *Public Administration*, Vol. 78, No. 4, 915–36.

Notes

1. This is a revised version of an article originally published in *Revista Internacional de Estudos Políticos*, September 2001, 93–111.
2. The original project was conceived by Frieder Naschold, Director of the Centre for Social Science Research Berlin, whose untimely and tragic death in 1999 is the main reason the final report and the publication of all findings has been delayed. The full title of the project is 'Central State Governmental Reform – International Best Practice Experiences for the Future Modernization of State and Administration in Germany'. The project was financed by a generous grant from the Hans-Boeckler Foundation, the foundation of the German trade unions.
3. The final report of the evaluation study is forthcoming.

4. Evaluating public management reforms in central government: Norway, Sweden and the United States of America[1]

Tom Christensen, Per Lægreid and Lois R. Wise

1. Introduction

This chapter focuses on the way public management reforms are evaluated in Norway, Sweden, and the United States. Elsewhere we have shown that the three countries vary in the extent to which they have been receptive to reforms in the new public management tradition, the alacrity with which they have embraced such changes, and the strength of alternative normative drivers of administrative reform (Christensen, Lægreid and Wise 2001, 2002; Wise 2002). Thus a next step is to study how they have evaluated the consequences of public management reform. This chapter will show that the three countries also vary in their receptivity to using evaluation as an instrument for understanding the consequences of planned changes as well as in their likelihood of using different types of evaluation research. Just as differences in cultural, political, and institutional contexts account for the way different nations receive and transform public management practices, countries can be distinguished by the way their cultures affect ways of knowing and reasoning processes, which in turn accounts for their willingness to use different methods of assessment and evaluation.

Polity features – political and administrative structural conditions – offer some potential for variation among the three countries. Norway and Sweden are consensus-oriented systems, typically characterized by negotiation and compromise in policy formulation. Their approaches to government reform can best be described as pragmatic and incremental (Olsen 1996). Compared with Sweden, responsibility for administrative changes in Norway has traditionally been sector-based and fragmented (Christensen and Lægreid 1998a). The US federal system, with its complex division of power among the levels of government and checks and balances among the branches, limits development of a uniform administrative policy. Certain structural features may shift evaluation efforts into a political, bargaining, and interpretative process. Complex reforms and unstable political contexts with shifting minority factions might have spillover effects on the evaluation process enhancing the bargaining and symbolic elements of evaluation. Evaluation is more than an objective fact-finding process, and it involves strategic use of politically significant information (Behn 1980; Olsen 1996; Brunsson and Olsen 1993; Gunvaldsen and Karlsen 1999).

Environmental factors – encompassing economic conditions, normative pressure for reform from allied countries and international organizations – also distinguish the three cases and may account for variations in their receptivity to different reforms and, in turn, to conduct evaluations (Ahlenius 2000). The national economic situation distinguishes the three cases; Sweden has experienced significant economic downturns and cutbacks in public spending in modern times, whereas no similar economic pressure was experienced in Norway or the United States. Fiscal stress may increase the salience of effectiveness information. These features may account for differences in the role central governments take in the evaluation of administrative reforms.

Moreover, the concept of cultural context provides insight into the differences among the three countries in their use of evaluative research. Culture affects reasoning processes and logic, as well as the extent to which behavior reflects a need for harmony with others and interpersonal relations prioritize groups or single individuals (Bennett 1990). Both Norway and Sweden can be classified as high-context cultures, whereas the United States is more accurately categorized as a low-context culture. This means, for example, that actors in the Nordic countries would be more likely to rely on intuitive understandings and less likely to rely on fact-based and analytical reasoning in making decisions or evaluating information than would members of a low-context, individualistic society like the United States. In contrast, among North Americans, meanings are less likely to be considered contextual, causality is more likely to be viewed as unambiguous, and relationships between cause and effect are more likely to be seen as a way of fact-finding. These cultural attributes would have the effect of making researchers in low-context, individualistic societies like the United States more receptive to evaluative research in general and to formal evaluation research designs in particular. Using the same framework, we might anticipate that critical evaluations of public policies or programs could be considered out of sync (or discordant) in collectivist cultures and the norm of remaining in harmony with others might reduce the frequency of critical research studies and evaluations. Critical evaluative research would be inhibited to the extent that a high-sync collectivist culture promotes the idea that once a decision is taken, criticism is no longer appropriate.

Cultural values in an administrative agency or society might undermine or enhance the value of 'objective' indicators as evidence of program-worthiness. Similarly, countries differ in their inclination towards rationalism and traditions for gathering information. Some of the more independent efforts from the research community, for example, could be more open-ended and unpredictable – and the findings could be available to different actors, who might use the results to promote their interests. Cultural contexts matter to the extent that context affects ways of knowing and the reasoning process. Cultural context might also explain why some actors would be more likely to rely on intuitive understandings and be less likely to rely on fact-based and analytical reasoning in making decisions or evaluating information.

If we think of evaluation as a political-administrative process, and not primarily as a technical one, different kinds of evaluations can be seen as fulfilling different functions (Vedung 1995). It is generally recognized that cultural and political forces influence whether or not evaluations are undertaken and, in turn, whether or not the findings of such efforts are put into use. There are many reasons formal evaluations of program impacts should not be undertaken. In cases in which the evaluators are compromised, the activity can merely manipulate symbols, whitewash activities, or try to present the administrative units in the best possible light. In some cases political and administrative leaders see control as the main purpose of evaluation efforts. Evaluations may create an environment or event that promotes efforts to negotiate between different political or administrative interests.

Before embarking on a review of evaluation practices in the three countries, we provide a brief discussion of approaches to evaluation as a framework for understanding differences among the three cases. The next section provides information about the extent to which each of three countries has used different evaluation mechanisms. The last section draws conclusions about evaluation practice in the three cases.

2. Approaches to evaluation

In none of these countries do we observe the sort of broad-based evaluation of a program of reform that Pollitt and Bouckaert describe in Chapter 2. The cases do provide examples, however, of the fact that evaluation of public reforms can take many forms and be organized and institutionalized in different ways. Some typologies of formal evaluation studies assume that all evaluation requires judgment and determinations of the extent to which specified objectives have been achieved, and characterize evaluation studies according to their validity and reliability (Suchman 1967). Evaluation studies can also be categorized more loosely: for example, into the two different types Thoenig suggests in Chapter 11. In this approach, the label 'quasi-evaluation' is applied to those studies that involve information gathering but do not judge success or cause and effect. Most performance audits and process evaluations would fall into the quasi-evaluation category. Process evaluation tracks the extent to which programs or practices were put into place as intended and monitors how implementation has progressed. From a political or administrative perspective, it may be useful to determine how efficiently activities are undertaken or resources are utilized, and process evaluations serve that purpose (Vedung 1997). A substantial amount of research activity appears to fall outside the range of either quasi- or true evaluation; these efforts involve studies that critically examine reform initiatives but meet neither the design standards of a formal evaluation research study nor the information-gathering requirements of so-called quasi-evaluations. But since they are so common and affect the way reform initiatives are interpreted, they should not be overlooked as an element in the body of knowledge of the consequences of public management reform.

Evaluation efforts can also be distinguished by the way they are executed, as Wollmann notes in Chapter 7. A standard distinction used in different countries is based on whether internal or external actors execute the evaluation. Independent government authorities may be responsible for auditing or evaluation activities. In Norway and Sweden a national audit bureau conducts studies of government-wide operations; in the United States the same responsibility is held by the General Accounting Office. Internal evaluations may be conducted within the agencies themselves or by other overseeing bodies. External evaluations can also be conducted by special commissions or committees, by independent research think tanks or private consultants, or by the research community. These activities might be sponsored by (or independent of) government agencies and public funds.

3. Examples of public management reform evaluation activities in three countries

This section reviews efforts to study and evaluate public management reforms in the three cases and provides some information about the forms of evaluation used in the different cases. By reform we mean planned change, and thus exclude other studies of administrative practice as well as studies of the strength of democratic and other normative values. We focus on empirical studies of the consequences of change in central government. As the summaries reveal, substantial differences exist among the three cases in the extent to which they use evaluation as an instrument.

Norway
Although auditing of public programs has a relatively long history in Norway, the use of social science methods to evaluate public programs is more recent. Since the mid-1990s there has been a revitalization of the National Audit Office (*Riksrevisjonen*), and it is now the biggest audit office in the Scandinavian countries: its two performance audit units comprise 125 positions. Performance-based auditing began to complement financial auditing in the national audit bureau during the 1990s (Gunvaldsen and Karlsen 1999). Performance auditing is controversial because it can be seen as interfering with ongoing political processes and influencing the relationship between the executive and legislative powers (Christensen, Lægreid and Roness 2002). On average, the National Audit Office submits ten performance audit reports per year to the *Storting* (Parliament).

In-house evaluation of reforms in Norway is very much connected to the functioning of the MBO (management by objectives) system, but other reforms such as structural devolution and the contract system for top civil servants have also been evaluated. One of the main agencies undertaking this kind of evaluation is the Directorate of Management (*Statskonsult*). This system is connected to the formal obligations of administrative units to draft yearly plans, to the formal letter they receive from the political and administrative leadership about goals and resources, to formal and informal meetings and dialogue about the plan, and to the monitoring system. An in-house evaluation of a new performance management reporting system in the post-1997 state budget, administered by the Ministry of Finance, concluded that this system has generally been too complicated and bureaucratized; it is now being simplified.

There is also a pattern of evaluation of sector-specific policy reforms initiated by the relevant ministry or the research council and conducted by external research groups or institutes. Examples are evaluations of different educational reforms and local government reforms (Baldersheim and Ståhlberg 1994; Bleiklie 1998; Kyvik 1999; Kvalsund 1999), as well as a research program set up to evaluate the ongoing reform of the Norwegian system of universities and colleges. Also, large institutional reorganizations have been evaluated: the establishment of the single Research Council of Norway was evaluated by an international group in 2002.

Norway experimented with local government home rule in the late 1980s, which was the focus of several scholarly studies. The Norwegian evaluation of free commune projects reputedly has been more systematic than that of any Scandinavian country (Baldersheim and Ståhlberg 1994). There is generally a tradition in Norway of evaluating different reforms on the local and regional levels rather than on the national level; these evaluations often are conducted by different research units located within the different regions. One example of this is a large research program conducted by the Research Council of Norway to evaluate the new Norwegian Local Government Act of 1992 (Bukve and Offerdal 2002).

Social scientists have contributed to the body of knowledge about administrative reforms. A broad external study of the MBO system seems to indicate that the goals of the reform were difficult to fulfill in practice (Christensen and Lægreid 1998a). Civil servants reported that the reform increased goal clarity and distinctions between means and results, but apart from that, few of the promised major changes were realized. Civil servants were particularly reluctant to accept some of the more typical market-oriented elements of NPM, which are connected to MBO and which focus on control of economic factors. Also, the system of management by objectives and results has been hard to fulfill in practice due to difficulties in isolating outcomes and rewarding good performance (Berg-Helgesen 2001; Ørnsrud 2000); furthermore, the relationship between structural forms of affiliation and different values are looser than promised by reformers (Grønlie 2001; Wik 2001). The conclusion drawn from evaluations by the research community is that the NPM proposition – that more emphasis on market and management leads to greater efficiency – has to be modified and specified. For instance, the new contract system for top civil servants has a weak empirical foundation and there is no robust and clear answer to the question of whether reform is really working as promised (Lægreid 2001).

Norway has no tradition of commissions evaluating the results and effects of public reform. However, the country has been judged as having a strong empirically-oriented tradition of independent researchers studying administrative reforms based on both organization and democratic theory, using both qualitative and quantitative data, and producing critical assessments of government performance (Christensen and Lægreid 1998b, March 1997). In the area of evaluative research, however, Norway was ranked third – after the United States and Sweden – by one comparative study (Derlien 1990). One of the main research strategies for external evaluations has been to put the reforms into a broader political-democratic context and to analyze the effects of administrative reforms on the political-administrative decision-making system (Christensen and Lægreid 2001).

Unlike the United States, Norway has no series of public employee attitudinal surveys; however, opinion research is undertaken by the research community and captures civil servants' beliefs and attitudes about the consequences of reform efforts. University-based research on public administration in Norway has challenged the one-sided economic analysis of public administration reforms, in which the private sector is so readily adopted as a model for public-sector organizations. Instead, the tasks of public administration have been characterized and analyzed on the basis of a democratic-political perspective, in which the value-, interest-, knowledge- and power-bases of the public-sector have been emphasized (Olsen 1996).

Normative standards used by researchers in political science for evaluating reforms have been linked to the questions of whether the definition of and relationship between political and administrative leadership roles are changing with the reforms, whether there is a real devolution of authority to lower levels and institutions in the governmental structure, whether change is apparent in the balance of influence towards economic and commercial arguments and signals, and to what degree the relationship between the civil service and some main actors in the environment (such as the parliament, interest groups or international actors) has been changed (Christensen and Lægreid 2001, 2002). Studies focusing on norms connected to political-democratic questions have, however, been supplemented with studies emphasizing other standards, such as whether the reforms are efficient (Sørensen et al. 1999).

The main picture of Norway is one of relatively little evaluation activity within government, late introduction of performance auditing, and reliance on critical assessments from the research community as a basis for understanding the consequences of administrative reform. This low level of emphasis on evaluation is consistent with expectations based on Norway's cultural context. Evidence of sector-specific evaluation activity is consistent with Norway's structural and political features and a sector-based reform implementation strategy.

Sweden

Audits of public agencies have a relatively long history in Sweden. Financial audits and process evaluations of public policies and programs have been common in Sweden at least since the 1960s and 1970s (Ahlenius 2000; Brunsson 1995; Wittrock 1984).

Several different agencies conduct evaluations within government. Two of these, the National Audit Board[2] (*Riksrevisionsverket [RRV]*) and the smaller Parliamentary Auditors (*Riksdagens Revisorer*), was merged into one agency (*Riksrevisionen*) reporting to the *Riksdag* (Parliament) in January 2003. The RRV, which currently reports to the government, has a staff of about 250 employees and conducts about 20 scheduled audits of agency- or ministry-level performance per year (Sweden National Audit Office 2002). During the 1990s, individuals with competence in social science research methods were increasingly brought into the agency and the scope of its research expanded beyond expenditure analysis. The Performance Audit Department within the RRV investigates and promotes efficiency and effectiveness in government activities. Its audit authority pertains to all state agencies and any companies or foundations financed or controlled by the government. The RRV independently decides which agencies or organizations to audit, as well as which questions are to be investigated and by what methods.

Evaluations and audits of public programs are also conducted by the Swedish Agency for Public Management (*Statskontoret*),[3] which defines its mission as conducting studies and evaluations at the request of the government and government agencies. Within this agency, the Department of Evaluation (*Enheten för utvärderingsfrågor [ESV]*) makes comparisons among national organizations – and between Sweden and other countries – and benchmarks performance.

The staff of the Ministry of Finance (*Finansdepartementet*), which has overall responsibility for coordinating public management reforms, are also engaged in evaluation efforts. The Swedish National Financial

Management Authority (*Ekonomistyrningsverket [ESV]*), which was established in 1998 and which has over 200 employees overall, has one unit that conducts financial and performance management audits using a specific rating system. ESV is undertaking a pilot program for benchmarking agency performance and is developing benchmarking networks within the public-sector.

Sweden received relatively high marks in a comparative study of evaluation activities in eight countries, including the United States and Norway (Derlien 1990). Comprehensive and formal evaluations have become more common, and higher interest in and knowledge of evaluation have increased the level of ambition (Rombach and Sahlin-Andersson 1995). But evidence of the use of rigorous evaluation research designs is slim (Sandahl n.d.; Sweden, Statskontoret 2000). The development of a body of evaluative research pertaining to public management reform may have been hampered both by a prevailing preference for economic theories over management theories as models for public administration research and by the strong preference among Swedish political scientists for local and regional government research (Jørgensen 1996). The long absence of a tradition of formal evaluative research on public management reforms may partly reflect the nature of a relatively small political state in which key stakeholders participate in the development of programs and policies and consider themselves knowledgeable about program implementation. Nowadays, demands for feedback and reporting have increased; this can be attributed in part to the introduction of the use of formal letters of regulation, which serve as written contracts between agencies and government and which typically contain requirements for reporting on agency performance. At the same time, as a consequence of decentralization, instead of overseeing program implementation, many national government agencies have been left mainly with the evaluative responsibilities for public programs (Wise, Amnå, and Sinclair 1994).

Some studies follow the implementation process for public programs and policies to provide assurance that measures are on track or to identify opportunities for course corrections. The great majority of 'evaluation' studies lack evaluative criteria and are merely accounts of implementation activities (Sweden, Statskontoret 2000). Similar assessments of evaluation rigor come from the National Audit Office (Sandahl n.d.). One interpretation of this pattern is that individuals are reluctant to make critical assessments (Jonzon and Wise 1989; Sandahl n.d.; Statskontoret 2000), which would be consistent with Bennett's theory of cultural context as presented earlier. An overview of existing research found that individual agencies are the greatest producers of reports on budget performance, but the Swedish Agency for Public Management (*Statskontoret*) is the most frequent author of studies involving evaluations of central administration or related areas, special commissions are somewhat less common, and external consultants the least common providers. The body of work can be characterized as largely descriptive accounts and audits leading to recommendations about future directions and best practices, with some critical assessments of policies or practices. One detailed analysis finds that expenditures drove management reforms, rather than the other way around (Sweden, Ministry of Finance 1997). As Pollitt and Bouckaert note in Chapter 2, saving money is one of the main motives of New Public Management style reforms.

During the mid-1990s, the Swedish Agency for Government Employers (SAGE) sponsored a series of empirical studies to explore issues related to different reform strategies and to assess the impact of implemented reforms from the perspective of different stakeholders. These studies looked for normative consequences of reform as well as effectiveness gains. One study found that assumed hindrances to public management reform were not perceived as significant deterrents to change by managers (Wise and Gallup 1995; Wise 1999). Studies grounded in psychology provided the impetus for training materials and events for managers with new responsibility for salary setting. The investigations also provided support for implementation of individualized pay as well as evidence that managers were using the discretion delegated to them to set pay, indicated change in the prevailing work culture and acceptance of pay reform among the majority of employees, and found little evidence of anticipated perceptions of inequality between the sexes (Wise and Gallup 1995, 1996). Differences in implementation strategies were found across branches of government and perceived inequalities related to agency size and resources were identified. SAGE attempted to respond to some of these issues by providing different means of access to information and consultation to smaller units, including employee mobility assignment.

An interesting evaluation approach is the use of reform laboratories in Sweden. For example, the 'Free Communes' initiative, which was in effect from 1984 to 1991 and devolved home rule to local governments, was implemented on an experimental basis and then made into law in 1992. A government-appointed investigator reported on the consequences of the experiment. As Häggroth (1994: 1860) notes, although it was not a formal evaluation, that documentation became part of the political evaluation, which led to the continuation of the experiment and subsequent revision of the Local Government Act. Similarly, beginning in 1985, budgetary reforms were implemented in a few agencies, then evaluated before being applied throughout government (Brunsson 1995); more recently, ESV has been testing an agency benchmarking system on a pilot basis.

The traditional research 'commission system' is a central part of Sweden's evaluation culture. Vedung (1997) labels the use of ad hoc policy commissions as a Swedish stakeholder model, in which the stakeholders conduct the evaluation and take responsibility for its results. The RRV is typically commissioned to conduct five or six special evaluations per year (RRV 2002). The parliament may establish commissions to evaluate a specific aspect of public management reform that may be executed by the Parliamentary Auditors or by external consultants. During the 1980s, the government undertook two national investigations concerning management and issues of democratic control that led to greater emphasis on results analysis and more demands for evaluation of state agency operations (Sjölund 1994). In 1995, the Public Administration Policy Commission was charged with the task of providing a review and evaluation of how public administration functions in Sweden. The evaluation served as the basis for the government's continuation of public management reform. A commission charged with evaluating the consequences of the 1994 reorganization that created the Swedish Agency for Government Employers recently reported its findings: the new policies for wage development have functioned well but the agency should be reorganized to play a more effective role in the bargaining process (Reberg 2002). A government commission, the Expert Group on the Public Sector (EFO), provides regular reports on productivity in government activities over time. These investigations are widely disseminated and typically become part of the debate on future steps in public management reform.

The research community also originates external evaluations that contribute to the body of knowledge, mainly through critical assessments of reform rather than formal research evaluation research designs. Scholars differ in their views of the appropriate criteria for studying the effects of public-sector reforms. On one side is a group that looks for indicators of increased productivity and inculcation of market-based principles in public-sector management. On the other side is a group that argues that indicators of legitimacy, transparency and public support of government institutions and programs are key criteria in determining the success or failure of these efforts (for example, Ahlenius 2000; Sjölund 1994; Vedung 1997).

We find evidence in recent years of a growing interest among the re- search community in social science-based evaluations of public man- agement reforms in general (Vedung 1997), and (as in Norway) in the areas of health care and education management reforms in particular (Aidermark 2001; Bentsen et al. 1999; Ekholm 2000; Nilsson and Wahlen 2000; Rombach and Sahlin-Andersson 1995; Segerholm 2001). As is true in Norway, there is an ongoing evaluation of higher education administrative reforms. Sjölund's (1994) comparative study of the early implementation of market-based pay in four government authorities demonstrated flaws in the implementation of the bonus schemes and ambiguity about the conditions under which bonuses would be re- ceived. A few studies examine the effect of reforms designed to intro- duce market mechanisms and expand competition at different levels of government (Kumbhakar and Hjälmarsson 1998; Neij 2001). Another study of market reforms in the public sector concludes that the reforms have a positive effect on the citizens' free choice of public services, but the efficiency effects are lower than assumed by the reform advocates and they have effects of 'creaming' and of creating social segregation (Blomqvist and Rothstein 2000). Studies in the health care field indi- cate that market reforms had some positive productivity effects in hos- pitals (Jonsson 1996) and that the introduction of performance auditing techniques was positively received by health professionals because it reduced ambiguity in performance appraisal (Aidermark 2001).

Some studies find that, as is true in Norway, the amount of reform actually implemented is less than expected (Ekholm 2000; Forssell 2001). Wise and Stengård (1999) show evidence of implemented re- form on three of Pollitt and Bouckaert's categories of reform (see Chapter 2). 'Minimization' occurred with sharp decreases in the num- ber of central government employees (although overall public-sector employee was not significantly reduced) and with activities closed and moved into the market (for example, the Swedish Institute for Personnel Development [SIPU] was disbanded and personnel were provided short-term mobility assignments in management consultant firms during the transition). 'Modernization' is evident in the creation of new organ- izational forms, a shift to budget outcomes in performance auditing, and substantial change in the terms of employment for civil servants (for example, the elimination of permanent posts and job security, and the implementation of market-based policies for setting pay). 'Marketiza- tion' is apparent in the shifting of significant government activity into the gray zone of public corporations (such as railroads, telephone, energy, and postal services) and establishing competition between hospitals and schools for clients. In contrast with Norwegian reform, 'maintaining' was not a main focus of Swedish management reform and the reform was not sector-based.

Sweden has a relatively long history (dating from the 1960s) of using auditing techniques in central government, and it was one of the first Western countries to adopt performance auditing (Derlien 1990; Sandahl n.d.). Compared to Norway, Sweden has a strong tradition of national government commissions and investigations with which to evaluate reforms at different levels of government. Within the central government, two authorities have evaluation as a major element in their portfolios and the agencies themselves have been delegated responsibility for executing or overseeing evaluation of their own activities. In recent years, it appears that more critical assessments and other forms of evaluation have been independently undertaken by the research community.

United States

Several different agencies of the US federal government have evaluation as a main component of their portfolio. These include both executive and legislative branch agencies. The General Accounting Office (GAO), which is similar to the national audit agencies of Norway and Sweden, conducts audits of public agency expenditures and program performance and is responsible to the US Congress. Movement towards more management and policy-based reviews have been evident in the GAO since the 1950s. The GAO has a well-established social science capacity as well as analysts trained in cost-benefit analysis (Chelimsky 1985).

Within the executive branch of the federal government, oversight and evaluation responsibilities are assigned to different authorities, and individual agencies and departments are responsible for conducting internal evaluations. The Office of Management and Budget (OMB), which reports to the United States president, also assesses performance. OMB sponsored the 1993 Government Performance and Results Act that requires performance auditing in federal agencies of the United States. In late 2001, under the Bush Administration, OMB put the Executive Branch Management Scorecard System into effect. This system can be seen as a form of oversight and ranks agency performance on five areas of management against stated criteria for success.[4] Audits related to public management reforms might also be undertaken by the

Office of Personnel Management. The effects of reforms on equal employment opportunity and political independence of the civil service
could also be investigated by the Merit Systems Protection Board (US
MSPB) or the General Accounting Office (US MSPB 1992).

Evaluation activities pertaining to public management practices and
reforms are also carried out internally by different agencies at the federal and other levels of government. Individual agencies often execute
their own evaluations using internal capacity, special units, or external
consultants. Since 1978, within each agency the Office of Inspector
General (OIG) has had responsibility for auditing operations to advance
efficiency and effectiveness and may execute special audits and evaluation studies (Newcomer 1998). Inspectors General themselves have
sought a more proactive role and in many agencies the scope of activities falling under their purview has expanded in recent years. The majority of Inspectors General indicate that they sometimes make changes
in report recommendations in response to the concerns of line managers
and other audited staff. About two-thirds of the Inspectors General
indicate that they 'almost always' follow up to see whether recommendations for corrective action were put into place (Newcomer 1998).
According to one government study, agencies are increasingly devolving program evaluation responsibility to program managers and seeking
ways to leverage scarce resources for expensive evaluation efforts, as is
true in Sweden (Kingsbury 2000). The same study found that all the
studied agencies demonstrated evaluation capabilities of their own and
had previous experience conducting program evaluations.

Overall, the federal government produces a large volume of evidence about program performance (Rainey 1994; US MSPB 1992).
Perhaps partly because of this internal capacity for evaluation, the
United States federal government is less likely to use commissions and
special investigations to evaluate implemented reforms than are some
other governments. More typically, such groups would be established to
make an assessment of existing conditions prior to reform implementation (the Grace Commission under the Reagan administration is one
example). Practices related to the use of commissions for evaluation of
public management, however, would differ at other levels of government.

External consultants may conduct evaluative research for the federal
government. Agencies can contract with consulting firms, research
institutes or individuals to conduct studies related to implemented reforms and other performance issues. Different agencies of the federal
government might contract the National Academy of Public Admini-

stration (NAPA), a free-standing association composed of both practitioners and academics and chartered by the US Congress, to conduct investigations. Some of these activities involve evaluation of implemented administrative reforms. For example, NAPA was hired by the Secretaries of Interior and Agriculture to evaluate the implementation of a multi-agency wildfire management program. Agencies affected by the policy are required to develop an administrative unit to evaluate the effectiveness of their programs. The NAPA study found that the evaluation component of the program had not been implemented.

As Wollmann notes in Chapter 7, a strong interest in, and use of, formal program evaluation research designs has existed in the United States since at least the 1960s, when those methods were used to assess the impact of the War on Poverty. The United States has been considered a leader in the use of evaluative research based on these early efforts (Derlien 1990). Citizen surveys and surveys of public employees also became popular in the 1960s and have remained a staple of evaluative research. During the 1960s and 1970s, researchers focused specifically on the methodology of formal program evaluation research and efforts to promulgate rigorous evaluative research studies of government performance (Weiss 1972; Wholey et al. 1970). The federal government provided funds for training government officials at all levels of government in the formal methods of program evaluation (see for example Hatry et al. 1973; Wise 1976).

Evaluation research requirements are often attached to legislation enacting new social programs or administrative reforms at all levels of government. Evaluation requirements, for example, were attached to the Civil Service Reform Act of 1978, as were authorizations to conduct and evaluate administrative reforms experiments in certain government agencies (Ban 1992). Many of these experiments pertained to systems of job evaluation and compensation. As a result of a required evaluation of the Performance Management and Recognition System for awarding pay bonuses to management, for example, Congress did not authorize the continuance of the policy (US GAO 1989). The US GAO (1996) assessed management reforms at 12 different sites that had been designated for reform experiments under the National Performance Review. The study identified different factors associated with the success of the reinvention experiment and found, for example, that both real and perceived regulatory barriers to reform impeded implementation (United States, GAO 1996).

Under the Government Performance and Results Act (GPRA), the US has a comprehensive system for auditing public-agency perform-

ance, including efficiency audits, program effectiveness and performance management capacity (Barzelay 1996). Inasmuch as agencies are
required under GPRA to identify how they will compare actual results
with the goals stated in their performance plans and to explain why
goals were not met, they promote formal evaluations of agency performance and impact on target populations (Newcomer 2000). This
standard creates both technical and resource challenges for many agencies, but in a report to the Congress, government researchers identified
specific agencies that had incorporated program evaluations and
evaluation methods in their 1999 annual performance report under
GPRA (Kingsbury 2000). Evaluation studies enabled these agencies to
improve their measurement of program performance and their understanding of causal relationships between performance and other factors
and, in turn, of how performance might be improved. Some of these
agencies also compared actual program results with predictions of what
might have occurred if the program did not exist, in order to estimate
the program's net impact or contribution to organizational performance
and goal achievement. It is customary for agencies involved in such
studies to have the opportunity to rebut findings in an appendix, which
is important since many studies are critical assessments. This pattern of
evaluation corresponds with the cultural characteristics of a low-
context, low-sync, fact-oriented, and confrontational society. But Newcomer's (1998) observation that Inspectors General typically indicate
some responsiveness to line managers' requests for changes in draft
reports provides evidence of cooperation. Newcomer (1998, 2000)
interprets these findings along with evidence of involvement of a
broader array of actors under GPRA as an indication that federal
evaluation activities are becoming more inclusive.

Although it may be that the volume of evaluation activity conducted
by the GAO has declined since the mid-1980s (US GAO 1998), activities are more widespread throughout the government and the tasks of
evaluation have become part of everyday administrative practice. The
extent to which government benefits from so much evaluation activity is
an open question. Some find that in comparison to other countries the
picture is positive (Rainey 1994). Some scholars of public management
reform call for formal evaluations as a method of advancing real change
(Downs and Larkey 1986). But Radin's (2000) broad review of the
Government Performance and Results Act concluded that vague rhetoric prevents one from determining which management activity should
be emphasized and where evaluative efforts should be concentrated.

The question of how much reform has been implemented in the US federal government remains. In a relatively early study of NPM-style reforms in the US and Sweden, Wise and Stengård (1999) concluded that substantially more reform had been implemented in Sweden. Later studies, however, found more evidence of change in the United States. Among these reforms are more flexibility in pay setting, more flexible hiring, more use of contractual relationships and different organizational forms, more simplified decision-making and procurement, downsizing of some parts of the federal bureaucracy, and shifting of organizational cultures towards a stronger consumer orientation (Kettl 1998; Light 2000; Milakovich 1998; Thompson and Sanders 1998). Conclusions about the amount of reform implemented in the US would differ if one examined local and state government. In fact, state and local governments can be seen as leaders and initiators of the movement to reinvent government (Brudney, Herbert and Wright 1999).

In spite of this, the many agency-level and committee-based evaluations of reform programs in the United States give limited overall understanding of the consequences of reform for the bureaucracy at large, and do not address problems systemic to public management. Similarly, the studies fall short in the extent to which observed changes could be attributed to the reform programs themselves rather than other factors such as leadership, technological change or historical events. Knowledge about effects of administrative reform is often ambiguous; some assessments are negative and others are positive, and the pool of research is not deep enough to provide insight into these inconsistencies.

4. Conclusions

Our examination of the use of evaluation techniques in the three countries provides some support for the notion that national context partly accounts for the differences among countries in the way they compile information about reform consequences. Based on differences in the cultural context, we anticipated lesser emphasis on facts and evidence in Norway and Sweden than in the United States and less reliance on fact-based and analytical reasoning in making decisions. Political and structural features such as Norway's more sector-based orientation might account for differences in the amount of national government evaluation initiatives. Cultural features associated with high-context collectivist cultures might account for the relatively small volume of evaluation activity in Norway and the more moderate amount of evaluation research in Sweden in comparison with the US. The desire to avoid giving negative feedback or to support existing programs and policies might undermine a willingness to participate in evaluation activities. In the case of the United States, the pattern of evaluation corresponds to the cultural characteristics of a low-context, low-sync, fact-oriented, and confrontational society. There is considerable evaluation capacity and activity within the central government. Evaluative studies appear more confrontational.

For Norway, we found less activity within central government to evaluate public management reforms and more reliance on ad hoc studies initiated by independent researchers. Within these studies the emphasis is on broad conclusions rather than on agency-specific results. For Sweden, we observed early adoption of performance auditing and substantial use of official commissions as a component of central government-initiated evaluation activities. Some early efforts to evaluate public management reforms on the part of researchers have been supplemented in recent years by more quasi-evaluations from the research community. The great majority of 'evaluation' studies are accounts of implementation activities, despite a great emphasis on compiling statistical information. Part of the difference in the amount of evaluation apparent in Norway and Sweden might be attributed to the fact that Norway's approach to reform was 'maintenance,' and thus there were fewer significant reforms to evaluate, whereas Sweden's approach has been more active. Overall, there is less evaluation of public management practice in Norway than in Sweden.

In both Sweden and the United States we observed more reliance on agency-based evaluations and a possible trend towards greater inclusion of different stakeholders in the evaluation process. We observed frequent use of citizen and employee surveys in the United States, but this practice also dates back to the 1960s, and use of citizen or employee surveys in Norway and Sweden must be categorized as ad hoc.

In all three cases we find, as Pollitt and Bouckaert anticipated in Chapter 2, little rigorous evaluation of pre-implementation conditions, control groups, and multiple post-implementation data points. Cause and effect relationships are therefore difficult to claim. Although NPM-style reforms emphasize accountability and evaluation and thus gain legitimacy through objective evidence, there appears to be little change in the pattern of evaluation practice that can be ascribed to the NPM reform wave. The arrival of performance auditing in Norway is one change that could be linked to NPM. Although efficiency-based criteria are frequently used to assess government performance, we find this is not a new trend and we note some reaction against efficiency standards and efforts to include qualitative and normative indicators of government performance. An alternative explanation for these changes could be based on the greater sophistication of information management technology, or the increasing number of people within government trained in social science methods, for example.

Organization-bound experiments on the one hand, and limited evaluative research on the other, undermine our understanding of the consequences of public management reforms in general and the impact of NPM as a reform wave in particular. Two common conclusions for all three cases are that there is little systematic knowledge about the consequences of these reforms for the public bureaucracy and that the effects studied are more internal, administrative and output-oriented than external, political and outcome-oriented. Few single studies offer a good understanding of the consequences of public management reforms for greater efficiency and the achievement of good government, and no broad conclusions about the consequences of reform packages are drawn.

Contextual factors pertaining to a country's political, cultural, and environmental features provide insight into whether or not evaluations of public management reforms are undertaken, how they are conducted, and what use is made of evaluation findings.

References

Ahlenius, I.B. (2000), 'Performance audits, evaluations and supreme audit institutions', *International Journal of Government Auditing*, 27[1], pp. 1–2.

Aidermark, L.G. (2001), 'The meaning of balanced scorecards in the health care organization', *Financial Accountablility an Management*, 17[1], pp. 62–73.

Baldersheim, H. and K. Ståhlberg, (eds) (1994), *Towards the Self-Regulating Municipality: Free Communes and Administrative Modernization in Scandinavia*, Aldershot, UK: Dartmouth.

Ban, C. (1992), 'Research and demonstrations under CSRA: Is innovation possible?', in P. W. Ingraham and D. H. Rosenbloom (eds), *The Promise and Paradox of Civil Service Reform*, Pittsburgh: University of Pittsburgh Press, pp. 217–35.

Barzelay, M. (1996), 'Performance auditing and the New Public Management: changing roles and strategies of central audit institutions', in *Performance Auditing and the Modernisation of Government*, Paris: OECD, pp. 15–56.

Behn, R. (1980), 'How to terminate a public policy: A dozen hints for the would-be terminator', in C. Levine (ed.), *Managing Fiscal Stress*, Chatham, US: Chatham House, pp. 327–42.

Bennett, C. I. (1990), *Comprehensive Multicultural Education: Theory and Practice*, Boston: Allyn and Bacon.

Bentsen, E.Z. et al. (1999), *Når styringsambitioner møder praksis*, Copenhagen: Handelshøjskolens forlag.

Berg-Helgesen, S. (2001), *Aktivitetsmåling og atferdskontroll*, Bergen: LOScenter, report 0102.

Bleiklie, I. (1998), 'Justifying the evaluative state: New Public Management ideals in higher education', *European Journal of Education*, 33[3], 299–317.

Blomqvist, P. and B. Rothstein (2000), *Välfärdsstatens nya ansikte*, Stockholm: Agora.

Brudney, Jeffrey, Ted F. Herbert and Deil S. Wright (1999), 'Reinventing government in the American states', *Public Administration Review*, 59[1], 19–30.

Brunsson, K. (1995), 'Puzzle pictures: Swedish budgetary processes in principle and practice', *Financial Accountability and Management*, 11[2], 111–25.

Brunsson, N. and J. P. Olsen (1993), *The Reforming Organization*, London and New York: Routledge.

Bukve, O. and A. Offerdal (eds) (2002), *Den nye kommunen. Kommunal organisering i endring*, Oslo: Samlaget.

Chelimsky, E. (1985), 'Comparing and contrasting auditing and evaluation', *Evaluation Review* 9[4], pp. 483–503.

Christensen, T. and P. Lægreid (1998a), *Den moderne forvaltning*,Oslo: Tano Aschehoug.

Christensen, T. and P. Lægreid (1998b), 'Public administration in a democratic context: A review of Norwegian research', in N. Brunsson and J. P. Olsen (eds), *Organizing Organizations*, Bergen, Norway: Fagbokforlaget.

Christensen, T. and P. Lægreid (2001), *New Public Management. The Transformation of Ideas and Practice*, Aldershot: Ashgate.

Christensen, T. and P. Lægreid (2002), *Reformer og lederskap: Omstillinger i den utøvende makt*, Oslo: Scandinavian University Press.

Christensen, T., P. Lægreid and P.G. Roness (2002), 'Increasing parliamentary control of the executive? New instruments and emerging effects', *Journal of Legislative Studies*, 8[1], 38–62.

Christensen, T., P. Lægreid and L. R. Wise (2001), 'Assessing public management reform in Norway, Sweden and the United States of America', *International Journal of Political Studies*, September, 41–70.

Christensen, T., P. Lægreid and L. R. Wise (2002), 'Transforming administrative policy', *Public Administration*, 80[1], 153–78.

Derlien, H.-U. (1990), 'Genesis and structure of evaluation efforts in comparative perspective', in Ray C. Rist (ed.), *Program Evaluation and the Management of Government: Patterns and Prospects across Eight Nations*, New Brunswick. US: Transaction Publishers.

Downs, G. W. and P. D. Larkey (1986), *The Search for Government Efficiency: From Hubris to Helplessness*, Philadelphia: Temple University Press.

Ekholm, M. (2000), 'Management models for schools in Europe', *European Foundation*, 32[3], 50–62.

Forssell, A. (2001), 'Reform theory meets New Public Management', in T. Christensen and P. Lægreid (eds), *New Public Management. The Transformation of Ideas and Practice*, Aldershot: Ashgate.

Grønlie, T. (2001), 'Mellom politikk og marked – organisering av statlig næringsdrift', in S. Tranøy and Ø. Østerud (eds), *Den fragmenterte staten*, Oslo: Gyldendal Akademisk.

Gunvaldsen, J. and R. Karlsen (1999), 'The auditor as an evaluator. How to remain an influential force in the political landscape', *Evaluation*, 5[4], 458–67.

Häggroth, S. (1994), 'Deregulation and decentralization', *International Journal of Public Administration*, 17[10], 1853–70.

Hatry, H. P., R. E. Winne and D. M. Fisk (1973), *Practical Program Evaluation for State and Local Government Officials*, Washington, DC: Urban Institute.

Jonsson, E. (1996), *Utvärdering av Stockholm stads konkurrensprogram – en sammanfattande precentation av resultaten*, Stockholm: Institutet för kommunal ekonomi, Stockholm Universitet, IKE 1994/48.

Jonzon, B. and L. R. Wise (1989), 'Getting young people to work: An evaluation of Swedish youth employment policy', *International Labour Review*, 128[3], 337–56.

Jørgensen, T. B. (1996), 'Changing European states; changing public administration', *Public Administration Review*, 56[1], 65–104.

Kettl, D. (1998), 'The battle over fixing the IRS', *Brookings Review*, 16[1], 2–3.

Kingsbury, N. (2000), 'Program evaluation-studies helped agencies measure or explain program performance', report to Congressional Committees, *FDCH Government Account Reports*, 29 September 2000.

Kumbhakar, S. and L. Hjälmarsson (1998), 'Relative performance of public and private ownership under yardstick competition: Electricity', *European Economic Review*, 42[1], 97–132.

Kvalsund, R. et al. (1999), *Videregående opplæring – ved en skilleveg? Forskning fra den nasjonale evalueringen av Reform 94*, Oslo: Tano Aschehoug.

Kyvik, S. (1999), *Evaluering av Høyskolereformen: Sluttrapport*, Oslo: Norges Forskningsråd.

Lægreid, P. (2001), 'Transforming top civil servant systems', in T. Christensen and P. Lægreid (eds), *New Public Management. The Transformation of Ideas and Practice*, Aldershot: Ashgate.

Lægreid, P. and P. G. Roness (1999), 'Administrative reform as organized attention', in M. Egeberg and P. Lægreid (eds), *Organizing Political Institutions*, Oslo: Scandinavian University Press, pp. 301–30.

Lægreid, P. and P. G. Roness (forthcoming), 'Administrative reform programs and institutional response in Norwegian central government', in J. J. Hesse, C. Hood and B. G. Peters (eds), *Paradoxes in Public Sector Reform*, Berlin: Duncker & Humboldt.

Light, P. (2000), 'Requiem for Reinvention', *Goverment Executive*, 33[2], 82.

March, J. G. (1997), 'Administrative practice, organization theory, and political philosophy: ruminations and reflections of John M. Gaus', *PS Political Science*, 30[3], 689–98.

Milakovich, M. (1998), The state of results-driven customer service quality in government', *National Productivity Review*, 17[2], 47–55.

Neij, L. (2001), 'Methods of evaluating market transformation programmes: Experience in Sweden', *Energy Policy*, 29[1], 67–79.

Newcomer, K. (1998), 'The changing nature of accountability', *Public Administration Review*, 58[2], 129–37.

Newcomer, K. (2000), 'Is GPRA improving the federal government?', *PA Times*, 23[1], 1–3.

Nilsson, K.-A. and S. Wahlen (2000), 'Institutional response to the Swedish model of quality assurance', *Quality in Higher Education*, 6[1], 7–18.

Olsen, J. P. (1996), 'Norway: Slow learner – or another triumph of the tortoise?', in J. P. Olsen and B. G. Peters (eds), *Lessons from Experience*, Oslo: Scandinavian University Press, pp. 180–213.

Premfors, R. (1991), 'The Swedish model and public sector reform', *West European Politics*, 14[3], 83–95.

Radin, B. (2000), 'The Government Performance and Results Act and the tradition of federal management reform: Square pegs in round holes', *Journal of Public Administration Research & Theory*, 10[1], 111–35.

Rainey, H. G. (1994), 'Rethinking public personnel administration', in B. Romzek and P. Ingraham, *New Paradigms for Government*, San Francisco: Jossey Bass, pp. 115–40.

Reberg, K. G. (2002), 'Statlig lönebildning fungera bra', *Rikdsag och Departementet* 14, 22.

Riksrevisionsverket (RRV) (2002), *Statling tillsyn* 22-2002-0164, 2002-05-06, Stockholm: Riksrevisionsverket.

Rombach, B. and K. Sahlin-Andersson (eds) (1995), *Från sanningsökande till styrmedel: Moderna utväderingar i offentlig sektor*, Stockholm: Nerenius & Santerus.

Sandahl, R. (n.d.), 'Budgeting, auditing and evaluation in Sweden – connected or separate activities?' Internal paper, Stockholm: The Swedish National Audit Bureau.

Segerholm, C. (2001), 'National evaluations as governing instruments: How do they govern? *Evaluation* 7[4], pp. 427–38.

Sjölund, M. (1994), 'Transition in government pay policies: The problem of legitimacy', *International Journal of Public Administration*, 17[10], 1907–35.

Sørensen, R., L.-E. Borge and T. P. Hagen (1999), *Effektivitet i offentlig tjenesteyting*, Bergen: Fagbokforlaget.

Suchman, E. (1967), *Evaluative Research*, New York: Russell Sage Foundation.

Sweden, Ministry of Finance (1997), *Public Sector Productivity in Sweden*, Stockholm: Budget Department, Swedish Ministry of Finance.

Swedish National Audit Office (2002), *Performance Audits 2001*, Stockholm.

Sweden, Statskontoret (1997), *Staten i Omvandling*, Stockholm: Fritzes.

Sweden, Statskontoret (2000), *Utvärderingar och politik – en kartläggning av utvärderingarna i budget propositionen*, Stockholm: Statskontoret:17.

Thompson, J. R. and R.P. Sanders (1998), 'Reinventing public agencies', in P. Ingraham et al., *Transforming Government*, San Francisco: Jossey Bass, pp. 97–121.

United States General Accounting Office (US GAO) (1982), *Program Performance Measures: Federal Agency Collection and Use of Performance Data*, Washington, DC: General Accounting Office.

United States General Accounting Office (US GAO) (1989), *Pay for Performance: Interim report on the Performance Management and Recognition System*, Washington, DC: General Accounting Office.

United States General Accounting Office (US GAO) (1996), *Management Reforms: Status of Agency Reinvention Lab Efforts*, Washington, DC: General Accounting Office.

United States General Accounting Office (US GAO) (1998), *Program Evaluation: Agencies Challenged by New Demand for Information Program Results*, Washington, DC: General Accounting Office.

United States Merit Systems Protection Board (US MSPB) (1992), *Civil Service Evaluation: The Role of the Office of Personnel Management*, Washington, DC: US MSPB.

Vedung, E. (1995), 'Utvärdering och de sex användingarna', in B. Rombach and K. Sahlin Andersson (eds), *Från sanningsökande till styrmedel: Moderna utväderingar i offentlig sektor*, Stockholm: Nerenius & Santerus, pp. 25–52.

Vedung, E. (1997), *Public Policy and Program Evaluation*, New Brunswick, US: Transaction.

Weiss, C. (1972), *Evaluation Research*, Englewood Cliffs, US: Prentice-Hall.

Wholey, J. et al. (1970), *Federal Evaluation Policy*, Washington, DC: Urban Institute.

Wik, M.H. (2001), *Verdier og tilknytningsformer*, Bergen: LOS-center, Report 0106.

Wise, C. R., E. Amnå, and T. Sinclair (1994), 'National administrative agencies in Transition: A Comparison of Sweden and the United States', *International Journal of Public Administration*, 17[10], 18–25.

Wise, L. R. (1976), *Evaluating the Impact of Public Programs*, Chicago: Midwest Intergovernmental Training Association.

Wise, L. R. (1999), 'The use of innovative practices in the public and private sectors: The role of organizational and individual factors', *Public Productivity and Management Review*, 23[2], 130–49.

Wise, L. R. (2002), 'Public Management Reform: Competing drivers of change', *Public Administration Review*, 62[5 (September/October)], 542–54.

Wise, L. R. and P. Stengård (1999), 'Assessing the impact of Public Management Reform', in H. G. Frederickson and J. Johnston (eds), *Public Administration Reform and Innovation*, Tuscaloosa, US: University of Alabama Press, pp. 145–65.

Wise, L. R. and Swedish Gallup Institute (1995), 'Pay policy in transition: Attitudes toward pay equity among employees & managers', Report to Swedish Agency for Government Employers, Stockholm, 19 May 1995.

Wise, L. R. and Swedish Gallup Institute (1996), 'Survey of central government employees: Changing work cultures in central government: Attitudes toward Public Management Reform, part 3', report to Swedish Agency for Government Employers, Stockholm, January.

Witrock, B. (1984), *De stora programmens tid*, Stockholm: Akademilitteratur

Ørnsrud, I. (2000), *Mye fristilling, men lite kontroll*, Bergen: LOS-center, Report 0001.

Notes

1. The authors are grateful to Stig Montin, Paul G. Roness, Harald Sætren, and Per Stengård for insightful comments and to Jennie Johansson for valuable research assistance.
2. Different English translations of *Riksrevisionsverket* appear in official documents. These include National Audit Bureau, National Audit Office, and National Audit Board.
3. *Statskontoret* is now translated as The Swedish Agency for Public Management, but was formerly called the Agency for Administrative Development in English.
4. A simple 'traffic-light' system (green, yellow, red) is applied to human capital management, electronic government, financial management, competitive sourcing, and the linking of performance to budgets.

5. Public-sector reform and evaluation in Australia and New Zealand

John Halligan

This chapter examines the reform agenda under what is termed the Anglo-Saxon model of public management (Wollmann 2001) and how evaluation has been used in its external and internal forms. The primary question is the use of evaluation in public-sector reform, and whether it informs us about the impact of strategies and measures. A second question is the extent to which evaluation is institutionalized in public management. In exploring these questions, the article examines two countries identified with new public management. Australia and New Zealand have been widely acknowledged as exemplars of both public-sector reform and public management (Halligan 1997; Christensen and Lægreid 2001; Pollitt and Bouckaert 2000). Their approaches to evaluation have been quite distinctive and different for much of the reform era, although convergence has become apparent.

Evaluation has had a chequered history, and has failed to attain the potential envisaged by its advocates. New public management models were seen as providing fresh opportunities for evaluation to become a more significant element. Yet the international experience remains mixed, and even where conditions might seem to be favourable, the evidence has been ambiguous (Pollitt and Bouckaert 2001; Thoenig 2001; Wollmann 2001).

The two systems examined here reflect this broader pattern, but with some qualifications that suggest that general expectations were unrealistic. It is argued that according public management systems special status ignores the reality of the environment, the immediate imperatives of managers and the changing objectives of public management reformers. Consideration needs to be given to the evaluation system – the sum of evaluative elements that resides in the system of government of each country over time.

The argument about the environment is centred on the relationships between public management, evaluation and the political environment within a given system. There is a tradition of differentiating between bureaucratic and political approaches to public administration (e.g. Rosenbloom 1986). One use of this identifies two broad schools (March and Olsen 1989): the first is derived from orthodox administrative theory – administrative design of structures and procedures to facilitate bureaucratic efficiency and effectiveness; the other, realpolitik, regards administrative structures as the product of interests, and reform as a political issue. The claims for some forms of evaluation may stem from a technocratic perspective that can be identified with the senior public servants who are responsible for cultivating and transmitting public management. This approach makes assumptions about public management and its handling in practice. The implication is that politicians understand and adhere to something called public management and amend their behaviour accordingly. However, where politicians' operating styles reflect a political approach, this environment has to be taken more explicitly into account (Halligan 2001a).

There are also questions about the role of different forms of evaluation in both reform and routine public management. Other means of clarifying the forms are to distinguish between episodic evaluation and institutionalised evaluation and their role within the evaluations system. In systems committed to public management, there has been evolution and refinement over time, and different modes of evaluation have been used internally and externally. Discontinuities and lapses – such as changing agendas and governments, and the fast-moving currents of public management – arise out of the normal routines of governing.

The approach is informed by the well-established understanding that the composition of public management reform is important because of potential contradictions among the components (cf. Aucoin 1990), and because systems exhibit different packages of features that reflect choices about priorities and have major implications for operations[1]. This points to a further set of issues about what happens to evaluations, for ultimately it becomes a question of the capacity and inclination to make use of the results. The efficacy of a management system depends on what is made of the resultant knowledge.

This article first examines modes of evaluation before examining the experience of several internal and external forms in Australia and New Zealand. In addition to political and bureaucratic actors, there are the relative roles of central and line agencies and the relative importance of being external and independent from internal evaluation. Finally, it addresses the relationship between public management and the political executive and looks at the continuing challenges of using the information acquired from evaluation systems.

1. Modes of evaluation

The forms and levels of evaluation in these two countries can be categorized in three familiar ways. The first dimension involves the distinction between internal (or in-house, agency-based processes) and external types, which range from formal government-sponsored to central agency, to other reviews within the broader system: that is, they vary according to whether they are within the executive branch (consisting of cabinet and the public service) or within the governmental system (involving other more independent institutions, such as parliament and the audit office). Associated are the breadth of the evaluation – whether it is systemic, sectoral or instrument-focused – and the respective roles of central and line agencies. The range of external evaluations is extensive across the two countries (Table 5.1 p. 98).

The second dimension differentiates between event (or one-off) and ongoing evaluation. The latter covers commitments to regular reviews, which may be annual in nature, and regular programme evaluation. The levels of evaluation range from major reform to specific instruments and programme review. A third dimension is the purpose of evaluation, ranging from the ideologically driven, through agenda setting, to basic reflective reviews[2].

The differences between old- and new-style reviews can be overdrawn, but in Australia and New Zealand there have been clear departures from traditional approaches (Halligan 2001b). Public management is associated with an instrumental approach to developing and implementing reform programmes. A traditional approach was to proceed with some type of formal inquiry (perhaps a royal commission or commission of inquiry, for example, RCAGA 1976), which would receive submissions, and which often had a considerable measure of independence. The new-style reviews have been inclined to dispense with much of that process, operating more as an instrumental task force. The sum of all these elements comprises the evaluation system, that is, it comprises both components that are susceptible to government influence and those beyond its control.

2. External evaluation

Two features stand out: the use of major systemic reviews and the range of devices for initiating and tracking change, monitoring progress and reviewing results.

Agenda setting
The agenda-setting reviews are the most controlled and usually the most ideological. They are devices for initiating major reform and/or providing the basis for an important shift in values and direction. In these cases the evaluative basis is inclined to be subservient to the goals of the government.

The most celebrated case of recent times was the New Zealand Treasury *Government Management: Brief to the Incoming Government* in 1987 (there was also a 1984 brief). The elements of a framework first expressed in the briefs laid the foundation for New Zealand's radical programme of reform of management structures and processes. The centrality of institutional economics derived from Treasury thinking at that time and the influence of the Chicago school (Treasury 1987; Boston et al. 1996; Scott 2001).

The Australian *Reforming the Public Service* (Commonwealth 1983) reflected the new Labor government's election manifesto in providing initial directions for a reform programme, but was developed by the public service and more muted in key respects. In contrast, the commission of audit was a device trialled by conservative governments at the state level before being employed by the new Coalition government in 1996. The National Commission of Audit (1996) included in its evaluation of the public-sector the core question of whether there was a role for government in all publicly-funded activities anticipating an agenda that promoted the redistribution of public activity to the private sector.

Systemic reviews
Both countries have produced major systemic evaluations of their reform programmes that have few competitors internationally. None have produced a comprehensive analysis, but there were considerable (if varying) measures of independence. New Zealand has regularly conducted official reviews of the impact of and deficiencies in its reform program. The early report of the Steering Group for Review of State Sector Reforms in New Zealand (Logan 1991) addressed several aspects, including the accountability relationship between ministers and chief executives and the role of strategic formation in government deci-

sion-making. This subsequently led to the development of strategic results areas.

The New Zealand model later received a major official evaluation (Schick 1996), which examined the main components and produced a fairly sophisticated report, which pronounced it to be sound, successful and better managed, but criticized some cherished economic principles that had accounted for the system's uniqueness. The US academic, Allen Schick, concluded that although the reforms were 'more comprehensive and rigorous than those introduced in other countries, they have been neither complete nor perfect'. There was a further need 'to debug' the less successful elements, and to make modifications that would allow further development (Schick 1996: pp. 1, 3, 54).

New Zealand returned to the limitations of its model in 2001, having failed to implement the Schick report, with the Ministerial Advisory Group *Review of the Centre* (MAG 2001). In this case the Advisory Group combined the three central agency heads and three outsiders (two consultants and the national secretary of the Public Service Association), and can hardly be deemed to be a conventional external review. The exercise is depicted as 'essentially a review of the public management system – of how well it responds to the needs and expectations of Ministers and of citizens'. The report was not a fresh and comprehensive investigation of the model because the received wisdom about the model's deficiencies were well-known, and it had received five years of careful attention by insiders and outsiders (including Schick 1996; Boston et al. 1996; State Services Commission 1998, 1999c, 1999d; Scott 2001). The Advisory Group concluded that the system 'provides a reasonable platform to work from, but some significant shifts in emphasis are needed to better respond to the needs of the future' (p. 4). It defined three major issues: the need for integrated service delivery, fragmentation, and improvements to state sector culture. In addition, there was overdue recognition of the need to act on the limitations of central agency responsibilities.

After a decade of intensive change, Australia undertook possibly the first extensive official evaluation of the new-wave reforms in one country. The exercise was indicative of the Australian concern with systematic review and performance: a commitment to evaluation had been a feature of the reform program. The review, partly inspired by a parliamentary committee, was undertaken by the Task Force on Management Improvement, a quasi-independent group of public servants subject to central mentors (TFMI 1993). The report was influential in setting agenda for the mid-1990s.

An external businessperson or academic was used for several of these reviews (another was the more limited Block efficiency review in Australia in 1986). The CEO of the Sydney Stock Exchange has twice been used by the current Australian government for focused reviews with systemic implications: a review of public enterprise and the more recent IT outsourcing review discussed below (Humphry 2000).

Policy advice
Both countries have examined the possibilities for evaluating policy advice provided to ministers. The New Zealand debate explored the limits of evaluation (Boston 1994; Hawke 1993). The NZ State Services Commission has systematically addressed effectiveness or impact evaluation (SSC 1999a, 1999b).

The evaluation of central agency policy advice was the subject of an Australian experiment called programme management review, involving the advice provided by central agencies. The purpose was to extend the programme evaluation, which was compulsory for line departments, to the centre, the logic being that consistency in standards should apply. However, the approach was to evaluate the policy process rather than the results: 'In policy advice the evaluation strategy had found the limits to evaluating program outcomes'. Di Francesco concluded that 'the onset of fatigue in the application of evaluation to policy advice finally acknowledged the *external* political constraints facing program evaluation at every level' (2000: 45–6).

Annual and ongoing
The ministerialization of research and policy units with quasi-independent status occurred in the Australian reforms of the 1980s. Today the Productivity Commission conducts inquiries as required by references on economic and social issues from the Treasurer. These can extend to evaluation of government programmes.[3]

The Australian Public Service Commissioner's 2000 annual report on the state of the service has produced a series of three documents which review the events and trends of the financial year and survey and comment at a general level on strengths and limitations in key areas, such as customer service.

Both countries have produced centrally organized series on contemporary issues. The Australian MAB/MIAC (numerous reports between 1991 and 1998) had a collective basis, consisting of departmental secretaries and members of the senior executive service (Campbell and Halligan 1992). The current Management Advisory Committee has addressed performance management (MAC 2001).

The NZ State Services Commission produced occasional papers 1998–99, which represent agreed Commission views at the time of publication. Examples were the *Assessment of the New Zealand Public Service* (SSC 1998), and several other documents with evaluative aspects (SSC 1999a, 1999b). The analysis of accountability (SSC 1999c, 1999d) reported several problems, including system complexity and expensiveness, gaps in information provided to politicians and short-term focus (MAG 2001: 47).

External to government
The most independent evaluations within the governmental system of both countries are undertaken by organizations responsible to or constituted under the authority of parliament. Many of these have registered significant impacts on operational management. Performance audits and the parliamentary reviews are considered part of the performance management framework in Australia.

The most independent work is conducted by the Auditor-General of each country; their reports seek to exercise relatively low-key influence on management practice (for Australia, ANAO 2000; for New Zealand, Auditor-General 2000, 2002). However, their strategic role within the overall system has expanded, as discussed later, because of the leadership vacuums left by central agencies and the lack of reflection on the implementation of reform measures.

Parliamentary committees may also be quite independent of government, particularly those of the Australian Senate and the non-partisan joint committees of the two Australian houses. An assessment of their importance cannot be included here, beyond noting that the Australian committees have produced over 3000 reports covering the last three decades (Halligan, Miller and Power 2000). These reports range widely across government administration – from minor items to fully-fledged evaluations of programmes, reforms and management systems. As such they have come to provide an integral component of the evaluation system.

3. Evaluation and internal management

There were fundamental differences in how the two countries approached evaluation and incorporated it in agency programmes. A distinctive aspect of the Australian reforms was the commitment to systematic evaluation, which, unlike New Zealand's, was mandatory and driven centrally. For several years stark contrasts were drawn between the different attitudes on either side of the Tasman Sea. The Australian approach which was 'characterised as "evaluating everything that moves" – paints a picture of evaluation overkill' (SSC 1999a, p. 20), and seen as simply promoting an evaluation industry. In contrast, New Zealand's obsessive concern with outputs and accountability was regarded as precluding other considerations, including evaluation. Following critique and reflection on their respective approaches, there appears to have been some convergence of the two countries' positions in the latter half of the 1990s.

Both management systems have been based on devolution to agencies and have assumed that some form of 'evaluation activity' must be performed in order to sustain performance and reporting requirements. Evaluation activity is a term commonly used (ANAO 1997; SSC 1999a), which suggests ambiguity. Without a comprehensive survey and analysis of agency operations, it is difficult to gauge the level and quality of this work, much of which is formalized and relatively transparent.

Australia

The Financial Management Improvement Programme (FMIP), an initiative that was designed to produce more efficient use of resources, dominated the reforms of the 1980s. The implementation of FMIP occurred through several spheres of activity including improving management systems, which centred on the 'managing for results' and covered evaluation (Keating and Holmes 1990; Campbell and Halligan 1992). Under FMIP, the task environment within which departmental managers operated underwent a radical transformation to provide a new framework for holding managers accountable, which included the evaluation of outputs and outcomes against predetermined objectives. Evaluation was seen as tying the loop in the management cycle. The Department of Finance pronounced it to be the 'crucial element' in managing for results, performing the essential function of linking policy development and programme implementation. It was defined as 'systematic analysis and assessment of the appropriateness, efficiency and effectiveness of all or part of a programme' (DoF 1988, p. 65; Keating and Holmes 1990).

The logic of the managerial philosophy propounded by Finance required the question of closing the cycle to be eventually faced. By the late 1980s, the need for evaluation was increasingly accepted. In 1988, an evaluation strategy was established that required the development of plans by all agencies, and provided for the systematic evaluation of all programmes over a five-year period, the strengthening of requirements for reporting evaluations, improving evaluation skills and portfolio evaluation plans to be submitted to the Department of Finance. The primary responsibility for evaluation lay with departments and agencies, but the central agency coordinated the strategy, acting as a catalyst and assisting departments in developing evaluation capacities.

Evaluation proved to be controversial and 'the most difficult element of a "managing for results" approach', the problems reflecting 'its multiple, but linked objectives – improving programme performance, assisting government decision-making, and as a quid pro quo for the devolution of authority to managers, thus contributing to accountability' (Keating and Holmes 1990: 174). Attitudes towards evaluation were mixed, with 'some concern, confusion and in some instances, outright resistance in the Public Service to the use of evaluation as a formal management tool' (ANAO 1991, p. 130).

Following an investigation of the implementation of programme evaluation, the Audit Office reported a significant increase in evaluation activity, but progress was still unsatisfactory. There was greater focus on systematic evaluation and reporting, but the pattern of activity continued to vary widely among departments (ANAO 1991). The Task Force on Management Improvement also reported an increase in quantity and quality of evaluation activity but that it varied among portfolios because of deficiencies in management information systems and staff skills, difficulties in evaluating some types of programmes and the level of support at senior levels, and it was costly. More significantly, most members of the senior executive service were not making much use of evaluation information in their work: 'ironically, there may be a tendency to focus on satisfying the requirement for evaluation ... rather than learning to use evaluation to improve programme outcomes' (TFMI 1993, pp. 363, 378–9).

The system was ultimately judged to produce 'a predominantly process oriented approach' and compulsory evaluation was discontinued in 1997. A new approach was developed by Finance that was 'designed to ensure that evaluation becomes an integral part of a broader performance management framework across the APS' (ANAO 1997, p. 6).

Australia has been operating under its second management framework of the reform era: the outcomes and outputs framework has been the main financial management feature in recent years. Agency heads are responsible for ensuring that their department produces the necessary outputs in order to reach the outcomes that have been the subject of parliamentary appropriations. Senior staff members have performance agreements against which they are assessed (with bonuses attached in some cases). Some form of review is built into the model and there are a number of inducements that encourage such activity: accountability, reporting and transparency requirements and expectations. The requirements of risk management plans, forward planning and internal audit mean that evaluation of some aspects is routine. The centrality given to outcomes under the management framework means that outcomes are integral to the system's performance.

Under the scheme, transparency is meant to be enhanced because the outcome and output framework is designed to focus on external scrutiny, effectiveness and output questions, and to improve performance information. The main external reporting occurs through portfolio budget statements, which indicate agency plans for the next year, and annual reports, which record the extent to which the plans are achieved in practice.

There is some evidence of variations in attitudes towards evaluation and in its application. For example, the emphasis on customer focus means that service-delivery agencies regularly test their products. According to the annual State of the Service Report, evaluation of delivery strategies is important, but agencies 'varied from ongoing monitoring to formal review. The emphasis on evaluation would depend on agencies' particular role in service delivery and the nature of their clients. It is of some concern, however, that 30 per cent of agencies provided no information including a few that reported no evaluation' (Public Service Commissioner 2000, p. 126).

A recent survey indicated that 'Few evaluations in agencies have collected data to enable evaluation of whether the systems have achieved their goals or outcomes, the nature of their impact on performance of individuals or groups, or the quality of the performance management discussions that have taken place' (PS & IPAA 2001, p. 56).

The study also reports that some senior executives reject 'evaluation of the impact of their performance management systems' and in many agencies, 'important issues about performance management are not being examined in evaluations because the assumptions on which systems are based have not been questioned' (PS & IPAA 2001, pp. 56–57).

New Zealand

Key features of the New Zealand system were the distinction between outputs and outcomes in the original model, and their assignment to chief executives and ministers, respectively. The focus has been on the chief executives and their extensive responsibilities for managing departments under contract, the specification of their responsibilities through performance and purchase agreements, and the annual assessment of their performance by the employer, the State Services Commission (Boston et al. 1996; SSC 1999c; Scott 2001).

Two limitation of the New Zealand model have been widely discussed. First, the output orientation emphasized managerial accountability at the expense of public and parliamentary accountability (Boston et al. 1996, p. 359). Second, the gaps in the system's capacity to learn from experience have been recognized, in particular the ability to make 'systematic, empirical evaluations of policies a matter of routine'. OECD advocated institutionalizing the process because these assessments sometimes embarrassed agencies or politicians, and commended the experiences of countries such as Australia, France, Canada and the United States in designing an evaluation policy (OECD 1996, p. 112).

The diagnosis of New Zealand's public management system was that 'while the current environment is not overly conducive to outcome evaluation, there is nothing inherent in the public management model that inhibits it' (SSC 1999a, p. 5). One problem was 'the short-termism inherent in the system' (SSC 1999a, p. 15). Another was that the system lacked an evaluation champion – for most of the 1990s, no central agency played an advocacy role. This was contrasted with the role of the Australian Department of Finance, which 'played a leading role in creating the expectation that programmes should be evaluated (albeit with a focus on efficiency rather than effectiveness)' (SSC 1999b, p. 29). As the SSC argues, 'developing a capacity for review ... involves an evaluation of outcomes. These were consciously sidelined in the original reforms' (SSC 1998, p. 32). A final consideration was that 'the focus on outputs while improving the accountability and transparency of government/departmental processes has not assisted decision-making' (SSC 1999a, p. 12).

The State Services Commission reported 'evidence of a good deal of evaluation activity, [but] most tends to be focused on process, implementation, and efficiency, and used for internal management purposes' (SSC 1999b, p. 25; 1999a). There have been exceptions, such as the Education Review Office and a few departmental units (Aitken 1997). At the same time, 'evaluation against outcomes is considered too hard.

Some of those interviewed felt that other tools – such as good information flows from operations – provided better information more easily, for example: "... feedback loops are more important than academic evaluations"' (1999a, p. 9). The State Services Commission argues that 'both ex-ante identification of the impacts of outputs on outcomes and the ex-post evaluation of the same, could be seen as a complement to the current accountability system' (1999a, p. 12). The Commission appeared to be picking up the roles of building evaluation expectations and promoting outcome evaluation (SSC 1999b, p. 33), and it has now acquired broader responsibilities from central agency strengthening (MAG 2001).

In the meantime, the Auditor-General addressed the incidence of impact evaluation, defined as 'a particular form of performance assessment' designed to determine the actual outcomes from implementation, compare actual and desired outcomes, and establish whether there is a causal link between means and actual outcomes (2000, p. 101). The Auditor-General's survey of impact evaluation indicated that departments were not conducting much of it, and they did not have a shared understanding of the concept. Evaluation activity was common and a range of evaluation techniques were being used (2000, p. 111).

4. Using evaluation and evaluation results

The Australian and New Zealand systems have been distinguished by their initial level of reform and their ability to sustain reform over time. The demands of comprehensive reform have produced systemic evaluations and other instruments for reviewing and setting new agenda. However, much still depends on the capacity and inclination of the political environment – the political executive and parliament – to make use of the results. At the agency level much depends on the design and operation of performance management. Both countries report problems of alignment within their management systems.

Cross-cutting agendas: Public management and the political executive

The political approach referred to earlier regards administrative structures as a product of interests and reform as a political issue (March and Olsen 1989). Politicians will seek to have their objectives and values realized. A political approach to public administration emphasizes values such as political responsiveness and accountability through elected representatives (Rosenbloom 1986). Public management does not emerge unadulterated by other contextual factors, such as political agenda and state traditions. Any major reform needs to be viewed against the backdrop of these conditions and circumstances.

There is no evidence that public-choice ideas played a direct role in shaping political thinking in Australia in the early 1980s. The political agenda derived from Labor's experience in the 1970s, when it failed to effect proper engagement of the public service in order to improve implementation of its policy. In New Zealand there are indications that public-choice ideas (or the economics of institutions, according to Scott 2001) played a role in shaping an elite climate of opinion. However, politicians there were less ardent about redefining their relationship with public servants (in the Australian sense of requiring greater responsiveness), and succumbed to ideas about changing the incentive systems for public servants and politicians (in order to reduce budget-maximizing behaviour and capture), leading to a reduction in their influence (Boston et al. 1996; Scott 2001).

Australia and New Zealand provide two distinctive cases (Halligan 2001a): the first involves direct engagement of the public service, thereby affecting the operation of the public management model; the second involves redefining the formal relationship and the problem of engagement between the two sets of actors.

An early priority of the Australian Labor government elected in 1983 was the reestablishment of ministerial control and greater responsiveness from the public service to government policies and priorities. This was part of a political framework that sought to increase 'democracy' by allowing the minister to have greater influence through ministerial advisers while diminishing the roles of the public servant. Measures were introduced to reduce permanency, the monopoly on advice to ministers, and independence (Halligan and Power 1992; Wilenski 1986).

This recurrent theme was affirmed by the second Labor prime minister of the reform era, who observed that a central reform objective was ensuring that the government belonged to the elected representatives, with ministers deciding priorities. For the departmental secretary and senior public service, the increasing reliance on contracts in the 1990s was to be instrumental in exacting responsiveness. The new public management paradigm complemented and served the politicians' interests, for it provided a basis for fundamental change and a redistribution of power. The Australian minister's capacity for direct influence has meant that 'political management' was a better means of characterizing the system (Halligan and Power 1992; Halligan 2001a). This has been an overriding agenda, even though successive Australian governments have been highly committed to implementing public management change for two decades.

The recent Australian case of IT outsourcing illustrates both political intervention in management and conflicts between government agenda, as the government's approach to outsourcing contradicted its public management model (Halligan 2001c). The resolution of the issue involved two forms of independent evaluation: an Audit Office report and a review commissioned by the government (ANAO 2000; Humphry 2000).

Under the IT Initiative, the prime minister prescribed outsourcing unless there was 'a compelling case on a whole-of-government basis for not doing so'. The infrastructure and telecommunications requirements of agencies were grouped and offered to the market[4]. By the end of 2000, five groups (covering 23 departments and agencies) had outsourced their IT infrastructure, and another six were in process (ANAO 2000; Humphry 2000).

Long before the evaluations, features of the IT Initiative were being publicly debated. This culminated in an Audit Office report, which canvassed deficiencies in the financial methodology; shortfalls in attaining minimum service levels; overstated savings; and underestimations of the complexity of the transition, transaction costs and implementation costs (ANAO 2000, Summary, 9.9–10). The government's quasi-independent inquiry (the Humphry Review) reported major problems with the implementation process, stating that it was the government's prerogative to set policies, but agency chief executives were responsible for implementation and management. It recommended, inter alia, that responsibility for implementation of IT outsourcing be devolved to chief executives; agency requirements should determine the appropriate outsourcing model and the extent of outsourcing, and the decision should rest with the agency, subject to government policy (Humphry 2000).

The IT reform process was notable for being compulsory and driven from the centre. This was a startling divergence from the government's reform programme. On the one hand, the IT Initiative was centrally driven by the Office of Asset Sales and Information Technology Outsourcing. On the other hand, the overall direction of the mainstream programme for the public service was decentralization to agencies and departmental secretaries. An otherwise highly decentralized reform programme was being overridden in significant respects by a highly centralist agenda.

The New Zealand public management model consisted of a number of elements – only some of which can be touched on here (Boston et al. 1996; Scott 2001). Two important distinctions were between inputs, outputs and outcomes (with the emphasis being on outputs), and the definition of government roles as either the purchaser of outputs from agencies or as the owner of agencies. One of the most startling innovations was the separation of political and managerial roles through the association of outcomes with ministers and outputs with chief executives, the minister selecting the outcomes, and purchasing the outputs from the chief executive who selects the necessary inputs. This arrangement was meant to allow the chief executives to be held accountable by the minister for departmental results. The relationship was seen as being contractually based: the government purchases outputs from departments, while at the same time being defined as the owner.

Some reforms in effect 'depoliticized' government activity (see Gregory 1998 on 'fencing off' politics and technocracy) and detached ministers from being held responsible for public actions. Managerial accountability was developed while the political responsibility of ministers became more tenuous. Politicians had, according to former ministers, lost decision-making and become 'underpowered' (Lange 1998; Upton 1999; Gregory 2001).

The New Zealand model, derived from economics but lacking a sure grounding in organizational and political reality, was the most ambitious case of public management. It is now understood that a crucial missing element was the impossibility of controlling for the political environment. A disappointment of proponents of the New Zealand model was the failure of politicians over time to make the most of the instruments it offered. The State Services Commission reported that 'Ministers have not necessarily acted in the manner envisaged by the ... model, either in terms of specifying outcomes or results, or in terms of operating as discerning purchasers of outputs' (1999c, p. 15).

During the initial tenure of the Labour government elected in 1999, the relationship between ministers and the senior public service in New Zealand was uneasy and indicated a lack of proper engagement.[5] Some coalition politicians were ideologically opposed to key aspects of the New Zealand model, although the official policy was not to dismantle it. On the one hand, the political executive continued to be concerned that the bureaucracy was insufficiently comprehending of, or responsive to, its preferences. On the other hand, the public service argued that the levers existed for ministers to employ in furtherance of their objectives. The review of the centre (MAG 2001) recorded a series of problems with political-bureaucratic relationships that had emerged under the New Zealand model.

System capacity and changing agency roles

The evaluative capacity of each system depends on the leadership at the three levels of central agencies, the operating agencies that function in devolved environments, and external, independent organizations.

In both countries, the emphasis moved from the traditional, centralized approach to being highly devolved. While both systems proceeded down this path in the 1980s, New Zealand moved more rapidly as it embraced a more radical model (Boston et al. 1996; Scott 2001). For many years its operations were heavily focused on the numerous ministries and departments. However, in both countries, agency commitment to evaluation has been variable and relatively low in terms of formal impact.

The central agencies roles sagged as they withdrew from more direct intervention when devolved management caught on, but again, most starkly in New Zealand. The centre began to ascend to greater prominence towards the end of the 1990s, as reassessment of the weaknesses of the centre proceeded, and the need for stronger roles emerged. In the Australian case, it was the Public Service Commission under the new Public Service Act; in New Zealand's case, it was the State Services Commission, because of the vacuum in the centre of the system.

This is not to say that major evaluations were not undertaken – as indicated above – but implementation did not necessarily follow. Meanwhile, central leadership was restrained and lacking. In lieu of effective attention to management issues across the service, the Audit-General partly filled the leadership vacuum for systemic issues by reviewing and offering best-practice advice. System capacity has received more attention as the State Services Commission acquires more responsibilities for the commanding heights. A greater balance between centre and sector is now likely.

Evaluation challenges

The challenges to evaluation of reform are numerous (Pollitt and Bouckaert 2001, Thoenig 2001). Successful reforms do not necessarily endure. In the reform era, reform succession is compressed: a decade after the new approach to Australian public management took shape, it was being replaced by a revised system; New Zealand continued to expand and refine, and, by the year 2001, was reviewing the reforms, even though a framework was laid down at an early stage. The compulsion to change is partly driven by the internal commitment to continuous improvement and constant responses to environmental pressures. The lesson to be learned from Australia and New Zealand during two decades of reform is that successful implementation does not resolve the need to change and to refine the instruments of management improvement (Halligan 2001d). In fact, many Australian managers have been frustrated by the frequent modifications to the performance management system (PS & IPAA 2001, p. 58).

External reviews have registered a great impact on thinking about public management systems, but this knowledge does not ensure implementation, as the New Zealand case, in particular, illustrates. Much of the Schick report (1996) was not implemented and the reform programme continued to drift during the latter half of the 1990s, despite much public reflection on the shortcomings (e.g. SSC 1998, 1999c). In addition, throughout the reform period, other agendas have focused the minds of public servants: restructuring of departmental systems, annual efficiency dividends, outsourcing and targeted cuts of staff numbers. Cutbacks in order to balance the budget take priority over creative reform. The current Australian government has placed a much higher priority on market testing of departmental responsibilities, and this could be seen either as a substitute for evaluation or as an overriding imperative.

There will continue to be debate about the constitution of public management systems and whether performance design is optimal. The New Zealand accountability system has been critiqued for inhibiting high performance, for being preoccupied with ex ante specification of activities and for being excessively complex because of a 'pattern of accretion [of documents that] is being driven by increasing information requirements to enable better assessment of performance'. Ministers cannot read or digest the numerous information sets and have difficulty appreciating a department's performance overall (SSC 1999c, p. 12). However, information gaps continue, and the available information may still be problematic for stakeholders. Due to deficiencies in the quality of reporting, the New Zealand Office of the Auditor-General published *Reporting Public-sector Performance* to highlight the need for a comprehensive model of performance, comprehensive external accountability and multiple reporting levels (from agencies through to whole-of-government) (*The Watchdog*, Issue 17, June 2001; Auditor-General 2002).

5. Conclusion

This chapter has examined the evaluation of public management reforms and the implications of those reforms for evaluation in two countries. Evaluation has been employed in a variety of ways in countries
that have adopted public management. For both Australia and New
Zealand, it has been important at the level of reviewing reform publicly
and systemically.

There have, however, been significant differences in how they have
otherwise approached evaluation. One sought to implement formal
evaluation (although later discarding the approach), while the other
maintained a model that was unsympathetic to evaluation (and experienced internal and external critique for ignoring it).

Some form of evaluation activity is built into the models (at least at
the level of management performance); their public management systems provide for monitoring, assessment and reporting, and there exist
incentives to encourage such activity. Both countries have sought to
evolve and refine their management systems over the last decade. There
has also been movement towards focusing on outcomes within their
models, and this stronger commitment requires the use of evaluation
activity for determining impacts. In evolving their management models,
a considerable measure of convergence between the two has become
evident.

However, the understanding of the level and quality of evaluation in
the two systems remains somewhat elusive. In a decentralized environment, agencies will continue to display variations in how they handle
outcomes, performance information and the use of systematic evaluation. It is also apparent that no matter how innovative a public management system, it cannot remain immune to the unpredictable element
provided by politicians' pursuit of their aspirations and contradictory
agenda, nor to their failure to make effective use of management tools.

Table 5.1 Australia and New Zealand: Selected evaluations 1983–
2000[6]

Date	Australia	New Zealand
	Labor government 1983–1996	
1983	• Reforming the Public Service	
		Labour government 1984–1990
1984	• Financial management improvement program	• Treasury, economic management, briefing to the incoming government
	• Budget reform paper	
1986	• Block Review (streamlining, efficiency scrutinies)	
1987	• Restructuring of central agencies and reduction in departments	• Treasury, economic management, briefing to the incoming government
1988	• Department of Finance, *FMIP Report*	
		National government 1990–1996
1991	• MAB/MIAC Reports 1991–1998	• Report of steering group for review of state sector reforms, State Services Commission
1992	• Task Force on Management Improvement evaluation of reform decade	
1993	• Policy Management Reviews 1993–1995	
1994	• Report of the Public Service Act Review Group (McLeod Report)	
	Coalition government 1996–	*Coalition government 1996–1999*
1996	• Report of National Commission of Audit	• Schick Report for the State Services Commission and the Treasury
	• Towards a Best Practice Australian Public Service (Reith Report)	
1998		• State Services Commission, Occasional Papers, 1998–1999
		• State Services Commission, *Assessment of the New Zealand Public Service*
1999	• Public Service Commissioner *State of the Service Report, 1998–99–2000–01*	• Auditor-General, Third Report for 1999 – *Accountability to Parliament*

	• IT Initiative – Whole of government outsourcing of IT	
		Labour Coalition government 1999–2002
2000	• Market testing of activities and services, commencing with corporate services • Audit Office Implementation of IT Infrastructure Outsourcing • Humphry Review	
2001	• Management Advisory Committee, Performance Management in APS	
2002		• Auditor-General, *Reporting Public Sector Performance* (2nd ed., 2002) • Ministerial Advisory Group, *Review of the Centre*

References

Aitken, Judith (1997), 'The way we carry out the Queen's business: Big issues to be dealt with over the medium term: Information and evaluation', Future Issues in Public Management, Conference Proceedings, March.

ANAO/Australian National Audit Office (1991), *Audit Report No. 23 1990–91: Implementation of Program Evaluation – Stage 1*, Canberra: Australian Government Publishing Service.

ANAO/Australian National Audit Office (1997), *Program Evaluation in the Australian Public Service, Audit Report No. 3*, Canberra: ANAO.

ANAO/Australian National Audit Office (2000), *Implementation of Whole-of-Government Information Technology Infrastructure Consolidation and Outsourcing Initiative, Audit Report No. 9*, Canberra: ANAO.

Aucoin, Peter (1990), 'Administrative reform in public management: Paradigms, principles paradoxes and pendulums', *Governance*, 3[2], 115–37.

Auditor-General (1999), *The Accountability of Executive Government to Parliament*, Wellington: Office of the Controller and Auditor-General.

Auditor-General (2000), *First Report for 2000: Health, School Board of Trustees, Impact Evaluation*, Wellington: Office of the Controller and Auditor-General.

Auditor-General (2002), *Reporting Public Sector Performance*, 2nd ed., Wellington: Office of the Controller and Auditor-General.

Boston, Jonathan (1994), 'Purchasing policy advice: The limits to contracting out', *Governance*, 7[1], 1–30.

Boston, Jonathan (2000), 'The challenge of evaluating systemic change: The case of public management reform', IPMN Conference, Learning from Experiences with New Public Management, Macquarie Graduate School of Management, Macquarie University, Sydney, 4–6 March.

Boston, Jonathan, John Martin, June Pallot and Pat Walsh (1996), *Public Management: The New Zealand Model*, Auckland: Oxford University Press.

Bridgman, Peter and Glynn Davis (1998), *Australian Policy Handbook*, Sydney: Allen and Unwin.

Campbell, Colin and John Halligan (1992), *Political Leadership in an Age of Constraint: Bureaucratic Politics under Hawke and Keating*, Pittsburgh, US: University of Pittsburgh Press.

Christensen, Tom and Lægreid, Per (eds) (2001), *New Public Management: The Transformation of Ideas and Practice*, Ashgate: Aldershot.

Commonwealth of Australia (1983), *Reforming the Australian Public Service*, Canberra: Australian Government Publishing Service.

Department of Finance (1988), *FMIP Report*, Canberra: Australian Government Publishing Service.

Department of Finance (1989), *Annual Report 1988–89*, Canberra: Australian Government Publishing Service.

Di Francesco, Michael (1998), 'The measure of policy? Evaluating the evaluation strategy as an instrument for budgetary control', *Australian Journal of Public Administration*, 57[1], 33–48.

Di Francesco, Michael (2000), 'An evaluation crucible: Evaluating policy advice in Australian central agencies', *Australian Journal of Public Administration*, 59[1], 36–48.

Di Francesco, Michael and John Uhr (1996), 'Improving practices in policy evaluation', in John Uhr and Keith Mackay (eds), *Evaluating Policy Advice: Learning from Commonwealth Experience*, Canberra: Federalism Research Centre, ANU and Commonwealth Department of Finance, 41–57.

Gregory, Robert (1998), 'New Zealand as the "New Atlantis": A case study in technocracy', *Canberra Bulletin of Public Administration*, 90, 107–12.

Gregory, Robert (2001), 'Transforming governmental culture: A sceptical view of new public management in New Zealand', in Tom Christensen and Per Lægreid (eds), *New Public Management: The Transformation of Ideas and Practice*, Ashgate: Aldershot, 231–58.

Halligan, John (1997), 'New public sector models: Reform in Australia and New Zealand', in Jan-Erik Lane (ed.), *Public Sector Reform: Rationale, Trends and Problems*, London: Sage, 17–46.

Halligan, John (2001a), 'Politicians, bureaucrats and public sector reform in Australia and New Zealand', in B. Guy Peters and Jon Pierre (eds), *Politicians, Bureaucrats and Administrative Reform*, London: Routledge.

Halligan, John (2001b), 'The process of reform in the era of public sector transformation: Directive and retrospective', in Tom Christensen and Per Lægreid (eds), *New Public Management: The Transformation of Ideas and Practice*, Ashgate: Aldershot, 73–89.

Halligan, John (2001c), 'The implications of the Humphry Report', *Canberra Bulletin of Public Administration*, 99, 1–4.

Halligan, John (2001d), 'Paradoxes in reform in Australia and New Zealand', in Joachim J. Hesse, Christopher Hood and B. Guy Peters (eds), *Paradoxes in Public Sector Reform*, Berlin: Duncker and Humbolt, forthcoming.

Halligan, John and John Power (1992), *Political Management in the 1990s*, Melbourne: Oxford University Press.

Halligan, John, Robin Miller and John Power (2000), 'The three committee systems of the Australian parliament: A developmental overview', paper presented at Australasian Study of Parliament Group, Annual Conference, Brisbane, 14–16 July.

Hawke, G.R. (1993), *Improving Policy Advice*, Wellington: Institute of Policy Studies.

Humphry, Richard (2000), *Review of the Whole of Government Information Technology Outsourcing Initiative*, Canberra: Commonwealth of Australia.

Keating, M. and Holmes, M. (1990), 'Australia's budgetary and financial management reforms', *Governance* 3[2], 168–85.

Laking, R.G. (1994), 'The New Zealand management reforms', *Australian Journal of Public Administration*, 53[3], 313–24.

Lange, David (1998), 'With the benefit of foresight and a little help from hindsight', *Australian Journal of Public Administration*, 57[1], 12–18.

Logan, Basil (1991), *Review of State Sector Reforms*, Wellington: Report of Steering Group for Review of State Sector Reforms in New Zealand, State Services Commission.

MAC (Management Advisory Committee) (2001), *Performance Management in the Australian Public Service: A Strategic Framework*, Canberra: Commonwealth of Australia.

MAG (Ministerial Advisory Group) (2001), *Report of the Advisory Group of the Review of the Centre*, Wellington: State Services Commission.

March, James G. and Johan P. Olsen (1989), *Rediscovering Institutions: The Organizational Basis of Politics*, New York: Free Press.

National Commission of Audit (1996), *Report to the Commonwealth Government*, Canberra: Australian Government Publishing Service.

Norman, Richard (2002), 'At the centre or in control? Central agencies in search of new roles in a decentralized public service', paper presented to the conference of the Structure and Organization of Government Research Committee of the International Political Science Association, Centre for Public Policy, University of Melbourne, June 3–5.

Organisation for Economic Co-operation and Development (1995), *Governance in Transition: Public Management Reforms in OECD Countries*, Paris: OECD.

Organisation for Economic Co-operation and Development (1996), *OECD Economic Surveys 1995–1996: New Zealand*, Paris: OECD.

Pollitt, Christopher (1997), 'Evaluation and the new public management: an international perspective', *Evaluation Journal of Australasia*, 9[1 & 2], 7–15.

Pollitt, Christopher and Geert Bouckaert (2000), *Public Management Reform: A Comparative Analysis*, Oxford: Oxford University Press.

Pollitt, Christopher and Geert Bouckaert (2001), 'Evaluating public management reforms: An international perspective', *International Journal of Political Studies*, September, 167–92.

PS & IPAA (People and Strategy and Institute of Public Administration, ACT Division) (2001), *Performance Management: A Guide to Good Practice*, Canberra: PS & IPAA.

Public Service Commissioner (2000), *State of the Service Report: 1999–2000*, Canberra: Public Service and Merit Protection Commission.

RCAGA/Royal Commission on Australian Government Administration (Chairman: H. C. Coombs) (1976), *Report*, Canberra: Australian Government Publishing Service.

Rosenbloom, David H. (1986), *Public Administration: Understanding Management, Politics, and Law in the Public Sector*, New York: Random House.

Schick, Allen (1996), *The Spirit of Reform: Managing the New Zealand State Sector in a Time of Change*, Wellington: State Services Commission and the Treasury.

Scott, Graham (2001), *Public Management in New Zealand: Lessons and Challenges*, Wellington: New Zealand Business Roundtable.

State Services Commission (1998), *Assessment of the New Zealand Public Service, Occasional Paper No. 1*, Wellington: State Services Commission.

State Services Commission (1999a), *Looping the Loop: Evaluating Outcomes and other Risky Feats, Occasional Paper No. 7*, Wellington: State Services Commission.

State Services Commission (1999b), *Essential Ingredients: Improving the Quality of Policy Advice, Occasional Paper No. 9*, Wellington: State Services Commission.

State Services Commission (1999c), *Improving Accountability: Setting the Scene, Occasional Paper No. 10*, Wellington: State Services Commission.

State Services Commission (1999d), *Improving Accountability: Developing an Integrated Performance System, Occasional Paper No. 11*, Wellington: State Services Commission.

TFMI/Task Force on Management Improvement (1993), *The Australian Public Service Reformed: An Evaluation of a Decade of Management Reform*, Canberra: Australian Government Publishing Service for the Management Advisory Board.

Thoenig, Jean-Claude (2001), 'Evaluating public sector reforms: Learning from practice', *International Journal of Political Studies*, September, 193–214.

Treasury (1987), *Government Management: Volumes I and II*, Wellington: Government Printer.

Upton, Simon (1999), 'Weaving the future: Looking in, looking forward', Minister of State Services' Address, State Services Commission 1999 Conference. 30 September. Wellington.

The Watchdog, Newsletter to approved auditors from the office of the Auditor-General, Issue 17, June 2001,
http://www.oag.govt.nz/homepagefolders/watchdog/watchdog7.htm.

Wilenski, Peter (1986), *Public Power and Public Administration*, Sydney: Hale and Iremonger.

Wollmann, Hellmut (2001), 'Public sector reforms and evaluation: Trajectories and trends – An international overview', *International Journal of Political Studies*, September, 11–37.

Notes

1. This chapter does not explore the difficulties with undertaking public management research, such as the problem of comparing the results of specific reforms with prior conditions (Boston 2000; Pollitt 1997; Halligan 1997; OECD 1996).
2. This discussion does not extend to special inquiries into individual departments and agencies, such as the Review of the Department of Conservation (1995) in conjunction with the Cave Creek episode in New Zealand, or private reviews of the New Zealand Department of the Prime Minister and Cabinet (2000) and Australia's Centrelink (2000).
3. Recent reports have included *Cost Recovery by Government Agencies* (2002) and *Independent Review of Job Network* (Draft Report, 2002).
4. The model had several features including the grouping or clustering of agencies for consistency and economies of scale; an end-to-end approach, producing a 'winner takes all' result for each group's successful tenderer; and a centralized approach.
5. This section draws on interviews conducted in Wellington in November 2000. There was some variation among respondents' perceptions.
6. Auditor-General reports were produced through this period, but only recent ones have been included. There were also relevant reports by parliamentary committees.

6. Evaluation and New Public Management in the Netherlands

Frans L. Leeuw

I. Introduction

Government and public-sector in the Netherlands

The Netherlands has three basic governmental levels: central government (13 ministerial departments and their advisory and implementing agencies), the 12 provinces and about 550 communities. The concept of 'decentralized-unitary state' may sound like a contradiction in terms; however, it illustrates the relations between the levels of government: lower levels are granted a certain level of autonomy where specific local and provincial tasks are concerned, as well as the authority required to implement national programmes ('medebewind'); however, central policy and legislation, supervision and control provides authoritative direction to policy-making and implementation on local and provincial levels. Additionally, there are several hundreds of quangos (Jenkins, Leeuw and Van Thiel 2003). These organizations carry out many tasks that are considered to be public functions (Bemelmans-Videc 2002).

This chapter describes the position of evaluation within the public-sector over the last 20 years and focuses in particular on links between new public management and evaluation. Quangos will not be discussed.

Evaluation

Although evaluation in the public-sector concerns the production and relay of information on the processes and results of policy implementation to principals, parliaments and society at large, there is a difference between evaluation research – which focuses primarily on applying social science methodology – and other 'evaluative activities'. Hence, evaluation activities in the Netherlands also can be described in terms of analytical procedures, such as (indicator-based) monitoring, results-based management, 'inspection' activities and performance auditing.

Indeed, a plethora of activities can be grouped under the umbrella concept of evaluation: inspection, performance auditing, organizational audits, impact assessment and oversight (activities).

Another distinction is that between evaluation of 'substantive policies' within the public sector (such as educational, environmental and economic policies) and evaluating the public-sector reforms as such (like de- or re-regulation and 'quango-cratization').

A third useful distinction is that between internal (or in-house) evaluation mechanisms and external evaluation procedures, which mostly are carried out by independent organizations such as national audit offices, universities or other 'knowledge firms'.

First, I will describe developments of (new) public management and internal evaluations in the Netherlands. Next, I will shift my focus to the recent history of external evaluations of policies, programmes and results. The fourth section explores to what extent more internal and external evaluations might have lead to (more) results-based management. The final section describes some of the challenges facing evaluation and public management.

2. New Public Management and internal evaluations

On performance budgeting and the Ministry of Finance

In the words of Van der Knaap (2001): 'Bridging performance management and policy evaluation is *en vogue*'. In Holland, the importance of pairing performance management with policy evaluation research was first acknowledged in the 1991 government position papers, 'Policy evaluation studies in central government' and 'Frame-of-reference for policy evaluation instruments' (Ministry of Finance 1994; updated in 1998). Along with (project-based) policy evaluations – which usually take place less frequently than once a year and focus on the net (societal) effects of policy programmes – and 'organizational auditing', systems of performance and effect indicators have been high on the Netherlands central government's agenda since the early 1990s. These systems provide periodic insight – or 'monitoring information' – into government performance and the extent to which policy-makers have achieved their aims.

Performance management, including results-based management, currently occupies centre stage. One of the earliest forms of performance measurement in the Netherlands was 'performance budgeting' (Sorber 1999). Since the 1970s, ministries have provided annual performance data in their budgets (Klaassen and Van Nispen 1998). The main functions of this approach to performance budgeting were to increase Parliament's insight into the budget estimates in order to improve decision-making on the appropriation of funds (the allocation and control function), and to increase the efficiency and effectiveness of various policy programmes (the management and control function).

These functions are still relevant today. The availability of reliable and timely information on government performance is of vital importance to the development of increased efficiency and effectiveness through transparency. Inspired by Osborne and Gaebler's principle, 'If you don't measure results you can't tell success from failure', one of the major efforts in the field of public management in the Netherlands Government in the 1990s was the systematic development of indicators of the performance and effects of government management and policy measures. To stimulate development, a step-by-step approach to good governance was used: expenditure control, efficiency and effectiveness (Ministry of Finance 1999). Up to and including the 1996 Budget, the emphasis was put on 'estimate key figures', that is, data that provide insight into the factors upon which budget estimations are based.

This information, however, was largely restricted to data on price and quantity aspects of budget estimates, the so-called 'P(rice) × Q(uantity) approach' (Sorber 1999). Relevant as they may be for budgetary purposes, estimated key figures only partially provide insight into actual government performance. According to Van der Knaap (2001), one reason for this is that they include either output or input factors (e.g. the number of civil servants employed). For this reason, in the preparations of the 1997 and 1998 budgets, the emphasis shifted to more substantive performance indicators. The inclusion of the costs and quality of government products and services allowed greater insight into efficiency, that is, the resources-performance ratio. The main criterion by which to assess efficiency is 'cost per unit output', combined with quality indicators. With comparisons over time, cross-sectional analysis (benchmarking) and comparisons to specific norms or targets, insight in efficiency improvement can be acquired (Ministry of Finance 1994, 1998). The addition of efficiency information to ministry budgets paralleled the introduction of the state agency model.

Agencification
Currently, there are some 20 agencies with an overall turnover of approximately NLG 3.5 billion. Personnel number approximately 27,500 – more than a quarter of the total number of public servants within the Netherlands' central government.

In 1998, the first steps were taken to develop key figures on effectiveness. The objective was to provide insight into the effects of policy measures within society. Currently, the objective is to gain insight into the pursued effects – and, ex post, achieved net effects of policy measures within society. In 1998 and 1999, ministries started to include target figures on the effectiveness of policy measures in their budgets. Nevertheless, information of this kind is still very rare. By putting the objectives of policy measures first, the new proposals on the structure, content and presentation of budget documents does correct this inadequacy' (Van der Knaap 2001). He goes on to say the following. 'In 1991, the agency model was introduced, intended to increase the efficiency within Central Government by means of results-oriented management.' These agencies are required to present annual data on costs and benefits. Most of them are confronted with sunset legislation, in the sense that, usually after some five years, an external evaluation of the functioning of the agency is carried out. With regard to financial management, the National Audit Office must conduct an independent annual review of the quality of the data. With regard to the quality of data concerning the efficiency and the impact of the agency's activities, this *can* be done by the national audit office, but usually not on an annual basis. Occasionally the audit office carries out a meta-evaluation of evaluations – ranging from energy conservation to the effectiveness of fiscal instruments – conducted by agencies and other public-sector organizations. The focus is primarily on learning and stimulating the organizations to increase the quality of their (internal) evaluations. Sanctions have not yet been implemented.

Organizational auditing

'Organizational auditing' resembles the application of 'operational auditing' to the public sector. Organizational audits explore whether or not management has done enough to safeguard an efficient and effective development and implementation of policies and programmes. Their focus is on provisions and operating procedures that must be installed to ensure adequate implementation. The role of the national audit office is important here, because in many of its investigations it has requested – over and over – that ministries install these provisions. However, in some studies (Bemelmans-Videc 1998; Leeuw 2000) it has been shown that a perverse effect of this emphasis is that government attention shifts from solving social and policy problems to creating procedural and administrative arrangements that are believed to be of relevance for solving social and policy problems.

3. New Public Management and external evaluations[1]

National Audit Office studies of evaluations and their impact

Important examples of (independent) governmental organizations that have been established to carry out external evaluations include 'planning bureaus', which hardly do any planning but instead evaluate and monitor,[2] and the National Audit Office. This office, which is several hundred years old, started its evaluation and performance monitoring work in the mid-1980s. Its most effective audit instruments were the Office's government-wide investigations into several policy instruments: subsidies, levies, information campaigns, laws, covenants, licences, contracts and internal evaluations, including the evaluation infrastructure of the ministries. A government-wide study was published in 1990. It described the ways in which evaluations were carried out by the departments, which results were used and how, how much public money was involved in evaluation, who was responsible for the studies and the results, and what were the intended follow-ups. In this government-wide investigation (Kordes et al. 1988; Leeuw 1998a) the audit office concluded that the evaluation function inside government was rather underdeveloped. In the wake of this (devastating) report central government declared its intention to issue legislation on systematic and periodic policy and programme evaluation.

In an official Cabinet reaction to this government-wide audit, government also endorsed the Audit Office's recommendations and Parliament's wishes. Systematic and periodic evaluation research was considered instrumental in reviewing policy programmes for their effectiveness and efficiency. In more operational terms this would mean that policy evaluation was to be part and parcel of the policy process, implying that there would be periodical review of all programmes; evaluations should be used to refocus existing policies or contribute to new policies; the evaluation function needed to be embedded in the existing departmental frameworks and structures in order to optimize linkages to existing policy and budgeting processes; the support and utilization in policy formation of evaluation research results would be primarily the responsibility of the department's political and civil service management; and evaluation results needed to be incorporated in budgetary decision-making.

These views were set in new legislation and instructions regarding the management and coordination of the evaluation function. First, legislation stipulated evaluation responsibilities: the departmental minister and his/her policy directorates would be primarily responsible for policy evaluation; within each ministry, the Central Financial and Economic Affairs Department has a stimulating and coordinating role in the evaluation functions of the various internal policy directorates; and ministers should timely inform the NCA of all its evaluation research and results. This information should aid the court in its performance audits (a meta-evaluation function).

Second, the Ministry of Finance's Directorate-General of the Budget would have a stimulating, coordinating role: issuing relevant budget instructions to all ministerial departments and checking their compliance.

Third, an annual budget report to facilitate policy evaluation was recommended. The departments were to indicate what evaluation research was proposed or in process, what were the results of that research and how these results had been used in budgetary decision-making.

Over the years the Audit Office has repeated a number of government-wide investigations. The watchdog role of the National Audit Office has become more important in the last quarter of the 20th century, although it has frequently been met with criticism (Leeuw 1998). The office has expanded its activities and its budget over the last ten years; in addition to legality and compliance investigations, it carries out performance audits and occasional meta-analyses of evaluations. Recently, its powers have expanded to allow the office to carry out compliance and performance studies within municipalities and regions in which EU-money is involved. This was impossible for decades.

Inspectorates

Another development concerns the growth of inspectorates. Most ministries have supervisory or inspection departments, such as the Health Inspectorate or the Education Inspectorate. Their duties also have evolved to include inspection and evaluation not only of process variables, but also of the actual effectiveness and regularity of output and outcome. These organizations, some more than 200 years old, became more involved in evaluations, quality assessments, and impact studies, in addition to their more traditional role of investigating compliance with law. Debates inside and outside Parliament on the independence of these organizations (most of them part of a government department) have taken place since the late 1990s. Sometimes, as was the case with the Education Inspectorate, this led to legislation on the oversight and evaluation of education, which regulated the evaluation function, the functional independence, and 'hearing both sides' procedures for this (200-year-old) office.

The role of Parliament

A recent development concerns the introduction of a day of parliamentary discussions focused on scrutinizing what the cabinet has accomplished during the previous year in light of the goals that were set for that year. Recently a very small 'congressional research bureau' has been established, which amongst others will review and use research by others on behalf of Parliament.

Parliament has also actively developed sunset legislation, that is, legislation implemented over a period of several years, after which an evaluation must be carried out in order to determine whether or not a law (or policy instrument or organization) should be continued. An interesting example is a new law on educational oversight and evaluations (to be implemented by 2003) that concerns the work of the (202-year-old) Education Inspectorate. Parliament wanted an (independent) evaluation of the Education Inspectorate after five years; this amounts to evaluating the evaluator. Furthermore, Parliament has been very active in parliamentary inquiry hearings, field investigation and commissioned research (typically) conducted by university professors.

The late 70s versus the early 2000s

Since Hoogerwerf made his 1977 address on the field of evaluations in the Netherlands' public sector, a big step forward has been made: there has been more measurement of processes and outputs – both on the basis of internal and external evaluations, more organizational provisions for this work, bigger budgets, a larger number of reports, and more institutionalization.[3]

Given all this, to what extent has the emphasis on evaluation, auditing and measurement in general and organizational prerequisites in particular led to more results-based management?

4. Evaluating and measuring performance- and results-based management: with special emphasis on the performance paradox

The concepts of performance monitoring and results-based management do not refer to the same phenomenon. Performance monitoring means measurement, analysis and reporting; these activities produce knowledge and information. Results-based management, however, boils down to steering, actions, implementing incentives and other instruments for (behavioural) changes.

A recent (external) evaluation – one that explored to what extent re-sults-based management is indeed practised in the central and lo-cal/regional government and that was based on empirical evaluations of the implementation of this type of policy and management – found that although measuring and monitoring have indeed strongly increased, results-based management and results-based policy-making have lagged behind (Van Gils and Leeuw 2000).

This study was sponsored by the Ministry of the Interior and was carried out jointly by a university and a policy research organization. The methodology used was document analysis; all empirical evalua-tions that have been carried out between 1990 and 1999, with a focus on the question to what extent evaluating and monitoring performance leads to results-based management, were inventoried and content-analysed. The study found that there is a long way to go before measur-ing results and costs could lead to managing with and for results in practice. The authors used as a baseline a 1990 study on the question of where the government was with regard to 'results-focused steering' inside governmental departments (as it was called in those days). They then used published and non-published evaluations wherever available. Findings therefore included education, social welfare and privatization but also health, waterworks and energy conservation.

A first explanation of their findings (Van Gils and Leeuw 2000) is that in most of the public-sector organizations, links between results achieved and costs involved on the one hand and human resources management, including incentives for officials and 'street-level bureau-crats', on the other hand, have not yet been developed, let alone imple-mented. Attention has been given to measurement, not to 'steering' on the basis of the measurement results. As the public-sector is a 'people's business', this is an important omission.

Second, even in organizations that carry out numerous evaluations and audits, almost no knowledge management has been put in place. As streams of data increase over increasing numbers of topics, knowledge management is needed to make the findings usable. In that respect, the world as described by Weiss, Bucuvalis and earlier students of evalua-tion utilization in the 1970s and 1980s has become somewhat irrele-vant, because results-based management produces streams of evalua-tions instead of single, large-scale evaluations such as the income main-tenance projects, and the Head Start project.

On the performance paradox
A third explanation is that results-based management produces its own unintended and negative side-effects, such as the performance paradox. Meyer and O'Shaughnessy (1993) have coined the concept of the 'performance paradox' and have demonstrated the validity of this concept on the basis of research in the private sector. Van Thiel and Leeuw (2002) have expanded the knowledge base to the public sector. Basically, the performance paradox is the simultaneous proliferation and non-correlation of performance measures, which are central to the idea of auditing. An organization which aims at safeguarding its performance through the application of performance measurement instruments is not necessarily an effective organization: 'Even though organizational performance measures tend to be weakly correlated with one another, performance measures have increased in number and sophistication over time and staff charged with monitoring performance have burgeoned correspondingly' (van Thiel and Leeuw 2002, p. 271). This has contributed to the growth of 'second order performance assessment by external auditors and financial analysts' (van Thiel and Leeuw 2002, p. 271). Perverse learning – how to 'deal' with monitoring (like 'teaching to the test' and 'window dressing') – is one cause of such a paradox. Another is an overemphasis on rules and procedures that must be in place in order to make policies and programmes auditable, but in the end often lead only to 'rituals of verification' (Power 1997; Leeuw 2000). One example is the emphasis by the European Union and many nation states and NGOs to produce logical framework analyses (LFAs). In order to make decisions on funding, LFAs are considered necessary as an ex ante evaluation instrument to help decision-makers. These frameworks specify which (policy) goals have to be realized, when and under which conditions, to what extent there are intermediary goals and whether or not there is a 'killer assumption' that must be addressed.[4] However, according to recent evaluations these LFAs in practice often produce only schematic and superficial information, resembling a 'tick-and-flick approach' or 'box-ism' (Gasper 1996). Among the remedies suggested are theory-driven and on-site evaluations that are able to identify causal mechanisms that underlie programmes and policies. The realist evaluation approach (Pawson and Tilley 1997) is particularly helpful here.

How to explain the change from the late 1970s to the present
What appear to be the most important factors explaining the difference? Bemelmans-Videc (2002) presents an initial answer. She is of the opin-

ion that the Netherlands is seen as a second-wave country: by the mid-1970s attempts at institutionalizing the evaluation function started. Sweden, the USA and Canada are considered first-wave countries, in which evaluation started in the 1960s. The different waves are explained by general social developments – both political and economic – and by constitutional differences. The specific nature of institutionalization was further linked to the intended uses of evaluation. For the first-wave countries (such as the USA and Canada) the crucial link was between evaluation efforts and interventionist programmes, while for second-wave countries, such as the Netherlands, the crucial link was between cutback management and budgetary review procedures. On the supply side there were developments in the basic (social) sciences, providing policy evaluation with a professional methodology.

Two other explanations are needed, however. The first concerns the role parliamentary inquiries have played in getting evaluation and results-based public-sector management going. Between the late 1940s and the early 1980s, no parliamentary inquiry has taken place. Inquiry is a powerful instrument; it allows members of parliament to develop their own problem formulation and 'theory'; it makes it possible to question everyone involved under oath; it contributes to an 'evaluation capacity' to do appropriate field study, and has as a proviso that central government must act upon its findings. In the early 1980s, Parliament suddenly reinvented this inquiry instrument and started large-scale investigations into a.o. housing subsidies and the administrative collapse of Dutch industrial policies. The results were devastating to ministers, but moreover, they opened the question of how these failures could have taken place. The parliamentary and societal debate was shifted from substantive issues to more structural ones, such as: Where were the controllers and accountants in these departments? Where were the audit committees of these departments? Why were there no independent evaluations before Parliament stepped into the picture? Will there be further administrative collapses?

The role of reinventing parliamentary inquiries as a trigger mechanism cannot be underestimated. It at least brought the National Audit Office into a position to start a series of government-wide audits in which it was shown, time and again, that policy instruments such as subsidies, contracts, public information campaigns, quangos, laws and certificates were not being evaluated adequately by the central government.

The second explanation concerns the question of why there is, in the year 2002, no backsliding in the attention paid to evaluation, auditing and control in the Netherlands' government; in fact the opposite is taking place, that is, an increased number of organizations doing evaluative work. The 2000 Volendam and Enschede disasters deserve mention.[5] Reports investigating how these accidents could have taken place revealed a number of factors, but two are of prime importance to our discussion. The first concerns the lack of knowledge of what went on in cafés that youngsters frequent and of what was stored in the fire-works factory. The second concerns the lack of compliance with rules and regulations in both situations. Government officials did issue warn-ings to the organizations but did not engage themselves in follow-up actions. Both factors help to prioritize evaluative activities, by both the central government and local governments. Knowledge sharing and compliance auditing had some benefit,[6] but for how long will there be no side-effects? That topic will be discussed in the final section.

5. New challenges: On side-effects and the law of diminishing returns

Are more evaluation activities always better? The assumption that evaluative activities are always beneficial to the public-sector and its management may run counter to common knowledge: there are unin-tended (negative) side-effects of good intentions; and the law of dimin-ishing returns.

Unintended side-effects do occur and the more evaluation there is, the greater the possibility of such side-effects. One side-effect has al-ready been mentioned: the 'performance paradox'. Smith (1995, p. 299) discussed several other unintended consequences. He illustrates that monitoring and auditing performance can inhibit innovation and lead to ossification: organizational paralysis brought about by performance measurement. He also pays attention to tunnel vision (Smith 1995, p. 284). 'Tunnel vision can be defined as an emphasis on phenomena that are quantified in the performance measurement scheme at the expense of unquantified aspects of performance'. Other unintended side-effects are 'sub-optimization', which is defined as 'narrow local objectives by managers, at the expense of the objectives of the organization as a whole' and 'measure fixation' ('an emphasis on [single] measures of success rather than [on] the underlying objective').

Fitz-Gibbon (1997, pp. 87–95) used Smith's approach in a survey of 104 head teachers of primary schools in the UK. One of the aims of this study was to find out to what extent monitoring, inspection and audits contribute to school effectiveness. She found that 'with the exception of ossification, each of these possibilities [i.e. unintended side-effects] was commented upon by head teachers in open-ended items in the question-naires. These are not theoretical problems but actual, already-perceived problems' (p. 87). What these studies reveal is that, despite the goals of audits and evaluations, they may end up producing perverse effects.

In addition, as the law of diminishing returns points out, at a certain point there are no increased benefits to increased evaluation. The cur-rent Dutch attention to evaluations might, in the not too distant future, reach such a point. Some already refer to 'evaluations' as the policy instrument par excellence, because it produces only knowledge. Others refer to the danger of 'analysis paralysis', where evaluation after evaluation is carried out without decisions being made. Furthermore, the concept of 'behavioural costs' (that is, transaction costs for the ones who are being evaluated) of evaluations is on the agenda. Dealing with these signals and developments in public-sector management is a seri-ous challenge. More is not always better.

References

Algemene Rekenkamer (2000), *Organisatie van Beleidsevaluatie*, Tweede Kamer, vergaderjaar 1999–2000, 27 065, nr. 2.

Bemelmans-Videc, M.L.(1998), 'De Algemene Rekenkamer: controlenormen en stijlen in een veranderende bestuurlijke context', in: M.L.M. Hertogh et al. (eds), *Omgaan met onderhandelend bestuur*, Amsterdam: Amsterdam University Press.

Bemelmans-Videc, M.L. (2002), 'The Netherlands', in Jan-Eric Furubo et al. (eds), *The Evaluation Atlas*, New Brunswick, US: Transaction.

Fitz-Gibbon, J. (1997), *The Value Added National Project: Report to the Sec-retary of State*, University of Durham, SCA: School Curriculum and As-sessment Authority.

Des Gasper (1996), 'Analysing policy arguments', *European Journal of Devel-opment Research*, vol. 8, pp. 36–62.

Ghoshal, S. and P. Moran (1996), 'Bad for practices: A critique of the transac-tion cost theory', *Academy of Management Review*, 21, 13–47.

van Gils, Ger H. C. and Frans L. Leeuw (2000), 'Outputsturing in de publieke sector: voortgang maar traag', *Beleidsanalyse*, 31, 3–14.

Hoogerwerf, A. (1977), *Effecten van beleid*. Inaugural address, University of Twente, Enschede.

Jenkins, W. I., F. L. Leeuw and S. Van Thiel (2003, in press), 'Quangos, evaluation and accountability in the collaborative state', in A. Gray, B. Jen-kins, F. L. Leeuw and J. Mayne (eds), *Collaboration in public services; the challenge for evaluation*, London, Transaction Publishers, Chapter 3.

Klaassen, Henk L. and Frans K. M. Van Nispen (1998), 'Policy analysis in the Netherlands', research paper, The Institute of Public Policy, George Mason University.

van der Knaap, Peter (1995), 'Policy evaluation and learning: Feedback, enlightenment or argumentation?', *Evaluation*, 1[2], October, 189–216.

van der Knaap, Peter (2001), 'Performance management and policy evaluation in the Netherlands: towards an integrated approach', Working Paper, Ministry of Finance, The Netherlands.

van der Knaap, Peter (2002), 'Policy evaluation in the Netherlands: Linking budgets to operations and results', Working Paper, Ministry of Finance, The Netherlands.

van der Knaap, P., H. Korte and R. van Oosterom (2001), 'The central government's financial management', working paper, Ministry of Finance, The Netherlands.

Kordes, F. G., F. L. Leeuw and J. H. A. van Dam (1991), 'The management of Government subsidies', in A. Friedberg et al. (eds), *State Audit and Accountability*, Jerusalem: State of Israel, Government Printer, Jerusalem, pp. 280–99.

Leeuw, Frans L. (1997), 'Prestatie-indicatoren in de publieke sector (Performance indicators in the public sector)', in *Overheidsmanagement*, 1997 [1], 8–12.

Leeuw, Frans L. (1998), 'Doelmatigheidsonderzoek van de Rekenkamer als regelgeleide organisatiekunde met een rechtssociologisch tintje?', *Recht der Werkelijkheid*, 14, 35–71.

Leeuw, Frans L. (1998a), 'The carrot: subsidies as a tool of government; theory and practice', in Marie-Louise Bemelmans-Videc (ed), *Carrots, Sticks and Sermons: Policy Instruments and Their Evaluation*, Comparative Policy Analysis Series, New Brunswick, US: Transaction, pp. 75–103.

Leeuw, Frans L. (2000), 'Unintended side effects of auditing: the relationship between performance auditing and performance improvement and the role of trust', in W. Raub and J. Weesie (eds), *The Management of Durable Relations*, Amsterdam, Thelathesis, pp. 95–96. [Available on CD-ROM.]

Leeuws, Frans L. and Gils, G. van (1999), *Outputsturing in de publieke sector: een analyse van bestaand onderzoek*, Den Haag, Ministrie van Binnenlandse Zaken en Koninkrijksrelaties.

Meyer, M. W. and Gupta, V. (1994), 'The performance paradox', *Research in Organizational Behavior*, 16, 309–69.

Meyer, M. W. and O'Shaughnessy, K. (1993), Organizational design and the performance paradox, in: R. Swedberg (ed.), *Explorations in Economic Sociology*, New York, Russel Sage Foundation, pp. 249–78.

Ministry of Finance (1994; 1998), *Frame-of-reference for Policy Evaluation Instruments*, The Hague: Ministry of Finance.

Ministry of Finance (1999), *Voorhoedeprojecten prestatiegegevens en beleidsevaluatie* (Vanguard projects performance indicators and policy evaluation), The Hague: Directorate of Budget Affairs.

Osborne, D. E. and T. Gaebler (1992), *Reinventing Government – How the Entrepreneurial Spirit is Transforming the Public Sector*, Reading, US: Addison-Wesley.

Parliament (1999), *Van beleidsbegroting tot beleidsverantwoording* (From Policy Budget to Policy Annual Account), The Hague: SDU.

Pawson, R. and N.Tilley (1997), *Realist evaluation*, Sage, London.

Power, M. (1994), *The Audit Explosion*, London: Demos.

Power, M. (1997), *The Audit Society*, Oxford: Oxford University Press.

Smith, P. (1995), On the unintended consequences of pubishing performance data in the public sector, *International Journal of Public Administration*, 18, pp. 277–310.

Sorber, Bram (1999), 'Performance measurement in the central government departments of the Netherlands', in Arie Alachmi (ed.), *Performance and Quality Measurement in Government*, Burke, US: Chatelaine Press.

van Thiel, S. and Frans L. Leeuw (2002), The performance paradox in het public sector, in: *Public Productivity and Management Review*, 25[3], pp. 267–81.

Notes

1   See also Bemelmans-Videc (2002), Leeuw (2000) and Leeuw (1997).
2   The first was established immediately after World War II (central economic planning bureau), the social and cultural planning bureau was established in the 1970s, and recently a planning bureau for housing was established.
3.   An example is *Van beleidsbegroting tot beleidsverantwoording* (From policy budget to policy accountability [*VBTB*]), which is an important movement comprising several organizational and institutional arrangements focused on making clear to Parliament (and society) which goals have been set by ministries and which have been realized.
4.   A killer assumption is an assumption underlying the project or programme that, when it is true, 'kills' the project or programme in its implementation stage.
5.   Volendam concerns the burning down of a café, which killed more than 10 children; Enschede concerns the explosion of a fireworks factory that destroyed a whole community.
6.   Although the disaster was of a completely different magnitude, one of the major critiques of the CIA and FBI regarding the 9–11 disaster concerns the lack of knowledge sharing and knowledge management of factors that might have served as warnings, if pooled together at the right time.

7. Evaluation and public-sector reform in Germany: Leaps and lags

Hellmut Wollmann

This chapter comprises essentially two parts. First, a cursory overview on the recent development of public-sector reforms will be given. Second, the development of evaluation will be addressed. Finally, some conclusions will be formulated.

1. Public-sector reforms in Germany since the early 1990s

Germany has been a conspicuous latecomer to international NPM-guided modernization discourse and practice. While the ideas and concepts conveniently summarized under New Public Management (NPM) (see Hood 1991) ran rampant in the international (largely Anglophone, if not 'Anglo-Saxon-centric') debate on public-sector modernization (see Wollmann 2001, p. 152), the German modernization debate and practice kept a conspicuous distance until the late 1980s. The reasons for this time lag are explained below (for more details see Wollmann 2000a, pp. 923 ff.).

First, the Federal Republic's intergovernmental administrative system traditionally has been characterized by a number of institutional features which, through NPM lenses, might be seen as remarkably 'modern':

1. In the basic constitutional setup of the Federal Republic's political and administrative system the federal level, *grosso modo*, is largely restricted to policy-making and legislation (with very few executive functions and, hence, with a comparatively small personnel body of its own[1]) while the implementation of federal policies and legislation

as well as of the administrative functions are left to the *Länder* (federal States).

2. At the same time, within the *Länder* the lion's share of the executive and administrative tasks is carried out by the local authorities,[2] which traditionally operate on a politically as well as (multi-)functionally strong local government model (see Wollmann 2000a, pp. 918 f.). Internationally Germany's local government system is counted, along with the Scandinavian countries, among those countries with strong local governments (see Hesse and Sharpe 1990). With regard to the vertical division of executive and administrative functions one could speak, in NPM parlance, of some kind of 'agencification' both in federal/*Länder* relations as well as in the *Länder*/local government interface.

3. Despite this wide scope of local responsibilities the *delivery* of the personal social services (kindergartens, homes for the elderly, etc.) has been left, under the traditional 'subsidiarity' principle, to a large extent to non-public not-for-profit (NGO-type) welfare organizations (*freie Wohlfahrtsverbände*) (Bönker and Wollmann 2000, p. 337). In this traditional feature one could see the NPM principles of restricting local government to an 'enabling' function and of outsourcing the delivery of services to NGOs.

These traditional constitutional and institutional peculiarities (multi-level government, decentralization, multi-functional local government system, and subsidiarity) might be interpreted as having already put in place some crucial NPM conditions.

Second, the German administrative sphere had a good record of administrative reforms over the years. This applies particularly to the (short-lived) *planning* era of the 1960s and 1970s, when significant administrative reforms were undertaken on the federal, *Länder* and local government levels, including the introduction of evaluation as an essential modernization tool (see Wollmann 2000a, pp. 920 ff.). The reform activities continued during the 1980s in a typically incrementalist and adaptive style (see Wollmann 1997, pp. 86 ff.). As a result, at least into the 1980s, Germany's public administration has gained the national and international reputation of performing well by international standards, particularly when it comes to legally correct and reliable conduct.[3] This widely-accepted assessment served as another cognitive and normative barrier against an easy adoption of the NPM discourse in Germany.

When, in the early 1990s, modernization discourse and practice in Germany finally (and surprisingly rapidly) opened up to NPM message, this dramatic shift was triggered by a number of factors, of which two in particular should be highlighted (for details see Wollmann 2001, pp. 160 ff.):

1. Skyrocketing public debts incurred by the financial burdens of German Unification and the pressure to meet the budgetary parameters set by the Treaty of Maastricht on the EU led all levels of government to turn to NPM as a panacea for their budgetary plight.

2. In rhetorical and practical terms the NPM movement took root at first at the local level, when KGSt (a municipally funded non-profit consulting organization under its director Gerhard Banner) formulated and propagated a managerialist modernization concept called New Steering Model (NSM; *Neues Steuerungsmodell*) (Banner 1991, Reichard 1994) which significantly drew on the NPM-guided concept then pursued in the Dutch City of Tilburg ('Tilburg model', see Hendriks and Topps 1999). NSM was originally meant to achieve two objectives: on the one hand, it was to reshape the relation between (local) politics (centring around the elected council) and (local) administration (hinging on its political and administrative leadership). On the other hand, it was to apply to the public-sector micro-economic (*betriebswirtschaftlich*) concepts and instruments borrowed from private sector and private business managerialism, such as global output-oriented budgeting, decentralized resource management, controlling and contracting in the intra-administrative setting, and provider/client relations, competition and quasi-markets in the external dimension.

In contrast with most other countries (particularly the unitary and centrally governed ones), Germany's modernization movement in the early 1990s showed a distinct bottom-up pattern, in that conceptually – as well as practically – it started at the local government level, was then taken up at the *Länder* level and, in the late 1990s, finally reached the federal government level.[4]

Although the story of post-1990s public-sector reforms would have to be told chronologically in a bottom-up sequence, we shall give a cursory account in the familiar top-down order.

The institutional transformation of East Germany

At this point mention should be made of the institutional transformation in East Germany which, following the German unification of 3 October 1990, amounted to nothing less than a revolutionary public-sector reform (see Wollmann 1996a, 1996b with references). As of 3 October 1990, the entire constitutional and legal structure of the old Federal Republic was transferred and expanded to East Germany, replacing the legal order of the former German Democratic Republic (GDR). Within a short time, the GDR's entire state-owned and state-run economy was dismantled and privatised. When the GDR's central government level ceased to exist after 3 October, the five East German *Länder* that had been abolished by the communist regime in the early 1950s were reinstalled, and their administrative structures had to be rebuilt from scratch. As German unification came as a total surprise and then unfolded at an unprecedented pace, the 'creative destruction' (*schöpferische Zerstörung*, a term coined by Joseph Schumpeter) of the GDR's Socialist state and the build-up of the new political and administrative structures, at least at the beginning, largely adopted the organizational blueprints of the old Republic in a kind of (exogeneously) imposed institution building (see Wollmann 1996a).

Federal government level

Parallelling the 'privatization' of the former GDR's Socialist state economy, the conservative-liberal federal government under Chancellor Helmut Kohl proceeded to 'privatize' the national railway and postal systems by turning the railway system, by January 1994, into a state-owned, but autonomously operated corporation; and by splitting up the postal system, by January 1995, into three companies – one of which became Deutsche Telekom (40 per cent of its stocks were sold to private investors).

For the rest, however, the conservative-liberal federal government dragged its feet on modernizing its governmental and administrative structures. Even after the Federal Parliament decided in June 1993 to move the greater part of the federal government from Bonn to Berlin, thus opening a window for restructuring federal government and administration, little actually happened (Jann and Wewer 1998). In 1995, towards the end of the conservative-liberal Kohl era, an Independent Experts Commission, under the title of 'Lean State' (*Sachverständigenrat Schlanker Staat*), was established. It produced voluminous guidelines on where and how to modernize the federal structures. But, in real terms, hardly any administrative reform measures were taken by the outgoing government (see König and Füchtner 1998).

Following the federal elections of September 1998, the incoming 'red-green' federal government coalition coined the term 'activating state' (*aktivierender Staat*) – a new 'red-green' reform shibboleth meant to oppose the conservative-liberal predecessor government's 'lean state' and to draw up a 'Third Way' strategy (see Wollmann 2000b, pp. 702 ff.). In December 1999, the red-green government finally put forward a modernization programme labelled 'Modern State-Modern Administration' (see www.moderner-staat.de). Making an unmistakable allusion to the Clinton/Gore rhetoric – recalling the vision of 'an administration which performs better and costs less' (Bundesregierung 2002, p. 15) – the programme proposed the introduction of 'modern management which creates innovation by delegating responsibility and creates scope for performance through results-oriented monitoring' (Bundesregierung 2002, p. 15). In the meantime the programme has made some noticeable progress:

1. Cost-to-performance accounting, or accrual accounting, has been introduced in 306 federal authorities, already covering 89 per cent of the federal staff (Bundesregierung 2002, p. 18).
2. 'Product budgets' were applied to some federal authorities in the 2001 federal budget and will be extended to some others in 2002 (Bundesregierung 2002, p. 19).
3. Inter-departmental (inter-ministerial) benchmarking has been initiated in a number of cases (Bundesregierung 2002, p. 21).
4. Ministries now use target-setting as a tool for steering their subordinate authorities. Target-setting is also used as an essential management tool for internal purposes within a given authority (OECD country report 2000, p. 3).
5. The use of modern information technology has been pushed. As a result of the 'BundOnline 2005 e-government initiative', citizens can access many government services via the internet.

Thus, it can be said that, after a late and slow start at the end of 1999, the federal government has moved fairly fast in putting some modernization measure in place. Its operations are still hampered by the fact that, due to the compromise decision which left some ministries and most of the rank and file officials in Bonn, the federal government still operates at two locations, that is, in Berlin as well as in Bonn.

Länder level

Since the early 1990s the *Länder* governments have significantly stepped up their public-sector modernization activities, at first by establishing (independent) reform commissions (usually made up of politicians, administrative experts, interest group representatives, and academics) and reform units (mostly in the ministries of the interior which are traditionally the ministries responsible for constitutional and administrative reforms [for details see Bürsch and Müller 1999, Konzendorf 1998]).

Within the great institutional variance of reform concepts and measures which typically shows in the reform activities of the *Länder*, two main groups of reforms can be discerned. On the one hand, some *Länder* have taken on reform issues which were addressed back in the 1960s and 1970s, but have remained unfinished business. The recent modernization momentum has created a 'window of opportunity' to reopen reform issues. For instance, some *Länder* (particularly Nordrhein-Westfalen and Rheinland-Pfalz) have finally undertaken the restructuring of the meso-level of district administration (*Regierungspräsidien*) which so far have withstood all attempts to abolish them (Fürst 1996).

On the other hand, in nearly all *Länder* steps have been taken, under the umbrella of the New Steering Model (NSM), to introduce elements of public management in various sectors of *Länder* administration (see Germany OECD country report 2000, pp. 7 ff.). In order to reduce administrative costs the *Länder* are testing procedures of output-oriented budgeting (see Germany OECD country report 2000, pp. 8). Furthermore, methods of accrual accounting are increasingly being applied.

So far, however, the modernization measures have been directed at reducing the costs and expenditures of administration rather than at increasing its performance (see Bogumil 2002, p. 8 for details and references, see also Konzendorf 1998, p. 64 for a sceptical assessment).[5]

Local government level

As was already mentioned, it was the local government level that was the launching pad for the New Steering Model-driven modernization movement in the early 1990s. In the meantime, a growing number of municipalities and counties have started employing management concepts (see Germany OECD country report 2000, pp. 11 ff., see Bogumil 2002, pp. 12 ff., Grömig and Gruner 1998),[6] whereby it should be noted that, with a time lag owing to reconstruction problems, the local authorities in East Germany have followed suit (Wollmann 2000). Budgeting and decentralized responsibility for resources (*dezentrale Resourcenverantwortung*) now serve as the basis for new product- and result-oriented controlling. Contract management and the obligation to report are meant to make things more transparent and allow personal responsibility for results on the basis of set targets. The cameralistic system is increasingly being replaced by commercial bookkeeping. Product-oriented accounting has been put in place, and sometimes is supplemented by accrual accounting.

In summary, it can be said that managerialist principles and tools, based on economic rationality and geared to (cost-)efficiency, have entered into – and have had an impact on – Germany's administrative world, in which public administration has been understood as primarily guided and held accountable by legal provisions (and, in the last resort, subject to judicial review). These no doubt are important (and lasting) institutional and also cultural shifts in economic thinking and managerial principles in German public administration; however, there are strong indications that the advances and impact of the latter will be contained and counterbalanced – not the least by the very *Rechtsstaat* principles which are institutionally and culturally entrenched in the country's tradition. Institutionally the *Rechtsstaat* finds its expression in the importance of the legal regulation of administrative activities and the application of law in the day-to-day operations of public administration, particularly on the lower implementation levels. This sets an institutional, cultural and normative limit to the adoption of managerialist principles (see Wollmann 2000c).

In a similar vein, the model of politically and functionally strong local authorities which characterizes the German local self-government tradition, and its concomitant principle of politically and democratically accountable local administration, marks an institutional, cultural and normative barrier to a full-blown (marketization-driven) outsourcing (or even 'quangoization') of public functions to single-purpose, economic rationality-bound (semi-public or private) organizations.

Both dimensions (*Rechtstaat* and strong local government traditions) may set current and future trajectories of public-sector modernization that are quite distinct from those of countries in which, in the absence of a *Rechtsstaat* tradition and a strong local government, the ground for managerialism and outsourcing may be more friendly and inviting.

The balanced assessment which follows from this argumentation falls in line with the appraisal which has been submitted by Christopher Pollitt and Geert Bouckaert. They came to classify Germany's current public-sector reform trajectory as a 'mixture of maintaining and modernizing' after comparatively analysing ten countries and applying the following criteria: minimizing (the public functions), marketizing (the public functions), modernizing (the internal structures by management tools) and maintaining (retaining traditional structures) (Pollitt and Bouckaert 2000, p. 178). It may well be that the modernizing dimension will still pick up further momentum, but the traditional profile, based on the *Rechtsstaat* and the decentralized local government model, will, in all likelihood, be retained and maintained.

2. Public sector reforms and evaluation

Definitions

As explained in our introduction (see Wollmann, Chapter 1 of this volume), our discussion of the institutionalization and employment of the evaluation function will depart from a general understanding of evaluation as any analytical procedure which aims at the collection of information pertinent to the assessment of public policy programmes and measures (see also Bemelmans-Videc 2002, p. 94). Monitoring procedures, which are meant to identify the changes effected by policies and measures without pursuing the 'question of causality', can be seen as typically evaluative. Vis-à-vis the inflationary terminology which has been mushrooming (performance audit, performance measurement, and result-oriented monitoring), a functional understanding of evaluation allows the discovery of the substantive meaning of these terms beyond their usage in fashionable terminology and parlance. We would exclude 'financial auditing' as an evaluative variant, as it is essentially directed at budgetary figures and date (see also Sandahl 1992).

Setting aside most of the definitions presented in the introductory chapter, we shall be guided especially by the distinction, relating to the institutional 'locus' (and 'ownership') of evaluation, between *internal* and *external* evaluation.

Internal evaluation is carried out by the operative unit that implements the pertinent programme/measure (in forms of self-evaluation or in-house-evaluation). In most cases this is done in a descriptive monitoring fashion rather than in a 'causal-analytical' exercise. The procedures of (intra-administration) controlling, performance monitoring and other feedback mechanisms would fall under this category.

By contrast, *external* evaluation can be seen as analytical activities which are initiated (and possibly also carried out) by an agency (or organization) outside the domain of the administrative unit operating the policy programme/measure under consideration (such as parliament, the court of audit, or a governmental unit distinct from the operating unit – such as the ministry of finance). In these cases the conduct of the (external) evaluation project, because of methodological and other complexities, is often commissioned or contracted out to self-standing (independent) research institutions ('contractual research', see Woll-mann 2002b). The operating unit itself may decide to undertake an 'external' evaluation of its activity by commissioning an (independent) research institution to carry out the evaluation.

Stages and 'waves' of evaluation

As was argued in the introductory chapter, over the past 30 years or so public-sector reforms and evaluation have been Siamese twins, as it were, in that the introduction of evaluation was intrinsically intertwined with the concepts and implementation of public-sector reforms. Because of this contextuality the specific conceptual and strategic thrust of the public-sector reform was interrelated with, and shaped the profile and the orientation of, evaluation.

In a widely accepted conceptualization (see Wagner and Wollmann 1986, Derlien 1990), the development of policy evaluation from the 1960s into the 1980s is seen as a sequence of 'two waves' which are linked ('twinned') with distinct periods of policy-making in general and of public-sector reform policy in particular (for an updated account of the development of evaluation in Germany, see Derlien 2002).

The 'first wave': The (late) 1960s and (early) 1970s

During the late 1960s and early 1970s the Federal Republic was, along with Sweden, among the European countries which embarked upon policy/programme evaluation as a new approach to analytically in-formed policy-making, following the lead of the US (for an early comparative assessment, see Levine 1981). In this 'first wave' the introduction of policy evaluation was conceptually and politically driven by the aspirations of the expansive welfare state and by the planning beliefs of the time, as evaluation was perceived as a pivotal information and feed-back link in the policy-cycle triad of policy formulation/ implementa-tion/termination. The (temporary) upsurge of policy evaluation directed at the 'scientification' of policy-making was evidenced by the spree of 'social experimentation' upon which the federal and the *Länder* levels embarked in the late 1960s and early 1970s (see Hellstern and Woll-mann 1983); at that time Germany probably went further than any country other than the US in terms of 'social experimentation' and the ensuing evaluation thereof.

The introduction and institutionalization of the evaluation function was expressed in significant changes (see Hellstern and Wollmann 1984 for an overview):

1. In many federal as well as *Länder* ministries, administrative units for planning and evaluation were established (see Derlien 1976, Wollmann 1989, pp. 244 f.). The high degree of autonomy which ministries have in the context of the core executive has led to a topical sectoralization and 'sectoral imbalance' (see Derlien 2002, p. 80) in the evaluation of policies.

2. Increasingly, budgetary resources that were allotted to the ministries and were earmarked for policy evaluation started to feed an expanding 'contractual money market'.

3. While the federal and *Länder* parliaments did not have any budgetary means of their own to commission external evaluation themselves, they pressed the governments to provide evidence-based reports on policies and measures. The ensuing stream of government reports did much to establish policy evaluation as a 'matter of fact' procedure in policy-making. By contrast, the (federal and *Länder*) courts of audit still largely followed their traditional restricted responsibility for 'financial auditing', that is, for checking the compliance of budgetary regulation, while refraining from engaging in policy evaluation (see Derlien 2002, p. 80).

With regard to the evaluation of *substantive* policies, the expansion of evaluation activities, including the volume of external (contractual) evaluation research, has been significant. Evaluation has arguably become a standard operational procedure in policy-making. By contrast, despite some significant administrative reform measures effected during the reform wave of the 1960s and 1970s, the evaluation of such institutional policies and measures was conspicuously neglected. For instance, the massive territorial reforms at the local government level, which were carried out by the *Länder* during this period and which fundamentally remoulded the territorial format of local government, were not evaluated by any of the *Länder* concerned; instead, they were finally studied by a major social-science research project funded by the (independent) Volkswagen Foundation and conducted by university-based research groups.

'Second wave' period of evaluation

In the mid-1970s, Germany entered its retrenchment phase, which, in the face of mounting economic and budgetary problems, was geared to cutback management and budgetary retrenchment. Instead of being directed at policy outputs (to support – and normatively improve – the attainment of policy goals), the focus and mandate of evaluation began to be focused on budget cuts and cost-efficiency. Despite the 'regime shift' from the social-liberal to the conservative-liberal federal government in 1982, evaluation continued on a comparatively high, albeit unspectacular level (see Wagner and Wollmann 1986, Wollmann 1989, pp. 258 ff.).

As a result of this development since the late 1960s, policy evaluation can be judged as having been anchored in the practice of policy-making and the country's evaluative culture.[7]

Evaluation and public-sector reforms since the early 1990s: towards a 'third wave' of evaluation?

When NPM – with the New Steering Model (NSM) as its German off-spring – made its entry into the German modernization discourse, the employment and direction of evaluation were given a new push and focus.

Internal evaluation (self-evaluation, in-house evaluation)

In its 'Modern State – Modern Administration' programme which the federal government put forward as late as December 1999, the installation of evaluative procedures, particularly internal evaluation, has been given prime attention. Ranging the entire gamut of management tools (such as 'guiding models, agreed goals, controlling, accrual accounting, budgeting, product budgets, as well as procedures for the ongoing improvement process' [Bundesregierung 2002, p. 15]), the federal government emphasizes that 'all the concepts ... set in motion a process which chooses measures oriented in line with strategic goals, monitors these for their effectiveness and leads to further improvements by a permanent comparison of actual situation with targets' (Bundesregierung 2002, p. 15; see also OECD country report 2000, p. 2). First steps have been taken to implement these intentions:

1. 215 federal agencies have started to establish controlling schemes.
2. Accrual accounting expands the view of government receipt-expenditure accounting by probing the internal process of the generation of performance in accordance with economic criteria. As a

result it allows the assessment of the cost of each project. This type of accounting permits a view of the efficiency of public production processes. Accrual accounting now covers 89 per cent of the staffing of federal administration (Bundesregierung 2002, p. 18).

3. As a further development in standard accrual accounting, one that is thus consistent with the product-oriented budget presentation, a basic model was developed to reproduce the accrual accounting data in the federal budget. Hence, a tool has been created for output-oriented monitoring in which the tasks, products and impacts of administrative activity are allocated the necessary resources at the outset (Bundesregierung 2002, p. 18).

Drawing on the work and the recommendations of the various reform commissions and expert groups which were set up in the early 1990s, the *Länder* have also moved towards establishing accrual accounting and indicator ('product')- and result-based controlling mechanisms as means of internal evaluation (see Bogumil 2002, p. 9).

At the local government level, reflecting the early lead which the local authorities have taken since the beginning of the 1990s in introducing management tools to local administration, the employment of cost-to-performance accounting and indicator-(or 'product'-)based controlling procedures is fairly far advanced. However, the initial focus of the New Steering Model on the definition of 'products' (that is, of specific administrative tasks) and on the lengthy 'product catalogues' as the key information tool of the entire new steering and controlling system, has proven a costly failure and was called a typically (because of its conceptual over-sophistication) 'German impasse' (Reichard and Wegener 1998, p. 41). In the meantime, conceptually less ambitious and more realistic institutional and instrumental versions of internal (in-house) collection, monitoring and utilization of indicator-based information on administrative operations have been put in place in a growing number of public authorities. Although such internal indicator-based steering and controlling mechanisms have gained ground in providing intra-administrative information flows – particularly between the lower operative and managing units and the upper executive level – similar information feedback and linkages which would allow local councils to improve their steering and controlling potential vis-à-vis the administration have yet to be implemented.

While the steady expansion of administrative process-generated data and the rapidly advancing computerization of public administration would suggest that indicator-based information and controlling systems be increasingly available in public administration, in practice such information potential is still insufficiently used for monitoring and evaluative purposes. There are indications that such usage is often evaded, if not boycotted, by rank-and-file staff who – in a period of ongoing budgetary squeeze and cost-reduction – suspect the internal controlling and evaluation mechanisms and loops to act, at the end of the day, as a 'job killer'.

Benchmarking

With the advent of NPM-inspired modernization concepts, benchmarking, too, has made its entry into the German administrative sphere. At the federal government level, within its (late in coming) modernization push, three inter-departmental benchmarking exercises have been established so far (see Bundesregierung 2002, p. 21).

Significantly, earlier and more extensive use has been made of the benchmarking approach at the local government level, where the first initiative was taken by Bertelsmann Foundation and then followed by KGSt's creation of 'intermunicipal benchmarking circles' (*interkommunale Vergleichsringe*). Such 'benchmarking circles' are joined by local authorities that are prepared to engage in such exercises on a regional basis and sectoral basis (such as social administration, city libraries, issuance of building permits and the like), combining indicator-based self-evaluation and quasi-competition (see Kuhlmann 2002).

By now comparisons between local authorities have become almost a matter of course; 85 benchmarking rings are already operating, and more than 600 administrations and over 3000 municipal employees are actively involved in benchmarking. A newly developed database (IKO network) contains comparative data on the participants and the sets of quantitative and qualitative indicators for all local authorities (see OECD country report 2000, p. 12).

External evaluation

A 'soft' understanding of external evaluation would also include the evaluation of modernization projects carried out by units at the local or meso-level and assessed by the ministerial level (as an outside actor). Some *Länder* governments have started some pilot 'soft' external evaluations in order to experiment with and test reform strategies and measures.

In *Land* Baden-Württemberg the *Land* government has, since the late 1980s, required ministries to 'report' on the conduct and the goal attainment of relevant reform projects. For instance, the Ministry of the

Interior conducted a survey of counties and municipalities in order to 'evaluate' the restructuring of the field offices of *Land* administration (see Baden-Württemberg 1999, p. 80). In *Land* Nordrhein-Westfalen the Ministry of Interior conducted a survey among the administrative authorities on the state of 'internal modernization'.[8] In October 2000, the city-state of Berlin compiled a remarkably comprehensive (and critical) report on the implementation of Berlin's reform legislation and programme, via a 'standardized survey' among the administrative offices, in order to explore the relevant reform goals (see Senat von Berlin 2000). Typically, such evaluative assessments have been undertaken by the central level 'lead' agencies on the basis of 'intergovernmentally' conducted surveys and reports (without resorting to social-science methods).

A noteworthy attempt at evaluation-oriented 'experimentation' was undertaken by a number of *Länder* in the mid-1990s, when some *Länder* initiated pilot projects which obviously drew on the 'free communes experiments' that were conducted in Scandinavian countries during the 1980s. In these *Länder*, under a legislative 'experimentation clause', the legal provisions regulating the budgetary and related activities of local government could be suspended for a four-year period. Originally the idea was to have these 'experiments' duly evaluated and to feed the results into future *Länder* legislation, but in practice the local projects were carried out without methodological rigour (let alone independent external evaluation). At the end, the final reports were largely inconclusive (Wollmann 2000b, p. 215).

Another example of 'experimentation' was a pilot project initiated and funded by the East German *Land* Brandenburg which was intended to promote NPM-/NSM-led reforms in a selected group of ten (small) municipalities. In this case the *Land* government commissioned an independent university-based research team to do the evaluation (Maaß and Reichard 1998). In sum, external evaluations have so far been extremely rare.

Complementary 'evaluative' empirical research
A useful body of evaluative information on the administrative reform activities at the local level stems from the municipal associations, particularly from *Deutscher Städtetag* (German Cities Association), which is the national association of large and middle-sized cities. *Deutscher Städtetag* has conducted a number of written surveys among its member cities – starting in 1994 and repeating them every two years, using largely the same questionnaire (see Grömig and Gruner 1998). So far,

however, the surveys have addressed the state of the institutionalization of the reform concepts and elements rather than the performance or results (outputs) thereof.

Applied academic research

Another body of useful empirical knowledge on the process of public-sector reforms stems from research conducted at universities and at other public research institutes. During recent years a community of political scientists has advocated and conducted empirical research on administrative reform measures and has at the same time taken an active part in the reform discourse, thus giving their work a distinct applied orientation.

The late Frieder Naschold was a leader in engaging in the reform discourse and of initiating and in conducting pertinent research, including influential internationally comparative studies (Naschold 1995). An important player in this reformist network has been the Hans Böckler Foundation (associated with the trade unions), which has been instrumental in funding (applied basic) research on public-sector modernization and, at the same time, has been actively involved in the reform debate.

As NPM-/NSM-induced reforms have so far been pursued primarily by the local government, most available research has focused on local level developments, whereas research on the upper government levels is still rare (see, for example, Engelniederhammer et al. 1999 on the administrative reform project started by the City State of Berlin in 1994). Since many of the reform projects have been put into place only recently, empirical research has – not surprisingly – dwelt on the (early) implementation phase and hence on the evaluative question of whether (and which) reform objectives (in terms of the intended institutional and instrumental changes) have been attained. In most cases, it seems to be too early to empirically assess their performance, let alone output and outcomes.

The few evaluation studies which explicitly tried to shed some empirical light on the performance and output/outcomes dimensions (Jaedicke et al. 1999, Kißler et al. 1997) exhibit typical conceptual and methodological problems, such as the still limited availability of viable indicators ('products') and the above-mentioned dearth of accessible administrative-process generated data (Jaedicke et al. 1999, p. 251).

Finally, a huge body of social science research has been conducted on East Germany's institutional transformation (Wollmann 1996a with references). Although many of the research projects conceived as implementation studies looked at the rate and results of the institutional transfer and change, some projects pursued the (evaluative) question (including an East German/West German comparison) of whether and how the institutional transformation has affected administrative behaviour and performance (Lorenz et al. 2000).

3. Concluding remarks

Due to the entry of NPM-inspired management concepts, performance-management tools and result-based monitoring and reporting into Germany's administrative sphere, internal evaluation has made conspicuous advances in the politico-administrative system. In the previous developmental stages ('waves') of evaluation, the evaluative focus was on policies (whether to maximize output in the planning-era 'first wave' or to minimize financial input in the retrenchment-era 'second wave'). Now, internal evaluation, including cost-to-achievement accounting, accrual accounting and controlling, is taking centre stage. This marks a decisive move from an input-guided model of public administration (that is, guided by legal provisions and an allocation-based budget) to an output-guided one (that is, oriented towards results). Hence, output- and result-orientation depends on 'steering' as well as on evaluation and feedback. It is because of this shift in the conceptual focus and institutional importance of evaluation that one might, as was suggested in the introductory chapter, speak of a 'third wave' in the development of evaluation.

External evaluation of public-sector reforms has so far been conducted infrequently. This stands in glaring contrast with the salience ascribed to the creation of transparency as an overarching goal and principle in the new modernization philosophy, which would require the exposure of public-sector reform policies and measures, their effectiveness and efficiency to external (independent) evaluation. The paucity of external evaluation is a greater paradox (if not, normatively and politically speaking, a scandal), as the governments and executives at all levels have been quite open-handed during the 1990s when it came to spending money on hiring and commissioning (usually expensive) consultants to prepare[9] and carry out modernization measures.[10] The time should have come to check whether these measures have achieved their goals and have produced 'value for money'; such 'transparency' and accountability through commissioning external evaluation still lacks voices and advocacy in the institutional and political setting. In Germany's multi-level and multi-actor system there is, generally speaking, no single level, let alone single actor, that would push for such evaluation.

Horizontally, at each level and in each agency, in line with the 'sectoralization' that has characterized policy-making as well as evaluation in the past (see Wollmann 1989, Derlien 2002, p. 80), administrative reforms are largely undertaken and 'owned' by the 'sectoral' units and actors – without an executive actor assuming the role of evaluation advocate. While in most cases (both on the federal and on the *Länder* levels) the minister of the interior has been assigned the task of being the government-wide leader in administrative reform matters, this has not ushered in noticeable evaluative measures and projects. Recently, the president of the federal court of audit suggested that the federal finance minister should request more frequent evaluation studies when preparing the budget (see Bundesbeauftragter 1990, Derlien 2002, p. 80). It remains to be seen whether the federal finance minister will take up this challenge and follow suit. On the *Länder* level, too, task forces set up in the ministries of the interior push for internal evaluation approaches (see Germany OECD report 2000).

In the development of evaluation of substantive policies (such as social policy, education, or infrastructural programmes), the federal as well as *Länder* parliaments have, in the past, been active promoters of policy evaluation, in that they have pressed the government to present evidence-based reports to them. In the field of administrative reforms, however, the parliaments have so far manifested remarkably little concern and interest. Perhaps the German parliaments still consider administrative reforms an executive prerogative to be respected by the lawmakers.

The courts of audit at the federal as well as at the *Länder* levels have so far played a conspicuously small role in policy evaluation in general, and in the evaluation on public-sector reforms in particular. They have retained their traditional focus on budgetary and bookkeeping review and have moved only cautiously towards looking into policy performance. There are recent indications, however, that both the federal and the *Länder*[11] courts of audit are moving towards paying more attention to administrative reform matters. However, it bears repeating that the active role the courts of audit in Sweden and the Netherlands (to say nothing of the United States) play in the evaluation of public-sector reform measures is a far cry from the German case.

Finally, it should be mentioned that increasing professional and public interest should provide some additional leverage for putting the evaluation of public-sector reforms on the research and political agendas.[12]

References

Baden-Württemberg (1999), *Verwaltung im Wandel. Zwischenbilanz der Verwaltungsreform*, Stuttgart.

Banner, Gerhard (1991), 'Von der Behörde zum Dienstleistungsunternehmen: Die Behörden brauchen ein neues Steuerungsmodell', *VOP*, 13, 37–64.

Bemelmans-Videc, M. L. (2002), 'Evaluation in The Netherlands 1990–2000: Consolidation and expansion', in Jan-Eric Furubo, Ray C. Rist and Rolf Sandahl (eds), *International Atlas of Evaluation*, New Brunswick and London: Transaction, pp. 115–28.

Benz, Arthur and Klaus H. Goetz (1996), 'The German public sector: National priorities and the international reform agenda', in Arthur Benz and Klaus H. Goetz (eds), *A New German Public Sector?*, Aldershot: Dartmouth, pp. 1–26.

Bogumil, Jörg (2002), 'Verwaltungsmodernisierung und aktivierender Staat', in *Perspektiven* DS, S., 2–20.

Bönker, Frank and Hellmut Wollmann (2000), 'The rise and fall of a social service regime: Marketisation of German social services in historical perspective', in Hellmut Wollmann and Eckhard Schröter (eds), *Comparing Public Sector Reform in Britain and Germany*, Aldershot: Ashgate, pp. 327–50.

Bundesbeauftragter für die Wirtschaftlichkeit in der Verwaltung (1990), *Erfolgskontrolle finanzwirksamer Maßnahmen in der öffentlichen Verwaltung*, Stuttgart: Kohlhammer.

Bundesregierung (2002), *Modern State – Modern Administration, Progress Report 2002*, Bonn (www.staat-modern.de).

Bürsch, Dieter and Brigitte Müller (n.d.), *Verwaltungsreformen in den deutschen Bundesändern*, Bonn: Friedrich-Ebert-Stiftung.

Buschor, Ernst (2002), 'Evaluation und New Public Management', *Zeitschrift für Evaluation*, 1[1], 61–74.

Derlien, Hans-Ulrich (1976), *Die Erfolgskontrolle staatlicher Planung*, Baden-Baden: Nomos.

Derlien, Hans-Ulrich (1990), 'Genesis and structure of evaluation efforts', in Ray Rist (ed.), *Program Evaluation and the Management of Government*, New Brunswick and London: Transaction, pp. 147–76.

Derlien, Hans-Ulrich (1996), 'Patterns of postwar administrative development in Germany', in Arthur Benz and Klaus H. Goetz (eds), *A New German Public Sector?*, Aldershot: Dartmouth, pp. 27 ff.

Derlien, Hans-Ulrich (2002), 'Policy evaluation in Germany: Institutional continuation and sectoral activation', in Jan-Eric Furubo, Ray C. Rist and Rolf Sandahl (eds), *International Atlas of Evaluation*, New Brunswick and London: Transaction, pp. 77–91.

Engelniederhammer, Stefan, Bodo Köpp, Christoph Reichard, Manfred Röber and Hellmut Wollmann (1999), *Berliner Verwaltung auf Modernisierungskurs*, Berlin: Sigma.

Fürst, Dietrich (1996), 'The regional districts in search of a new role', in Arthur Benz and Klaus H. Goetz (eds), *A New German Public Sector?*, Aldershot: Dartmouth, pp. 119–36.

Furubo, Jan-Eric and Rolf Sandahl (2002), 'A diffusion-perspective on global developments in evaluation', in Jan-Eric Furubo, Ray C. Rist and Rolf Sandahl (eds), *International Atlas of Evaluation*, New Brunswick and London: Transaction, pp. 1–26.

Grömig, E. and K. Gruner (1998), 'Reform in den Rathäusern', *Der Städtetag*, 8, 581 ff.

Hellstern, Gerd-Michael and Hellmut Wollmann (eds) (1983), *Experimentelle Politik*, Opladen: Westdeutscher Verlag.

Hellstern, Gerd-Michael and Hellmut Wollmann (1984), 'Evaluierung und Evaluierungsforschung: Ein Entwicklungsbericht', in Gerd-Michael Hellstern and Hellmut Wollmann (eds), *Handbuch zur Evaluationsforschung*, Bd. 1, Opladen: Westdeutscher Verlag, pp. 17–93.

Hendriks, Frank and Piter Tops (1999), 'Between democracy and efficiency: Trends in local government reforms in the Netherlands and in Germany', *Public Administration*, 77[1], 133–53.

Hesse, Jens Joachim and J. L. Sharpe (1990), 'Local government in international perspective', in Jens Joachim Hesse (ed.), *Local Government and Urban Affairs in International Perspective*, Baden-Baden: Nomos, pp. 603–21.

Hood, Christopher (1991), 'A public management for all seasons?', *Public Administration*, 69[1], 3–19.

Jaedicke, Wolfgang, Thomas Thrun and Hellmut Wollmann (1999), *Modernisierung der Kommunalverwaltung. Evaluierungsstudie zur Verwaltungsmodernisierung im Bereich Planen*, Stuttgart: Bauen und Umwelt.

Jann, Werner and Göttrik Wewer (1998), 'Helmut Kohl und der "schlanke Staat": Eine verwaltungspolitische Bilanz', in Göttrik Wewer (ed), *Bilanz der Ära Kohl*, Opladen: Westdeutscher Verlag, pp. 229–66.

Kißler, Leo, Jörg Bogumil, Ralh Greifenstein and Elke Wiechmann (1997), *Moderne Zeiten im Rathaus?*, Berlin: Sigma.

Klages, Helmut and Elke Löffler (1995), 'Administrative modernization in Germany – a big qualitative jump in small steps', *International Review of Administrative Sciences*, 61, 373–83.

König, Klaus and Natascha Füchtner (1998), *Schlanker Staat*, Baden-Baden: Nomos.

Konzendorf, Götz (1998), *Verwaltungsmodernisierung in den Ländern*, Speyerer Forschungsberichte, Nr. 187, Speyer.

Kuhlmann, Sabine (2002), 'Kommunales Benchmarking', *Verwaltungsarchiv* (forthcoming).

Levine, Robert A. (1981), 'Program evaluation and policy analysis in western nations', in Robert A. Levine, Marian A. Solomon, Gerd-Michael Hellstern, and Hellmut Wollmann (eds), *Evaluation Research and Practice*, Beverly Hills and London: Sage, pp. 12–27.

Löffler, Elke (1997), *The Modernization of the Public Sector in International Comparative Perspective: Strategies in Germany, Great Britain and the United States*, Speyer: Forschungsinstitut für öffentliche Verwaltung.

Lorenz, Sabine, Kai Wegrich and Hellmut Wollmann (2000), *Kommunale Rechtsanwendung im Umbruch und Wandel*, Opladen: Leske + Budrich.

Maaß, Christian and Christoph Reichard (1998), 'Von Konzepten zu wirklichen Veränderungen?' In Grunow, Dieter and Hellmut Wollmann (eds.), *Lokale Verwaltungsreform in Aktion*, Basel etc.: Birkhäuser, pp. 267–85.

Naschold, Frieder (1995), *Ergebnissteuerung, Wettbewerb, Qualitätspolitik: Entwicklungspfade des öffentlichen Sektors in Europa*, Berlin: Sigma.

Nordrhein-Westfalen, Innenministerium (2001), '*Bericht zum Stand der Verwaltungsmodernisierung*', mimeo, Düsseldorf.

OECD (2000), *Germany OECD Country Report 2000* (www.staat-modern.de).

Pollitt, Christopher and Geert Bouckaert (2000), *Public Management Reform. A Comparative Analysis*, Oxford: Oxford University Press.

Reichard, Christoph (1994), *Umdenken im Rathaus*, Berlin: Sigma.

Reichard, Christoph and Alexander Wegener (1998), 'Der deutsche Weg des Produktkatalogs – eine Sackgasse?', in Deutscher Städtetag (ed.), Produkte im Mittelpunkt, DSt-Beiträge zur Kommunalpolitik, 23, 41–50.

Röber, Manfred (2003), 'Public sector reform in Germany', in Munshi, Sundra et al. (eds), *Good Governance in Democratic Societies: Cross-cultural Perspectives*, London, New Dehli etc.: Sage (forthcoming).

Sachverständigenrat 'Schlanker Staat' 1998, Abschlußbericht, Bonn.

Sandahl, Rolf (1992), 'Evaluation at the Swedish National Audit Bureau', in J. Mayne et al. (eds), *Advancing Public Policy Evaluation*, Amsterdam: Elsevier, pp, 115–22.

Schmidt-Eichstaedt, Gerd (1999), 'Autonomie und Regelung von oben', in Hellmut Wollmann, Hellmut and Roland Roth (eds), *Kommunalpolitik*, 2. Auflage, Opladen: Leske + Budrich, pp. 323–37.

Schröter, Eckhard and Hellmut Wollmann (1997), 'Public sector reforms in Germany: whence and where?', in Hallinon Tutkimus, *Administrative Studies*, 3, 184–200.

Senat von Berlin (2000), *Vorlage über die Umsetzung des Verwaltungsgrundsätze-Gesetzes*, mimeo, Berlin.

Wagner, Peter and Hellmut Wollmann (1986), 'Fluctuations in the development of evaluation research: Do "regime shifts" matter?', *International Social Science Journal*, 108, 205–18.

Widmer, Thomas (2002), 'Staatsreformen und Evaluation. Konzeptionelle Grundlagen und Praxis bei den Schweizer Kantonen', *Zeitschrift für Evaluation*, 1, 101–14.

Wollmann, Hellmut (1989), 'Policy analysis in West Germany's federal government', *Governance*, 2[3], 233–66.

Wollmann, Hellmut (1996a), 'The transformation of local government in East Germany: Between imposed and innovative institutionalization', in Arthur

Benz and Klaus H. Goetz (eds), *A New German Public Sector?*, Aldershot: Dartmouth, pp. 137–64.

Wollmann, Hellmut (1996b), 'Institutionenbildung in Ostdeutschland: Neubau, Umbau und "schöpferische Zerstörung"', in Max Kaase, Andreas Eisen, Oskar Niedermayer and Hellmut Wollmann (eds), *Politisches System*, Opladen: Leske + Budrich, pp. 47–153.

Wollmann, Hellmut (1997), 'Modernization of the public sector and public administration in the Federal Republic of Germany – (mostly) a story of fragmented incrementalism', in Michio Muramatsu and Frieder Naschold (eds), *State and Administration in Japan and Germany*, Berlin: deGruyter, pp. 79 ff.

Wollmann, Hellmut (2000a), 'Local government modernization in Germany: Between incrementalism and reform waves', *Public Administration*, 78[4], 915–36.

Wollmann, Hellmut (2000b), 'Staat und Verwaltung in den 90er Jahren', in Roland Czada, and Hellmut Wollmann (eds), *Von der Bonner zur Berliner Republik*, Opladen; Westdeutscher Verlag, pp. 694–731.

Wollmann, Hellmut (2000c), 'Comparing institutional development in Britain and Germany: (Persistent) divergence or (progressing) convergence?', in Hellmut Wollmann and Eckhard Schröter (eds), *Comparing Public Sector Reform in Britain and Germany*, Aldershot: Ashgate, pp. 1–26.

Wollmann, H. (2001), 'Germany's trajectory of public sector modernization: continuities and discontinuities', *Policy & Politics*, 29[2], 151–69.

Wollmann, Hellmut (2002a), 'Contractual research and policy knowledge', *International Encyclopedia of the Social and Behavioral Sciences*, 5, 11574–11578.

Wollmann, Hellmut (2002b), 'Verwaltungspolitik und Evaluierung: Ansätze, Phasen und Beispiele im Ausland und in Deutschland, Evaluation und New Public Management', *Zeitschrift für Evaluation*, 1, 75–101.

Notes

1. As of 1994, after the privatization of federal rail and federal post/*telekom* was effected, the federal personnel made up some 11.9 per cent of the total number of public employees which is remarkably little by international standards, certainly when compared to unitary countries (such as New Zealand with 89.7 per cent, France with 48.7 per cent and the UK with 47.7 per cent), but also as compared to other federal countries (such as the US with 15.2 per cent and Canada with 17.1 per cent).
2. It has been estimated that between 70 and 85 per cent of the federal and *Länder* legislation (as well as of the growing body of EU law) is being implemented by local authorities (see Schmidt-Eichstaedt 1999, p. 330).
3. For the controversy on this issue, see Wollmann 2000a, p. 923 with references.
4. For (English-language) accounts on public-sector reforms in Germany, see Klages and Löffler 1995, Benz and Goetz 1996, Derlien 1996, Wollmann 1997, Schröter and

Wollmann 1997, Löffler 1997. Pollitt and Bouckaert 2000, pp. 235 ff., Wollmann 2001, and Röber 2003.

5. Further information can be accessed through the websites of the respective reform units in each of the 16 *Länder*, see the list of the websites in: Germany OECD country report 2000, p. 10.

6. Grömig and Gruner 1998 present and interpret the findings of a survey which the German Association of Cities conducted among its member cities.

7. See Furubo and Sandahl 2002, p. 10 for the ranking of 'evaluative cultures' which they tried to establish on the basis of nine indicators in 21 countries. Germany ranks among the upper third of the countries, taking seventh place.

8. See VM-Impulse, 2002/ no 1 (www.im.nrw.de/inn).

9. *Land* Nordrhein-Westfalen, for instance, has commissioned 88 analyses and studies on the entire range of its administrative structures (see Nordrhein-Westfalen 2001).

10. See Wollmann 2000b, p. 95 FN 46 with some figures.

11. For instance, the court of audit of the city-state of Hamburg has explicitly put the evaluation of public sector reforms on its future agenda. See Wollmann 2002b, p. 95 with references.

12. As indications of this, the (German) Evaluation Society put its 2001 annual conference under the 'Public sector modernization and evaluation' theme, and the newly-founded *Zeitschrift für Evaluation* (journal of evaluation) devoted most of its first issue to the evaluation of public-sector reforms in Germany and in Switzerland. See Wollmann 2002b (on Germany) and Buschor 2002 and Widmer 2002 (both on Switzerland).

8. 'As a voluntary choice or as a legal obligation': Assessing New Public Management policy in Italy

Andrea Lippi

1. Introduction

The doctrine of New Public Management (NPM) has become pervasive in recent years, standardizing the political agendas of reformers and producing a 'globalizing' transformation of the bureaucratic administrations of Western countries (Peters and Savoie 1998). Nonetheless, reforms intended to introduce NPM have pursued goals, made choices and adopted methods of a highly diverse nature, giving rise to different and unlikely consequences. The case of Italy is distinctive in its originality and in the light that it sheds on *unintended* consequences.

In the most important cases, the reasons for implementation of an NPM strategy have been extremely clear, stemming either from the ideological background of the government opting for the strategy (as in the UK, Australia and New Zealand) (Hood 1995) or from the economic necessity to control public expenditure in the welfare state (as in continental Europe, Sweden and Norway) (Olsen and Peters 1996).

In both cases – in the 'original' neo-liberalist version as well as in the spillover effect one – NPM strategies have been deliberate political choices. In contrast, Italian reforms geared to the introduction of NPM began unobtrusively, adding innovative elements to former reformist tendencies, without major political decision-making. Italian reform displays a pattern whereby innovations have been introduced one at a time, disjointedly and incrementally. Hence, policy is implemented as a voluntary choice – from the bottom up – or a legal obligation – from the top down (Oliva and Pesce 2001).

How, then, can we assess this reform? We can undertake analysis of the policy process (agenda-setting, decision-making, implementation) and describe the purposes and the results of the reform.

2. Agenda-setting reform policy

Reform of the public-sector in Italy has moved through a sequence of cycles which have affected the country's institutions since World War II. Each of these cycles has seen the formation of new political coalitions and the invention of specific rhetorics with which the reformers have defined the problem and proposed solutions (Battistelli 2002). Analysis of this sequence of cycles permits an understanding of how and why Italy has come to formulate an NPM-oriented policy.

Capano (1992: 307–10) has identified three historical cycles – to which I add two more – which led to Italy's recent shift towards NPM (Table 8.1). The first cycle was that of the postwar reconstruction carried out by the Christian Democrat (DC) party government. The rhetoric behind these reforms concerned the adjustment of the public-sector to the democratic principles set out in the new Constitution. The second cycle was marked by the rhetoric of efficiency and planning adopted by the centre-left government (DC and socialists) in the 1960s. Both phases of reform relied on a Napoleonic ideology centred on modernization of the bureaucracy and its adaptation to the problems raised by social and economic development. Both phases of reform belonged to the tradition of administrative law, which was the only type of competence used for organization of the state.

These public-sector reforms were defined by political optimism and the confidence that changes could be made within the public-sector. In contrast, the third cycle (1979–83) was marked by profound pessimism and political emergency. The political arena in this period was greatly influenced by a Parliament-commissioned report on the state of public administration – Giannini Report of 17 November 1979[1] – that was harshly critical of the public-sector. The report not only denounced the failure of previous reforms, but went so far as to declare the illegality of many informal practices and to emphasize the dramatic problem of excessive public expenditure. It described the state of the public-sector as one of degeneration of authority, since 'the disconnection between the public powers and citizens' with their individual and collective interests placed the latter in a 'condition of subordination' and the former in a position of 'uncontrolled supremacy'. Thus, it 'permitted to public power what was forbidden in private life' (Giannini 1982).

Table 8.1 The cycles of public-sector reforms in Italy

Cycle of reform	Reform rhetoric	Political coalition
1948–1957	*Reconstruction* in accordance with the principles of the democratic constitution	Party government (DC)
1961–1972	*Planning* and *efficiency* (*modernization*)	Centre-left (DC and PSI)
1979–1983	*Reorganization* and *recovery* of bureaucratic rationality (*modernization*)	Pentapartito (a five-party coalition comprising the DC, PSI and three minor moderate parties)
1988–1995	*Implicit NPM orientation* (rationalization, decentralization, transparency)	Pentapartito (1988–1992) followed by the so-called 'technocrat governments' (1993 and 1995) headed by experts (Ciampi and Dini) voted into office by Parliament.[2]
1996–2001	*Explicit NPM orientation*	Centre-left (Ulivo)

The next phase of reforms sprang from the recommendations of the Giannini Report, in an endeavour to overhaul the bureaucracy and reorganize the public-sector according to principles of efficiency and effectiveness. However, scholars agree that this cycle of reforms was the least successful of them all (Capano 1992; Melis 1996). The Giannini Report was applied only to a partial and unsatisfactory extent; when reform was implemented, it was thwarted by a lobby made up of the trade unions of the public-sector, ministry officials and politicians, and both the majority coalition and the opposition. Moreover, the cultural resistance – more subtle than political resistance but more effective – raised by civil-service executives further hindered implementation of the reforms (Melis 1996).

At the end of the 1980s, however, further reports and studies documented the crisis besetting the public administration – a crisis that Cassese has called 'maladministration' (1992).[3] Intellectuals and scholars pushed for at least some of the Giannini Report's recommendations to be adopted, and called for the bureaucracy to be restored to its democratic role; they denounced its corruption (Cazzola 1988), its cultural backwardness (Cerase 1988), and its excessive spending and inefficiency (Cassese 1992).

It was these ideas that characterized the fourth cycle. In particular, the failure to implement earlier policies gave rise to a new interpretation of the purpose of reforms, with the issue of public-sector reform being incorporated into two new rhetorics. The first was of rationalization. According to this rhetoric, a project of simplification, reduction and transparency should be pursued, the essential idea being to impose order on a chaotic situation by achieving efficiency, effectiveness and equity in the public-sector.

The rationalization project mixed the principles of a social contract with vaguely NPM-flavoured principles regarding the improved use of resources, management by objectives and privatization. In other words, this was an 'enlightened' approach that sought to inject a number of exogenous competences into the bureaucratic tradition. The main difference between the modernization and rationalization rhetorics was that the former asserted that the solution to bureaucracy was 'better bureaucracy', while the latter called for 'less bureaucracy'.

The second rhetoric adopted during this phase was that of decentralisation. The debate was driven by frustrations deriving from the experience of regional government. According to observers, the regional administrations – created about twenty years previously – had failed in the implementation phase (Putnam, Leonardi and Nanetti 1985). It was on this basis that the principle of the 'decision-making autonomy' of local governments came into being: the task of decentralizing the Italian state passed from the regions to the communes (municipalities) and the provinces.

The reforms of the fourth cycle (1988–92) were thus formulated in an intellectual environment partially external to political arenas. Initially the moderate political coalitions of the *pentapartito* (a five-party coalition comprising the DC, PSI and three minor moderate parties) responded to pressure from leading intellectuals and scholars. When in 1992 these coalitions – headed by Amato – were overwhelmed by corruption scandals, the reforms were carried forward by those same intellectual leaders, who were co-opted into the 'technocrat governments' headed by Ciampi (1992–94) and Dini (1995–96). The protagonist was law professor Sabino Cassese, who in his capacity as Minister for the Civil Service[4] surreptitiously mixed the principles of the Giannini Report with ideas on NPM imported from the UK. Under the banner of decentralization and rationalization, Cassese implicitly initiated a project for NPM in Italy.

Finally, the fifth cycle saw Italy's explicit commitment to the NPM programme, once again in a climate of considerable political optimism.

This came about under the new centre-left government coalition (1996–2001), called *L'Ulivo*, which undertook a radical policy of reform. Another professor of law – Franco Bassanini, who was Minister for the Civil Service like Cassese before him – completed the process of importing NPM principles from Europe. Bassanini's programme of reforms was even more radical and explicit than his predecessor's, and it sought to tackle the following:

1. the problem of public expenditure, which had become financially unsustainable for the state and intolerable for public opinion at a time when numerous politicians were under investigation for corruption; and
2. the Euro-Community commitments to cuts in public expenditure, later known as the Maastricht parameters (Capano 2000).

The NPM rhetoric attendant on the reforms promoted by Bassanini marked an important turning point in the reform process, because it succeeded in issuing provisions that were qualitatively more incisive and quantitatively more numerous where others had failed. The NPM rhetoric provided the centre-left majority with an important symbolic basis on which to 'save' the public-sector: it interpreted NPM principles as 'democratic' and followed the Giannini Report's recommendations for 'the restoration of a citizenship contract' between the state and the Italian people (Bassanini 2000).

However, the transition from reforms aimed at modernizing the bureaucracy to NPM reforms did not happen suddenly, but occurred gradually during the late 1980s and early 1990s. The profound crisis of the political class in the early 1990s, and the 'technocrat governments' of those years, informed the discussion, conception and formulation of policy by intellectual leaders who incorporated a new language into the previous rhetoric of modernizing the bureaucracy. In fact, a number of important changes came about. The culture of reference was decreasingly legal and increasingly one of business economics. Reforms were backed increasingly by such leaders of legal culture as Giannini, Cassese and Bassanini – less and less by political coalitions. The contents of reforms were no longer an exclusively Italian product, but the continuation of a globalizing political process in Italy.

Italy has never experienced a substantial shift between the rhetoric of modernization and that of NPM; instead, it has undergone a progressive and moderated approach. Nevertheless, the NPM programme has never been unambiguous and it has never been explicitly produced by a specific ideological mobilization. For the last ten years, NPM has been a part of the decision-making agendas of numerous different coalitions, but the agenda-setters have never created a direct linkage with the British NPM political and intellectual milieu.

Instead, NPM agenda-setting in Italy has been the result of cultural mediation by an intellectual elite (Gherardi and Jacobsson 2000). The reform programme approved by Parliament was drafted by a select group of insiders – 'soft translators' of NPM international experiences imported from other countries. This academic elite has constituted the policy community for most of the measures, and even today it comprises three distinct groups:

1. the academic community of experts on administrative law – the heirs of Giannini (as well as Cassese, Bassanini, and others) – who incorporated the principles of NPM and business economics into the traditional language of the law, and sought to modernize the bureaucracy by applying the logic of productivity;
2. the (powerful) academic and professional community of business consultants that adapts for-profit managerial knowledge and strategies to the non-profit sector;[5] and
3. 'the community of practice' (Gherardi and Lippi 2000) made up of professional associations and informal networks of academics, civil servants and specialist professionals who discuss and experiment with the innovations promoted by the reforms. These are often sectoral associations that specialize in evaluation, public communication, information technology, management, outsourcing and so on.

In short, NPM in Italy is the result of a slow process of approximation, at first implicit and only recently made explicit by the centre-left government. Cultural mediation, first by ministers and then by communities of practice and consultancy agencies, has established continuity between the rhetoric of modernizing the bureaucracy and the rhetoric of NPM, ushering in reform laws of unusual quality and quantity.

3. Reform legislation and evaluation practices

Public-sector reform in Italy has arisen from legislative arenas through numerous incremental, sometimes minor, acts of legislation consisting mainly of laws issued by the government on delegation from Parliament (*Decreto Legislativo,* henceforth D.Legs.), but also laws enacted by Parliament (henceforth L.) and guidelines issued by Ministries (*diret-*

tiva, henceforth D.). Rebora has classified these legislative acts into two groups: general and sectoral (1999:54). General acts address strategic issues of privatization, relations between politics and public management, top management role, organisational structures, job contracts and personnel management, and structural downsizing. Sectoral acts involve the reorganization of specific areas of the public-sector, such as universities and schools, the health system, regional administrations, local governments and social services.

An additional important form of cross-sectoral legislation is evaluation and control system acts, which have replaced the previous system of controls. These three groups of acts (general, sectoral, evaluation and control system) pursue eight crucial goals (see table 8.2): (1) renewal of the state–citizen relationship in terms of the greater democracy and transparency of administrative activities; (2) improved administrative management and human resources development; (3) the downward decentralization of decision-making power in the administrative structure, including the creation of a governance network and territorial decentralisation; (4) the separation of political decision-making functions from managerial ones; (5) the outsourcing of activities through privatization; (6) contracting out and the adoption of subsidiarity criteria both vertically and horizontally; (7) the simplification of administrative procedures and the reduction of structures; and (8) assessment of results (DFP 1993).

Table 8.2 Types of Italian reform laws

General acts	Sectoral acts	Evaluation and control system acts
Privatization and outsourcing	Local governments	Reduced legitimacy controls
Privatization of the employment contracts	Regions	State Auditors
Organizational downsizing	Health sector	Management control
Top management	Schools and universities	Assessment units
Simplification of procedures	Ministries	Customer satisfaction
Citizens' charter, URP	Bodies controlled by Ministries	Assessment of structural funds

General acts

The most important actions of the public-sector reform are those general acts intended to introduce radical changes in the traditional structures of the state bureaucracy by injecting them with a 'business' logic: (1) privatization and outsourcing; (2) job contract privatization; (3) organizational downsizing, top management, senior management, political administrative relationships; and (4) simplification, transparency, reduced bureaucracy, and 'client democracy'.

A first major innovation has been the privatization of entire public organizations, an undertaking that has reversed the process of nationalization which began in the 1950s and was completed about 20 years later. The privatisation of the public-sector has come about in two phases (see table 8.3). The first involved the largest amount of legislation, and it centred on the decision to privatize certain parts of the state. Privatization began in 1990, when Parliament enacted a law that dismantled the nationalized system of state-owned enterprises; it continued between 1992 and 1993, when the Amato government sought to restore the public accounts by issuing numerous decree-laws which privatised a first part of that system; and it concluded in 1994 when Parliament instituted authorities to supervise the liberalized sectors and the state's 'golden share' in them. The second stage began in 1995 and continues today. It consists of further measures to privatize the enterprises remaining in public ownership and the progressive sale of stock in those that were privatized before 1994.

Since 1990 there has been practically no interruption in the sale of entire parts of the public-sector, including both services and state-controlled enterprises (Zanetti and Alzona 1998:92). These privatizations have been accompanied by a broader strategy of outsourcing public activities and services, the purpose being to reduce the operational workloads of administrations. Outsourcing has been used mostly by local governments, regions and healthcare structures. The outsourcing strategies can be arranged along a continuum with contractual formulas used by the local governments to maintain their predominant position at one end, to marketization solutions at the other: (1) contract works; (2) agreements; (3) consortia; (4) contracting out to the non-profit sector; (5) creation of foundations; (6) creation of stock companies (where the administrations are the majority shareholders); (7) transformation into a private company; and (8) sell-off to a private company (Rebora 1999).

Table 8.3 Privatization of the public-sector in Italy

Phase	Year of privatization[6]	Organization privatized	Sector
First	1990	IRI (first part)	Industrial: steel, engineering, glass, chemicals, food
(1990–1994)	1992	ENEL, ENI	Electricity and petroleum
	1992	IMI, EFIM	Publicly-owned credit institutes and financial companies
	1992	PT	Post and telecommunications
	1992	BNL; Comit, Credit	Banks, public credit system
	1993	Ferrovie dello Stato	Railway transport
Second	1995	IRI (second part)	Industrial: steel, engineering, glass, chemicals, food
(1995–2001)	1997	Telecom	Telephony
	1998	Alitalia	Air transport
	1998	Monopoli di Stato	Tobacco production and processing
	1998	ANAS	Road construction and maintenance

The privatization of public-sector employment contracts is the central pillar of the Italian reform. It was initiated in 1993 by D.Lgs no. 29, subsequently extended by L. 87 in 1994 and by two further D.Lgs (nos. 80 and 387) issued by the government in 1998. NPM is at the core of this legislation:

1. the hiring of senior managers on private, five-year contracts rather than on public, open-ended ones (1993);
2. the introduction of general managers in the stead of officials ('secretaries') responsible for merely formal controls on legitimacy (1993);
3. the replacement of a hierarchical career system based on years of service and strictly regulated by law with one based on performance-related advancement (1993);
4. performance-related pay scales for senior management;
5. the equalization of public- and private-sector contractual categories[7] (1998);

6. the introduction of fixed-term contracts for routine jobs and the opportunity to hire external consultants (1993);
7. disputes on contracts no longer adjudicated by a special court (administrative court), but by regular courts, as are private-sector disputes (1993);
8. changes to public competitive examinations, to examinations based not only on legal knowledge but also on technical and professional expertise (1994).

These various measures apply to the public-sector as a whole. Each subsector has been subsequently regulated by specific applications. Points 1 to 4 have been implemented mainly in the health sector, the regional administrations and local governments. All others have been implemented throughout the public-sector.

Changes in the employment relationship have also had an impact on wage bargaining and on the role of the trade unions. Bargaining units tend increasingly to resemble their private-sector counterparts. Wages are defined both at the national level and through local-level negotiation between trade unions and administrations. Furthermore, the State has set up an ad hoc agency (*Agenzia per la Rappresentanza Negoziale per la Pubblica Administrazione* [ARAN]) which negotiates the collective part of the contract.

Another major change concerns organizational structures. Basically, each administration must adopt the organizational structure best suited to achievement of its goals. Administrations have consequently been allowed to alter the structure of offices according to such criteria as flexibility and user needs, facilitating communication and information sharing.

Since the introduction of general directors, the main developments have been the creation of new structures and the recruitment of professionals skilled in the areas of information technology, marketing, public relations, strategic control and evaluation. The potential for changes to be made to organization charts expanded apace during the 1990s and enabled political decision-makers to mould their structures and choose personnel to suit their purposes.

A further legislative change has been the different formulation given to the relationship between political decision-makers and administrative executives. This is mainly a public-sector transformation, one which seeks to eliminate both the co-opting of public officials by politicians and the strong resistance raised by officials and their informal power accruing from ritualism. The new configuration of public powers imposes a strict separation of responsibilities, instead of the former pre-eminence of the bureaucracy. The separation of roles has given politicians the power to determine only political strategy and set goals as the 'purchasers' of administrative implementation. Officials, for their part, have for the very first time become 'visible' and accountable for their decisions on the managerial strategies and on means with which to achieve those goals. This new system therefore envisages two distinct types of accountability: political and managerial.

Nearly all administrations have seized the opportunities that the implementation of this legislation offers, but to varying extents and with differing degrees of success. The provisions which have met with most cultural resistance and uncertainty are those concerning senior managers and their relations with politicians. Each side, in fact, tends to encroach on the competences of the other: the politicians are reluctant to settle for a merely decision-making role that precludes their involvement in implementation, whereas managers find it difficult to assume 'visible' accountability, accustomed as they are to remaining in the background (Dente 1999; Lippi 1999).

The last important general innovation concerns procedural simplification and structural reduction. This is a strategy linked to the bureaucratic structure and to the codex juridical system. Innovations have been based on two main principles: re-democratization of the relationship between state and citizens, and simplification of the rules that will make the administration more effective and efficient.

The legislative process began in 1990, when Parliament enacted L. no. 241 – thereby following the recommendations of the Giannini Report, which referred to legislation that had not previously been implemented. Law no. 241 had a revolutionary impact in terms of the democratization of the bureaucracy. It enabled citizens to participate in administrative procedures, introduced transparency, allowed self-certification and public access to databases, and provided for the bundling of information services and the issue of documentation through 'unified desks' which linked different administrations.

In 1994, Cassese obtained and had translated into Italian the Citizen's Charter introduced by the Major government in Britain, producing a document – more symbolic than legislatively significant – which envisaged a form of 'client democracy'. In the previous year the government had introduced an office of public relations (*Uffici Relazioni con il Pubblico* [URP]) which involved the collection of consumer requests and complaints with a view to the improvement of services. The URPs' functions were not restricted to public relations but also included public marketing, transparency, participation in administrative procedures, self-certification and public access to databases and, in some cases, customer satisfaction. Initially adopted and promoted by local governments, URPs have now been established in all public administrations, with a weak coordinating central structure at the Department for Civil Service.

Finally, in 1997 Bassanini gave further impetus to these developments with a decree D.Lgs based on a model proposed by American Vice-President Al Gore. The legislation provided for the creation in all administrations of work groups charged with simplifying regulations by eliminating those deemed obsolete or useless, streamlining procedures, and eliminating bureaucratic bottlenecks (NPR 1993).

At present, all public authorities have URPs, but they are not as effective in relations with citizens as the law intended. The simplification and streamlining of bureaucratic procedures has strong symbolic value, considering that more than two hundred thousand laws have been enacted since the unification of Italy in 1860 (Cassese 1998). However, a great deal of work remains to be done, and interest in the issue has dwindled.

Sectoral acts

Sectoral reforms have consisted of laws, or groups of laws, designed to introduce business principles into specific areas of the bureaucracy. They initially targeted certain areas of the public-sector, and later were extended to the others. They first involved the local governments (from 1990 onwards), then universities (1993), the health service (from 1995), social services (1995), and schools (1998), as well as administrations of lesser importance to the general public – such as civil defence (1992), chambers of commerce (1995), opera companies (1998), and the CNR (1999).[8]

Between 1997 and 2001, the government issued more than 40 D.Lgs designed to reduce, rationalize and innovate the above-mentioned sectors; these also were applied to central government ministries (1997–2000) and bodies controlled by them, most notably (in 1999): *Comitato Olimpico Nazionale Italiano* (CONI; the state agency which coordinates Olympic sports), *Ente Nazionale Energia Atomica* (ENEA; the state atomic energy board), the *Istituto Poligrafico dello Stato e la Zecca* (government printers and the Mint), FORMEZ (institute for socioeconomic research and development of southern Italy), the *Scuola Superiore di Pubblica Amministrazione*[9], the *Cassa Depositi e Prestiti* ('bank for deposits and loans'), and many others.

Provisions to reform the ministries have not followed a single pattern but have been formulated to suit the individual ministry, or even certain of its features or activities, which accounts for the plethora of minor ad hoc norms enacted. Although implementation of innovative legislation in the ministries has only just begun and is in an experimental phase, in many local governments and regional administrations, the implementation is complete. Moreover, the majority of the innovations introduced by sectoral reforms in the ministries and the bodies controlled by them are replicated at the central level; in the state-controlled bodies, the reforms made to the local governments and regional administrations, the health system, and the universities and schools, consists of the systematic and homogeneous application of the general reforms described earlier.

Local governments (communes and provinces) were the first to be affected by NPM reforms, and therefore served as proving grounds for ministerial reforms (Dente 1991). After 1990, there were innovations designed to alter the relationship between elected officials and local public servants, to change the role of management, to introduce general directors and professional personnel, and to promote outsourcing, merging and cooperation between communes. In 1993, local governments undertook a profound transformation of their operational procedures when they adopted planning and results assessment, budgeting, financial autonomy for up to 60 per cent of their resources, and diversified managerial strategies for public services. Today, local governments exemplify the most advanced public-sector reform in Italy.

Similarly, regional governments undertook major reforms (1997–98), either by adopting innovations tried out in communes and provinces or by introducing new ones. All of them (regions, provinces and communes) made significant electoral reforms that led to the direct election of mayors (in communes) and presidents (regions and provinces) as well as introducing a system of election by majority vote. This process heightened the potential of public-sector reform by granting broader margins of decision-making freedom to the executive organs, rather than the legislative powers. Thus empowered, the executives were able to make a larger number of discretional decisions, thereby strengthening the logic of decision-making autonomy.

Local executive power has thus grown to a greater extent than local legislative power. Indeed, as Europeanization proceeds, regions have come to act as the intermediaries between the state and local governments, and between the latter and the European Union. As was true of local governments, the purpose behind reform of the regional governments is to foster decision-making autonomy and to implement vertical subsidiarity. The regions must therefore adopt the same managerial innovations that have worked for communes and provinces – namely changing the role of senior management and creating general directors – and planning and results assessment are being introduced as a consequence.

It should be stressed, however, that the most significant development is the reorganization presently being undertaken by regions assigned new duties and new political and administrative functions. These changes are set out in two important laws enacted in 1998 and 2001. The regions have become the centre of political action, and have acquired unusual policy-making potential from the central administration. Implementation of this strong regionalization of the Italian state has only just begun; nonetheless, the new institutional structure has already given unprecedented decision-making discretion to local policy makers, and to public managers an exceptional level of managerial responsibility based on results assessment.

Local government has not been alone in undergoing NPM-style transformations, however. In 1995 a strategic D.Lgs. directly addressed the healthcare system. The decision by the government to replace the *Unità sanitarie locali* (USL; Local Healthcare Units – the old national and full state system) with *Aziende sanitarie locali* (ASL; local healthcare enterprises) and *Aziende ospedaliere* (AO; hospital enterprises) consituted a clear, and not merely nominal, attempt to 'marketize' the health service. In the past six years, both ASLs and AOs have been able to implement entrepreneurial philosophies that have not only prioritized such principles as decentralization, effectiveness and rationalization; they also have taken a minimizing approach by reducing services and cutting human resources expenditure. The reform of the healthcare system has adhered especially closely to NPM principles. Healthcare reform, in fact, has placed strong emphasis on budgets and reduced public expenditure since its inception (Maino 2000).

Transforming the healthcare system into a set of enterprises has, therefore, entailed the overt transplantation of business strategy into the public-sector, given that the main purpose of the reform has been to cut costs. Healthcare facilities consequently changed rapidly in the 1990s, adopting the same NPM characteristics as local governments and regions but placing a more radical emphasis on costs analysis.

The push for decision-making autonomy undertaken by the Italian public-sector has also involved the educational system, especially the universities (Capano 1998), which since 1986 have been obliged to have their own statutes, to act with relative financial autonomy (1993, L. 537) and to reorganize their teaching programmes according to a tri-level European system (D.Lgs. 5, 1998). The reform of the educational cycles in 1999 completed the process by extending reform, at least partially, to primary and secondary education.

The principle underlying this reform is progressive 'functional autonomy' (Rebora 1999:64), which follows three lines of action: political autonomy in terms of the selection of instructors, subjects taught, and materials used; financial autonomy in terms of both spending and fund-raising, including corporate funds and sponsorships; and autonomy in results assessment.

These innovations transformed the university from being a subordinate of the ministry into an autonomous and competitive organization. Important changes were made to management, including contracting and hiring systems, office organization, effectiveness and efficiency management criteria, adoption of budgets, human resources' performance evaluation, and selective incentives (Mazza and Quattrone 2002).

To a lesser extent, schools later underwent progressive transformation that culminated in the reform of educational cycles in 1998 and 1999 by two D.Lgs. (nos. 59 and 253). Decisions to reduce costs by unifying elementary and secondary schools were linked with NPM-oriented provisions such as transforming school principals from emanations of a centralized bureaucracy into autonomous managers (D.Lgs. 59/98), giving schools partial financial autonomy, and introducing new appraisal methods and individual incentives for teachers. The most evident changes, however, were didactic autonomy and differentiation of the curricula offered by schools.

Evaluation and control system acts

The public-sector in Italy has been historically based on a system of antiquated and ubiquitous controls designed to determine the legitimacy of administrative action and organized according to the functional logic of the bureaucracy, which requires the presence of an external vetting body to verify compliance with the law. In Italy, as in all countries with code-regulated bureaucracies, control has been exercised by bodies which verify the lawfulness of decisions and their implementation, accounting conformity, and disciplinary compliance by public employees. The most important organ of control in this system of formal supervision is the *Corte dei conti* ('court of accounts').

During the 1990s, Parliament and (especially) governments set about flanking this system of external controls (based on conformance) with a second one (based on performance) that consisted of internal controls. Legislation passed between 1990 and 1999 to introduce this system of internal controls was haphazard and incremental, because the laws and the legislative decrees issued by the government contained provisions that were often incomplete and opaque; it was therefore necessary to produce numerous minor instruments (circulars, memoranda, ministerial directives), which were intended to clarify matters but did nothing of the sort. The problem lay in the use of the term 'control'. This was an unfortunate choice of terminology because the word 'control' harked back to the bureaucratic tradition and thus fostered a tendency towards inspection and hierarchical authority. The word 'internal' was not enough to resolve the ambiguity. Additional rules were introduced in 1995 and 1997 by the government. Finally, in 1999, D.Lgs. 286 replaced 'internal' with 'strategic' (Dente and Azzone 1999). The words 'strategic control' finally enabled the bureaucracies to avoid cultural resistance.

During the same period, the government issued further D.Lgs to dismantle the system of external controls by substantially relaxing formal verification of the legitimacy of decisions by local governments, abolishing the municipal and provincial secretaries, and restricting the vetting powers of the *Corte dei conti* and the ministries. The system of external controls did not entirely disappear, however. A law enacted by parliament in 1996 offset the Corte dei Conti's diminished inspectorial powers by increasing its authority to audit financial and assets management, the use of European Union funds, and public spending and budgets. The *Corte dei conti* now assesses 'the opportuneness of public expenditures in accordance with the standards of efficiency, effectiveness and economicity' (Righettini 2001: 66).

This transformation of the role of the *Corte dei conti*, which now performs both a reduced (old) function of inspective control and (a new) one of financial audit, has introduced a transitional phase in the legislation on internal and external controls. From a legislative point of view, this has given rise to an ambiguous situation, because internal and external controls are still confused by practitioners, and both systems require further laws to separate them definitively. On this basis, the present situation combines a considerably reduced external system with a system of internal (assessment) controls which fall into two main categories: performance management (Davis 1999), and ex ante and ex post appraisal of structural funds.

In addition to these two assessment systems there is the sporadic ex post evaluation of policies implemented by individual ministries or other central government agencies (for example, evaluation of environmental impact). This has been the practice for years, although it has never been 'officialized' by specific legislation.

Performance management was legally defined as 'strategic control' by the government in 1999. It consists of three different activities: *controllo di gestione* (management control), *nuclei di valutazione* (evaluation committees), and customer satisfaction. *Controllo di gestione*[10] was intended to be a management monitoring system which evaluated performance, and it was considered by legislators to be the best example of business-oriented evaluation and an ideal decision-making support for policy makers. *Controllo di gestione* is the most widely-used form of performance evaluation in the Italian public-sector. It has been introduced gradually in the manner already described: first in the municipal and provincial administrations, then in the local health boards and the universities, and finally in the ministries.

In the public-sector the *controllo di gestione* has been adapted by legislators to suit the non-profit sector, although it is an awkward fit, not least because their managements have bureaucratic procedures very different from the exigencies of management control. Since the local-level experimentation with *controllo di gestione*, in fact, the government has sought to define its aims and methods in the public-sector. Given the difficulties encountered by municipal and provincial administrations in its implementation, new laws have been necessary. As a consequence, *controllo di gestione* has been fully redefined five times: first in 1990 by Parliament, and then in 1993, 1995, 1997 and 1999 by the government.

If the legislative formulation of *controllo di gestione* has been complex, even more so has been its implementation. Studies have shown that the performance indicators vary widely (Lippi 2000). Indeed, in practice, diversity has prevailed over homogeneity: each administration has adapted the dispositions of the law in a heterodox manner, by adopting either an 'efficiency-oriented' approach which uses *controllo di gestione* to assess the efficiency of public services using unitary costs indicators for each branch of welfare provision (kindergartens, nursing homes, social services, libraries, etc.); or an 'effectiveness-oriented' approach which uses *controllo di gestione* to assess the achievement of management goals and the effectiveness of policy planning.

The *nuclei di valutazione* are three- to five-member committees of experts commissioned to conduct specific appraisals for decision-makers. Their principal activity is the annual assessment of executives, who are judged on their achievement of annual targets and on their budget spending. The purpose of these committees is to advise general management on wage incentives, but they may also commission research on users, customer satisfaction and the marketing of services.

The majority of the *nuclei di valutazione* draw on the results of management controls, so that the two activities are complementary. In fact, however, several studies have reported that the assessment is unsystematic, that the data used are often incomplete, and that the use of effectiveness and efficiency indicators is unclear. These problems spring largely from an innovation which is in many respects pioneering. Creating the *nuclei di valutazione* was probably not difficult, but their members are often not experts in assessment, and in many cases they lack information support and management controls furnishing suitable data. The spread of the *nuclei di valutazione* has been much more rapid and problem-free than that of the *controlli di gestione*, which have required as much as two to three years to establish, but their actual capacity to conduct reliable assessments is still in doubt because of the cultural gap.

Finally, customer satisfaction is a sector now in rapid expansion, although its gestation was rather slow. It originated with adoption of the *Carte dei servizi* (Citizens' charter) in 1994. Since this charter was not a law but a ministerial document, the majority of administrations did not regard it as mandatory and did not carry out any sort of quality control. In 1995, the *Carte dei servizi* was incorporated into health service reform, and as a consequence the ASLs began to establish standards for individual services. After a period of inaction, during which the idea was more a matter of political debate than concrete reality, D.lgs 286/99 reprised the theme of customer satisfaction and recommended that the principles of total quality management should be extended to the public-sector in its entirety.

The legislation proposed a form of client democracy, and individual administrations began to conduct this form of assessment with considerable enthusiasm, especially in the health service and the local and regional governments, because they regarded it as a source of legitimacy for the public services. For this reason, customer satisfaction has spread spontaneously from the bottom up, often without the use of correct methodology in devising assessment instruments and adopting standards. This, however, does not reduce the symbolic value of, and the enthusiasm for, this kind of assessment (Lo Schiavo 1996; Ruffini 1999).

The cases of the *nuclei di valutazione* and *controllo di gestione* reveal a high degree of experimentalism and a certain heterodoxy with respect to the idea of customer satisfaction as embraced by businesses. One notes particular disconnectedness between the policy and the assessment of satisfaction, as if there were no relation among objectives, standards and indicators. There is a tendency to construct rather rudimentary indicators, with little concern for the internal coherence of instruments. In this case the Citizens' Charters have by no means been welcomed by practitioners, being regarded as yet one more law, and as mere theory, whereas the political and managerial intent – especially in the regional administrations, local authorities and the health service – has been to undertake concrete activities. This pragmatic approach – not always correct methodologically – is also reflected in the strategies of total quality management adopted, which have been little used, as if quality control amounts solely to verifying whether or not the user is satisfied, without any effect on planning, objectives and standards.

By way of summary, performance management is arousing enthusiastic endorsement in practice, but it is often somewhat improvised, without systematic and uniform implementation. The current tendency is to conduct assessments that yield immediate results, with scant consideration of their methodological correctness or their managerial coherence. In short, this is a 'pioneering' phase in which an innovative culture is spreading and being put into practice.

A second evaluation practice was promoted by European Union requirements. Structural funds evaluation has been forcefully implemented by the Ministry of Economics, which has obliged the regions to set up ad hoc project evaluation groups (ex ante evaluation) and results evaluation groups (ex post evaluation), according to EU requirements. Evaluation groups are the most recent prescription introduced, being set up by regional administrations between 1999 and 2001 (Merati 2001). These groups assess the use of structural funds in conformity with the European Community legal framework. Their activities are often perceived as a duty which regions must perform to gain access to financial provisions from the European Commission (Stame 2001a).

4. Assessing public-sector reform

In Italy, neither the scientific community nor the institutions have sought to evaluate public-sector reform policy, largely because the process is still ongoing: institutions are still making their decisions, and implementation is still in progress. Ex post evaluation of the outputs and outcomes of the reform project as a whole would therefore be inevitably incomplete. Furthermore, it is difficult to identify a homogeneous unit of analysis for such a pervasive phenomenon; thus, the use of experimental or quasi-experimental evaluation methods is an extremely complex undertaking.

There is also a cultural reason for this difficulty. The predominant attitude of public opinion towards the public-sector has not changed: it is still one of scepticism, at most indifference, towards a sphere of public life that most Italians ignore. Even specialist publications of recent years carry titles that do not prompt optimism; rather, they discourage any kind of evaluation and propound a rhetoric of pessimism: they describe 'a blocked administration' (Cerase 1988), 'an unlikely reform' (Capano 1992), 'the elephants' dance' (Arcuri, Ciacia and La Rosa 1994), 'an entrepreneurial administration?' (D'Albergo and Vaselli 1995), 'a difficult innovation' (Bifulco and De Leonardis 1997), or even 'the unfindable State' (Cassese 1998).

Although it is true that besides these studies there have been surveys aimed at evaluating specific aspects of the reforms (Rebora 1999; Capano 2000; Gherardi and Jacobsson 2000; Battistelli 2002), there has been no explicit and methodical endeavour to assess them. This essay has sought to respond to this need for evaluation by analysing the only aspect that at the moment lends itself to assessment: decision-making and implementation. On the basis of the descriptions given above, I shall seek to answer the following two questions: (a) Is the process achieving institutional change? and (b) has the process to date obtained the results intended?

Decision-making

Italy has never experienced a unitary decision-making phase; rather, it has undergone an uninterrupted sequence of micro-decisions. In Italy, unlike other countries, it is impossible to single out a political statement or an initial decision that sets coherent, internally ordered and systematic reform in train. Instead, what one finds is a sequence of minor rules which can be interpreted in the light of three different features.[11]

First, Italian governments (that is, the ministers of Civil Service) have always preferred to adopt a 'step-by-step' strategy so that they can progressively define stakes, stakeholders, objectives and resources, thereby broadening consensus during implementation and addressing doubts and difficulties about competences and technical and managerial solutions when they arise.

Second, limited and frequent decisions have been of crucial importance in avoiding resistance to change in the parliamentary arenas by guaranteeing advantageous discretion for reformers. It is evident that an 'all-inclusive' initial law would never have been politically acceptable to Parliament and would have taken even longer to gain approval.

Third, decision-making has been conducted mainly on the basis of legal procedures. The legal decision-making process has therefore consisted of a large number of specific laws followed by regulations, memoranda and ministerial circulars. The latter aspect is only apparently formal: indeed, it has been crucial because reformers have paid more attention to law enactment than to goal achievement. This distinctive characteristic of Italian decision-making has given rise to its ironic description as a 'change by decree' (Panozzo 2000). The consequences for the decision-making process have been the following:

1. a complex translation into Italian legalistic terms of English NPM principles, the uprooting of which from their original cultural context has made them misleading to implementers;
2. an excessive degree of detail in the law, which has introduced rigidity instead of flexibility, the fundamental requirement of NPM;
3. a superfluity of laws on the same subject enacted at different times, which has generated greater ambiguity rather than reducing it.

The decision-making process has thus acquired the feature described by Lindblom (1965) as a disjoint incrementalism: numerous small, strongly bargained and disjointed decisions. Objectives have been defined and redefined. There has been no pattern for reforms, which have been a hodgepodge of sectoral and general acts, and at times have been introduced without the necessary precedents.

All of this has had major repercussions. First, the lack of a unitary project has created uncertainty in the definition of purposes, objectives and implementation tools. An abundant set of NPM-oriented laws suggests that top-down implementation without intermediation has taken place: each individual public-sector organization has been required to enact the reform only by reading the relative law, which is rather difficult, even at the decision-making level. The laws are numerous and diverse and contain many innovations to be implemented almost simultaneously; furthermore, NPM innovations require competences and skills that did not exist in the public-sector, and which cannot be inferred from the laws, especially laws as cryptic as these.

Finally, an incremental public policy made up of single events is not as trenchant as a straightforward project. Hence, these innovations attack the problem from all sides, but haphazardly and without real effect on the core of the bureaucracy. They treat innovations as if they were independent from one another and unconnected to an overall project; furthermore, they allow the institutionalization of NPM within the structural and cultural framework of the bureaucracy, that is, they permit the grafting-on of extraneous accessories.

Implementation

Faced with a variety of disjointed and incremental objectives, implementation has had predictable effects. First, it has been – for the most part – slow and susceptible to local initiatives and to the influence of the senior management of each administration involved. It has thus transferred the conflict between innovators and conservatives to the organizational level, and has predicated the result of the reform on the outcome of this underlying conflict. Consequently, where political leaders and senior managers have been favourable to the reform, or knowledgeable about the innovations required, a bottom-up implementation process has occurred. Where these actors have been resistant to change, implementation has simply ground to a halt.

The regional administrations, the health service and local governments, in particular, have suffered from this phenomenon. Hence, it has created clear differences among local governments according to their size: minuscule, small, medium or large. Medium-sized bodies (towns or the smaller provinces) have benefited the most, whereas metropolitan cities and larger provinces have seen increased slowness in local decision making (Lippi 2001). Small and tiny administrations have suffered quite the opposite problem, for they do not have sufficient resources with which to stimulate and support change in a timely and continuous manner. Furthermore, each sectoral act has been implemented differently in the centre-north and centre-south regions, which has resulted in some active regions and other more passive ones.

A second major feature displayed by the implementation of reforms enacted in such legalistic manner has been a creeping, yet very real, posture of compliance with change whereby administrative organizations only pretend to have changed. This is a typical characteristic of Italian public-sector reform policy, seen over and over again in reforms labelled as 'modernizing', and it is extensively documented in the specialist literature. The strongly formalistic tone used by decision-makers adopting changes has met with a similar response from implementers. Some administrations have only formally adopted and imposed changes, approving the legal requirements in formal terms but without effectively enacting the measures. This is a behaviour known as 'apparent implementation' (Gherardi and Mortara 1988).

A third distinctive feature is a lack of the coordinated organization of implementation, particularly as regards actions involving local governments, regions and peripheral state administrations. In general, the central government has enacted only weak coordination in the implementation of specific rules; a weakness partly due to the multiplicity of central structures involved in coordinating change: Civil Service Department, ministries and also the _Corte dei conti._

Nonetheless, the most important factor is that coordination has been inadequate. Central bureaucracies have often played a secondary role, not having been legitimized by other administrations that do not welcome central intervention. Furthermore, especially in cases involving highly innovative and business-oriented NPM elements, organization has been the responsibility of coordinators who lack the necessary competences or who know nothing more than those being coordinated. In certain cases, intervention has turned into top-down action which has, de facto, 'centralized' implementation and provoked resistance without an integration and knowledge cycle between coordinators and the coordinated.

At the same time, intervention enacted by governmental departments and ministries has acquired strong symbolic value by resorting to knowledge campaigns on innovation. The most important of these campaigns has concerned the state–citizen relationship and citizenship rights (procedure simplification, unification of service counters, citizen's charter, and transparency). This symbolic mobilization, coupled with conferences, meetings[12], workshops and the creation of best practice awards, has facilitated the understanding and dissemination of an innovation culture, but it has not yet led to the coordination of implementation.

A final feature has been the heterogeneity of accomplishments. Apart from general acts, in fact, most innovations – especially sectoral innovations intended to foster decision-making autonomy – have given rise to very different and creative bottom-up solutions, resulting in a set of local innovations that are sometimes heterodox but always different from what is set out in the text of laws.

In short, this weak and failing top-down coordination generated a pervasive bottom-up implementation at the organizational level, at which people tried to implement laws by choosing wholesale from various NPM ideas. Therefore, there are numerous unexpected results indicative of a variety of management solutions. Implementation has thus been achieved at the organizational level through the mobilization of local competences, organizational cultures, ideas and consultants in an endeavour to find specific and diverse solutions to problems. The role of the three groups of cultural mediators (see Section 2) is even more pronounced in the implementation of policy than in its formulation. The business consultants that convey their experiences into the public-sector, the jurists 'converted' to NPM and the associations of practitioners that concern themselves with specific issues exert a decisive influence in this bottom up process.

Hence, bottom-up implementation has enabled administrations to adjust innovations to their specific needs, and to bring into effect a reform plan intended to enhance their decision-making autonomy. Almost paradoxically, therefore, top-down implementation has been more symbolic than real. On the other hand, bottom-up implementation has been concrete – albeit in an experimental and rather haphazard manner.

Results

It is rather difficult to draw conclusions about this policy process, particularly because it is still largely ongoing. I seek to specify the main results by answering the questions with which the section began: (a) Is this process achieving institutional change? and (b) has the process to date obtained the results intended?

Firstly, institutional change is still incomplete and slow; nevertheless, it is in progress. General acts are more visible. Privatizations are proceeding apace, and outsourcing in its different forms is undoubtedly a success. Similarly, progressive changes are being made to privatization of employment contracts. Less use is made of senior-management bargaining, which remains a minor phenomenon, and the recruitment of general directors is problematic. The progress of simplification, transparency and access is more complex because these innovations have encountered greater resistance, and have at times been more symbolic than real.

Sectoral acts have had a markedly diversified impact. Local governments display wide disparities in the pace of change, thereby creating an evident cleavage between those who are 'in step' and those who are 'latecomers'. A similar phenomenon can be observed in the universities and in the school system, which initiated reforms even later. The health system has undergone the most profound change: its transformation into a set of 'local enterprises' most closely replicates a 'business' pattern.

Finally, evaluation practices are still suspended between a pragmatic approach, methodologically not always correct and the ambiguity of the double role of the *Corte dei conti*. Performance management has been widely perceived as a resource providing important decision-making support. By contrast, ex post policy evaluation is still lacking a political demand.

The results expected have only partially been achieved. More importantly, the processes described have generated numerous unintended consequences, some of which have been highly undesirable, such as formalism, cultural resistance and only apparent change. Other unintended consequences – for instance, social learning and knowledge sharing among administrations, working groups and networks – have in fact been a blessing in disguise. All are innovative elements representative of important change. This bottom-up change has been greatly desired, and it springs from an interpretation of reform aimed at increasing decision-making autonomy. Unfortunately, this knowledge capital will be lost if it is not adequately integrated at the national level into a shared learning process that covers the entire country, not only isolated (sectoral or geographical) settings.

To conclude: even though Italian reform policy is sometimes a contradiction (as a 'voluntary choice or a legal obligation') of top-down and bottom-up tendencies, the institutionalization displays positive unintended consequences. Best practices and the fruitful implementation of decision-making autonomy are emerging in some areas of the Italian public-sector, along with the increasing importance of evaluation practices. However, these advances are still too limited.

Better integration is required. Closer coordination of each ministry, the sharing of individual experiences, and more effective networking among administrations are highly recommended. The reform process is in need of greater institutionalization. Integration between institutional top-down implementation and the increasing role of learning in bottom-up networking approaches could become a new policy goal. I submit that this is the real challenge now facing reform policy in Italy.

References

Arcuri, F., C. Ciacia and M. La Rosa (1994) (eds), 'Pubblica amministrazione e cambiamento organizzativo: "la danza degli elefanti"', *Sociologia del Lavoro*, 54.

Barzelay, M. (2000), *The New Public Management: Improving Research and Policy Dialogue*, Los Angeles: University of California Press.

Bassanini, F. (2000), 'La riforma della pubblica amministrazione in Italia: un bilancio a fine 2000', workshop Unioncamere, 'Le autonomie per lo sviluppo economico', Rome, December 13.

Battistelli, F. (2002) (ed.), *La cultura delle amministrazioni tra retorica e innovazioni*, Milan: Angeli.

Bifulco, L. and De Leonardis, O. (1997) (eds), *L'innovazione difficile: studi sul cambiamento organizzativo nello Pubblica Amministrazione*, Milan: Angeli.

Capano, G. (1992), *L'improbabile riforma*, Bologna: Il Mulino.

Capano, G. (1998), *La politica universitaria*, Bologna: Il Mulino.

Capano, G. (2000), 'Le politiche amministrative: dall'improbabile riforma alla riforma permanente?', in G. Di Palma, S. Fabbrini and G. Freddi (eds), *Condannata al successo? L'Italia nell'Europa integrata*, Bologna: Il Mulino, pp. 153–98.

Capano, G. (2002), 'Le riforme degli anni Novanta. L'adattamento reattivo del paradigma egemonico', in F. Battistelli (ed.), *La cultura delle amministrazioni tra retorica e innovazioni*, Milan: Angeli, pp. 47–69.

Cassese, S. (1992), '"Maladministration" e rimedi', *Foro italiano*, V[September], 243–50.

Cassese, S. (1998), *Lo Stato introvabile*, Rome: Donzelli.

Cassese, S. (2002), *La crisi dello Stato*, Bari: Laterza.

Cazzola, F. (1988), *Della corruzione. Fisiologia e patologia di un sistema politico*, Bologna: Il Mulino.

Cerase, F. P. (1988), *Un'amministrazione bloccata. Pubblica amministrazione e società nell'Italia di oggi*, Milan: Angeli.

Cerase, F. P. (1999) (ed.), *La nuova dirigenza pubblica*, Rome: Carocci.

D'Albergo, E. and P. Vaselli (1997), *Un'amministrazione imprenditoriale?*, Rome: Seam.

Davis, I. C. (1999), 'Evaluation and performance management in government', *Evaluation*, 5[2], 150–59.

Dente, B. (1991) (ed.), *L'efficacia dei poteri locali*, Bologna: Il Mulino.

Dente, B. (1999), *In un diverso Stato. Come rifare la Pubblica amministrazione italiana*, Bologna: Il Mulino.

Dente, B. and G. Azzone (1999) (eds), *Valutare per governare*, Milan: Etas.

DFP (Dipartimento della Funzione Pubblica) (1993), *Indirizzi per la modernizzazione delle amministrazioni pubbliche*, PCM, Rome: Ist.Poligrafico dello Stato.

DFP (2001), *Lo stato dell'amministrazione pubblica a venti anni dal Rapporto Giannini*, Rome: Ist.Poligrafico dello Stato.

D'Orta, C. (1994), 'La dirigenza pubblica tra modello burocratico e modello d'impresa', in G. Cecora and C. Cecora (eds), *La riforma del pubblico impiego*, Bologna: Il Mulino, pp. 53–114.

Fedele, M. (1998), *Come cambiano le amministrazioni pubbliche*, Bologna: Il Mulino.

Gherardi, S. and B. Jacobsson (eds) (2000), 'Managerialism as the latin of our times: Reforming Italian public sector organisations', *Scandinavian Journal of Management*, 4, special issue.

Gherardi, S. and A. Lippi (eds) (2000), *Tradurre le riforme in pratica. Le strategie della traslazione*, Milan: Cortina.

Gherardi, S. and V. Mortara (1988), 'Può il concetto di cultura organizzativa contribuire allo studio della Pubblica amministrazione?', *Rivista Trimestrale di Scienza dell'Amministrazione*, 1, 39–58

Giannini, M.S. (1982), 'Rapporto sui principali problemi dell'Amministrazione dello Stato. Trasmesso alle Camere il 16 Novembre 1979', *Rivista Trimestrale di Diritto Pubblico*, 3.

Hood, Ch. (1995), 'The new public management in the 1980s: Variations on a theme', *Accounting, Organizations and Society*, 20[2/3], 93–101.

Lindblom, Ch. (1965), *The Intelligence of Democracy: Decision Making through Mutual Adjustment*, New York: Free Press.

Lippi, A. (1999), 'Il sindaco "amministratore" e il burocrate "manager": Un bilancio del rapporto tra politica e amministrazione dopo un decennio di riforme', *Le istituzioni del federalismo*, 6, 1237–74.

Lippi, A. (2000), 'One theory, many practices. Institutional allomorphism in Italian reorganization of local government', in S. Gherardi and B. Jacobsson (eds), 'Managerialism as the Latin of our times: Reforming Italian public sector organisations', *Scandinavian Journal of Management*, 4, 455–77.

Lippi, A. (2001), *Valutazione e controlli di gestione nei governi locali italiani. Una teoria, molte pratiche*, Turin: Giappichelli.

Lo Schiavo, L. (1996), 'La carta dei servizi nel cestino dei rifiuti', *Rivista trimestrale di scienza dell'amministrazione*, 4, 243–70.

Maino, F. (2000), *La politica sanitaria*, Bologna: Il Mulino.

Mazza, C. and Quattrone, R. (2002), 'Dall'organizzazione del sapere al sapere organizzativo? Il sistema universitario italiano alla prova del mercato', in F. Battistelli (ed.), *La cultura delle amministrazioni tra retorica e innovazioni*, Milan: Angeli, pp.149–64.

Melis, G. (1996), *Storia dell'amministrazione italiana: 1861–1993*, Bologna: Il Mulino.

Merati, I. (2001). 'Il mercato della valutazione attivato dalle nuove politiche strutturali dell'Unione europea', in N. Stame, *Valutazione 2001: Lo sviluppo della valutazione in Italia*, Milan: Angeli, pp. 21–47.

Munari, F. (2002), *Privatizzazioni ed innovazione. Nuovi aspetti proprietari ed investimenti*, Rome: Carocci.

NPR (National Performance Review) (1993), *From the Red Tape to Results*, Washington DC: NPR.

Oliva, D. and F. Pesce (2001), 'Aggiungi un posto a tavola: la valutazione come scelta volontaria o come obbligo di legge', in N. Stame, *Valutazione 2001: Lo sviluppo della valutazione in Italia*, Milan: Angeli, pp. 48–61.

Olsen, J. P. and B. G. Peters (1996), *Lessons from Experience: Administrative Reforms in Europe*, Oslo: Scandinavian University Press.

Panozzo, F. (2000), 'Management by decree: Paradoxes in the reform of the Italian public sector', in S. Gherardi and B. Jacobsson (eds), 'Managerialism as the latin of our times: Reforming Italian public sector organisations', *Scandinavian Journal of Management*, 4, 357–74.

Peters, B. G. and D. Savoie (1998) (eds), *Taking Stock: Assessing Public Sector Reform*, Québec: Canadian Centre for Management, McGill University Press.
Putnam, R. D., R. Leonardi and R. Y. Nanetti (1985), *La pianta e le radici*, Bologna: Il Mulino.
Rebora, G. F. (1999), *Un decennio di riforme*, Milan: Guerini.
Righettini, M. S. (2001), 'L'evoluzione del sistema dei controlli in Italia', in M. Morisi and A. Lippi,. *Manuale di scienza dell'amministrazione: La valutazione*, Turin: Giappichelli, pp. 53–94.
Ruffini, R. (1999), *La carta dei servizi*, Milan: Guerini.
Stame, N. (2001a), 'Evaluation in Italy: an inverted sequence from performance management to program evaluation?', in J. E .Furubo et al. (eds), *Evaluation Atlas*, New Brunswick, US: Transaction, pp. 127–160.
Stame, N. (2001b), *Valutazione 2001: Lo sviluppo della valutazione in Italia*, Milan: Angeli.
Stame, N. (2002), 'La cultura della valutazione tra iper – istituzionalizzazione e pragmatismo', in F. Battistelli (ed.), *La cultura delle amministrazioni tra retorica e innovazioni*, Milan: Angeli, pp. 131–47.
Tomassini, M. and M. Bonaretti (2002), 'Le comunità di pratica nei processi di innovazione nella pubblica amministrazione', in F. Battistelli (ed.), *La cultura delle amministrazioni tra retorica e innovazioni*, Milan: Angeli, pp. 265–82.
Zanetti, G. and G. Alzona (1998), *Capire le privatizzazioni*, Bologna: Il Mulino.

Notes

1 The report is named for director and distinguished law professor Massimo Severo Giannini.
2 This phase was interrupted by the first Berlusconi government (1994), whose tenure, however, was too brief to permit any reform of the public sector.
3 Maladministration [bad administration] is an Italian-English neologism which emphasizes the inadequacy of the Italian public sector in an international context (that is, the increasingly Anglophone NPM rhetoric of institutional change).
4 The Minister for the Civil Service (*Ministro per la Funzione Pubblica*) is responsible for the public sector as a whole and is the head of the Civil Service Department, a branch of the Prime Minister's Office.
5 This community comprises a wide range of organizations centred on the private Bocconi University of Milan, which specializes in business administration.
6 This is the year of the legislation, while the actual privatization of each organization took place in five instalments over the next five years.
7 Although equalization has happened in theory, wages and benefits still differ greatly between the public and private sectors, with wages being higher in the latter.
8 CNR is the Comitato Nazionale delle Ricerche, an autonomous body that coordinates scientific research.

9   A school to train public functionaries, modelled on the French École Nationale
    Supérieure – but of less prestige and quality.
10 *Controllo di gestione* is a translation of the French *contrôle de gestion*, where *ges-
    tion* is the French for 'management'; both terms derive from the Latin verb *gerere*,
    'to lead'.
11 Only two documents (issued in 1992 by Amato and 1997 by Bassanini) have set out
    a political programme.
12 One of them, the Public Administration Forum ('Forum P.A.') has become an impor-
    tant national event.

9. The late and sudden emergence of New Public Management reforms in Japan

Michio Muramatsu and Jun Matsunami

1. Introduction

This chapter analyses administrative reforms in Japan in the last quarter of the twentieth century, and examines why the Japanese government was at first slow to engage in reforms falling under the rubric of New Public Management (NPM) but was quick to implement decentralization, outsourcing, and similar reform measures once NPM had been embraced in the late 1990s. While a multiplicity of factors is likely to have influenced public-sector reforms in Japan, we argue that fiscal pressures and globalization have been the driving forces. In our estimation, the 'bubble economy', that is Japan's seemingly ever-growing economy, at first delayed the Japanese government's serious reform activities; following the burst of the bubble, the economy accelerated and precipitated the government's response expressed in some kinds of reform in the late 1990s.

The LDP Government began to reform various segments of the public-sector in 1981, establishing the Second Provisional Administrative Reform Commission (SPARC) to cope with the fiscal imbalance. Japan's rate of bond issuance had become the highest among the OECD countries. However, deficit financing of general expenditures ended in 1990 due to increased revenue, generated in part by the bubble economy. The burst of the bubble, scandals and the realignment of the party system followed. These developments brought the issues of government deficit and fiscal imbalance to the forefront. However, the government resumed public-sector reforms only after a hiatus of several years. Fiscal spending was strongly advocated by the Neo-Keynesians in government from 1995 to 2000.[1] In their view, spending would stimulate the economy and the ensuing GDP increase would gradually solve the nation's economic problems, especially the numerous non-performing loans held by Japanese banks. The absence of strong government leadership after the LDP stepped down from power in 1993, however, elicited a lack of disciplined spending, thus encouraging excessive fiscal outlays.

This chapter will focus on the debate on public-sector reforms conducted in recent decades and on public-sector reforms undertaken since 1996. However, before turning to the administrative reforms pursued in the past 20 years in the context of NPM-related ideas, it is worthwhile to analyse the First Provisional Administrative Reform Commission.

2. The First Provisional Administrative Reform Commission of 1962

The First Provisional Administrative Reform Commission was modelled after the Hoover Commissions that were established in the United States in the 1940s and 1950s to promote public-sector reforms. The Commission was made up of seven members, including a former highest-ranking bureaucrat, and advocated a broad range of reforms. It advanced, for example, the establishment of special cabinet advisers who would serve a function similar to that of presidential aides in the United States. The Commission also wanted to transfer the responsibility for compiling the budget from the Minister of Finance (MOF) to the Cabinet Office. Although many of these reform recommendations were never realized, two important proposals were implemented. First, the Total Staff Number Law (*sō teiin hō*) concerning the size of the public-sector work force was enacted in 1969. This law limited the total number of civil employees in the Japanese central government and even stipulated a decrease. While most other OECD countries significantly increased the number of central government employees during the 'expansionist' 1970s, Japan refrained from such increase in strict compliance with the 1969 law. Secondly, based on another of the Commission's recommendations, the Sato cabinet abolished some twenty bureaus (the highest organizational units within the ministries) in 1968, in pursuance of the principle of abolishing one bureau in each ministry (*issho ikkoku sakugen*). It is noteworthy that in the 1970s the performance of the traditional prewar-styled higher civil service was not questioned, despite the scrutiny other components of central government received. Similarly, almost no attention was paid to policy evaluation. Our interpretation is that Japanese modernization – or 'catching up' –

was still a priority and that the (traditional) bureaucracy was deemed the best way to achieve it.

3. The Second Provisional Administrative Reform Commission (SPARC) of 1981

The Japanese economy continued to develop throughout the mid-1970s, and the government was able to maintain a balanced budget. The situation changed after two oil price shocks in the 1970s led to large deficits. By 1979, Japan had the highest ratio of accumulated deficits to GDP among the OECD countries (Mabuchi 1994, pp. 4–13). In 1979, Japan relied on the issuance of bonds for 34.7 per cent of its budget. In order to balance the budget, Japan faced a difficult choice: a tax increase or a budget cut. Prime Minister Ohira advocated the introduction of the consumption tax and was later defeated in the general election. The Suzuki cabinet opted for budget cuts, and organized the Second Provisional Administrative Reform Commission (SPARC) in 1981.

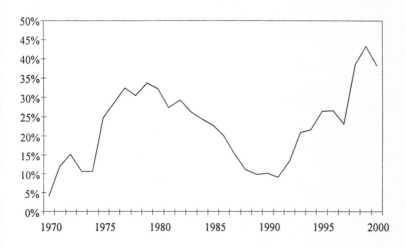

Figure 9.1 Percentage of National Bonds to the Budget

The aim of the Commission was to reconstruct finances without a tax increase (*zōzei naki zaisei saiken*), and this official slogan was used to persuade the public of the merits of the strategy (Ito 1997, pp. 63–69; Kumon 1984, pp. 143–7). One of the successful reforms was the privatization of Japan National Railways (JNR). JNR received annual subsidies from the general budget, but accumulated deficits. Consequently, it became a prime reform target for SPARC, eliciting intense political conflicts and negotiations among the major actors. The JNR reform bills were passed by the Diet in 1986, and JNR was divided into six regionally-based passenger train companies, one freight company and other organizations, resulting in a large number of layoffs in 1987. JNR privatization was modelled on the reorganization of the electric industry in the immediate postwar period. Until 1951, a single power company had monopolized the electric industry in Japan. It was argued that smaller units would improve productivity and weaken the influence of militant trade unionists (Kusano 1989, pp. 62–66).

After privatization, the productivity of the former JNR railway companies was evaluated. According to a Ministry of Transport study, the productivity of JNR was roughly one third that of privately-owned railways in 1980, but started to improve rapidly immediately before privatization; by the mid-1990s, the productivity of former JNR companies nearly equalled that of the privately-owned railways (Ministry of Transport 1997, pp. 52–53). At the same time, in 1985, two other large public corporations (a cigarette producer and a telecommunications firm) were privatized.

Table 9.1 Subsidy and tax to and from JNR (Ministry of Transport 1997, p. 90)

Year	Tax	Subsidy	Total (billion yen)[2]
1982	35.2	729.4	-694.2
1983	38.3	701.8	-663.5
1984	46.3	647.4	-601.1
1985	47.8	600.1	-552.3
1986	50.1	377.6	-327.5
1987	233.8	193.7	40.1
1988	264.8	211.0	53.8
1989	230.1	633.0	-402.9
1990	299.4	157.1	142.3
1991	444.3	108.2	336.1
1992	245.5	99.0	146.5
1993	252.4	91.7	160.7
1994	201.9	83.4	118.5

Deregulation was an equally important reform target of the SPARC under Nakasone, who seems to have been influenced by neo-liberal economic theory, as were British Prime Minister Margaret Thatcher and US President Ronald Reagan. However, the results were different from the privatization proposal. The latter materialized, but implemented only incrementally, which meant that, unlike the United States and United Kingdom, the Japanese government-industry relations did not change much, except the policy areas where privatization had happened, such as telecommunication. Still, SPARC was largely successful in decreasing bond issuance (See Figure 9.1).

4. Administrative Reform Commissions

The LDP government evaluated the reform results as follows. First, in order to carry on the reform momentum, the government subsequently established the new Administrative Reform Commission (ARC) in 1983, as a successor to the SPARC. Many policy areas and institutions that SPARC itself had not been able to address remained on the reform agenda. Thus, the First Administrative Reform Commission had two aims. The first was to research and advocate administrative reforms in areas that the SPARC had not. The other was to monitor the implementation of SPARC recommendations. At the end of the First Administrative Reform Commission's term, the Second Administrative Reform Commission was established to advocate new administrative reforms and to monitor the implementation of previous recommendations, including those of the SPARC and the First Administrative Reform Commission. Further Administrative Reform Commissions (ARCs) were formed one after another until 1996, when a new wave of administrative reform discussions emerged.

The SPARC and ARCs comprised business, labour and academic representatives and a former high-ranking civil servant. Evaluation of the reforms – a major mission of the ARCs – was carried out in part by external evaluation, but was a largely in-house evaluation: evaluation documents were prepared by the Secretariat's office, which was composed of bureaucrats dispatched from various ministries. Furthermore, one might argue that the evaluation results of the ARCs were not a meaningful part of the reform process in that they did not improve the quality of policies or government management. In the 1980s and early 1990s, Japanese officials failed to perceive the seriousness of bubble-induced problems. The general perception in Japan at that time was that everything was going well and that Japan was not facing financial troubles. Consequently, government officials prioritized spending policies over public-sector reforms, even though the nation had already run a large deficit. In fact, national loans dropped to 9.5 per cent of the budget in 1991. Soon after this pause in the expansion of the deficit, however, the Japanese government was forced to face the serious financial difficulties brought about by the end of the bubble economy.

Administrative reforms advocated by ARCs were implemented only gradually, and with a smaller impact than expected. Excepting only a few years the balance of governmental revenue and expenditure was not in good shape. The deregulation did not happen as the ARCs had planned. The bubble economy put the policy makers in the mist where they were not able to see the reality and then the burst of the bubble made it difficult for the government to implement deregulation and other policies due to the political turmoil caused by government scandals.

The state of party politics also proves relevant here, for it provides insight into why politicians in this period were preoccupied with activities other than administrative reform. Until the mid-1990s, Japanese political leaders were concerned, first of all, with the search for coalition partners to form the cabinet, since the LDP was unable to command a majority in both houses. A new situation had emerged, in which all parties had the opportunity to participate in cabinet formation. Several new parties, including Morihiro Hosokawa's Japan New Party, gained many seats in the House of Representatives. Morihiro Hosokawa was elected prime minister in 1993, and the old anti-LDP parties and the new parties formed the majority of the House of Representatives. In 1994, a once unimaginable LDP and Socialist Party coalition formed and was in office for four years. While politicians were absorbed by these new political developments, the political salience of public-sector reforms only gradually became apparent. By the late 1990s, however, these reforms re-emerged as the number one political issue, as deficit financing severely stretched the limits of government capacity. It was at this point that Hashimoto organized and served as chair of a new public-sector reform commission. Thus, it took several years for Japanese leaders to recognize that managerialism and NPM were important devices for reforming the Japanese government.

5. Public-sector reforms under the new LDP governments

In our view, substantial public-sector reforms have been introduced in response to the economic and financial crisis broadly perceived in the late 1990s. At both national and local levels, politicians and civilians have been committed to far-reaching public-sector reforms. The reorganization of central government ministries and agencies, decentralization, outsourcing, civil service and related reforms made a sudden entrance onto the political agenda after the 1996 general election. New research findings on NPM promoted this sudden and forceful movement towards public-sector reforms. Reform targets have even included the 'high-flyer system' in the civil service, a topic that had not been addressed in reform discussions until the early 1990s. Under the umbrella phrase of 'reorganization,'[3] many NPM tools were introduced. These encompass agencification, outsourcing and programme evaluation. The most notable component of the reform proposals is the reorganization of the government ministries, a move that threatens some ministry bureaucrats. Because officials entered these ministries at an early age – typically immediately after graduation from university – and expected lifetime employment, their loyalty to their respective ministries was particularly strong.

Prime Minister Hashimoto implemented four noteworthy reforms: increased power to the cabinet; reorganization of the central government; reformation of the civil service system; and outsourcing. The idea of granting more power to the cabinet and the prime minister was welcomed widely. Because the bureaucracy was the target of heavy criticism, the proposal to increase the influence of politicians in the policy-making process also was positively received. Under the guise of 'outsourcing,' public corporations became the object of scrutiny that seemed to indicate eventual abolishment of these organizations. The number of ministries was reduced from 22 to 13. Agencification of the service delivery component of public administration has also taken place through the establishment of Independent Administrative Institutions (IAIs), which are similar to British agencies.

The agencification concept is particularly interesting as an example of Japan's adoption of new ideas from abroad. Sixty IAIs – employing several thousand civil servants – now exist in Japan. Four differences exist, however, between British and Japanese agency systems. First, while British agencies are part of the state administration, their Japanese counterparts have independent legal status and are separate from the state. Second, the British idea of establishing a contract between the Secretaries of State and the agency manager has been transformed into a 'goal-setting and implementation plans' scheme, in which ministers establish the mid-term goals and aims of the agency and the agency itself formulates the implementation plans. The results are evaluated according the goals and the implementation plans. Third, each ministry in Japan must establish a committee to evaluate the agencies under its jurisdiction, whereas British ministries conduct these evaluations themselves. Fourth, Japanese agencies are not always engaged in the delivery of services under the pertinent ministry's jurisdiction. Instead, in keeping with a longstanding practice, the most important implementation tasks are delegated to local governments. Most IAIs are small public organizations such as research institutes or national museums. We would like to add, however, that the targets of the agencification are increasing. The postal services and the national universities are scheduled for agencification in a few years. Recently, large public corporations such as Japan International Cooperation Agency (JICA) and National Space Development Agency (NASDA) were added to the list, despite the fact that the results of agencification have not yet been observed. Politicians interested in administration find the 'Japanese-style' agency to be a useful policy tool for monitoring the administrative system. We have observed that the momentum is the key to continued administrative reform. Given current fiscal conditions, politicians – regardless of party – are obliged to declare themselves reformers of governmental organization.

Decentralization is another case that sheds light on the nature of reforms undertaken in the 1990s. While the Murayama administration formally put decentralization on the political agenda, the 1993 formation of the non-LDP coalition government under Hosokawa actually raised the political prominence of this issue. The Hosokawa-Hata Cabinets (1993–94) pushed decentralization as a public-sector reform. Murayama then put it on his agenda by passing the Decentralization Promotion Act (*chihō bunken suishin hō*) of 1995. However, decentralization should not be regarded as an NPM-guided reform. In the minds of the majority members of the Administrative Reform Commission, the aim of decentralization was not to improve the effectiveness of government management, but to realize the longstanding 'progressive' dream of enhancing local autonomy. The argument for decentralization entered mainstream political debates for the first time under the socialist Murayama administration. However, when the decentralization proposal entered the stage of legislative drafting, the justification for decentralization shifted from strengthening local autonomy to raising the effectiveness and productivity of the Japanese government as a whole. The changed fiscal situation was the catalyst for this change in the primary objectives to be achieved by decentralization.

Deregulation is another reform initiated for one purpose but later associated with another. In our view, deregulation is more a by-product of

US–Japan negotiations than it is a result of efforts to reform the public-sector. Deregulation originally was meant to curtail the leadership of the Ministry of International Trade and Industry (MITI) in industrial policies, but it has come to be associated with the promotion of public-sector effectiveness. This shift reflects a change in political climate since the 1990s. In this way, the deregulation and decentralization movements share a similar dynamic.

We should note that a policy evaluation procedure has been introduced. Before the Hashimoto reform proposal, the Board of Audit (BOA) and the Management and Coordination Agency (MCA) performed separate functions with regard to the evaluation of government activities and auditing. The MCA evaluated the efficiency and economy of government activities, whereas the BOA checked the accounts of government agencies. The 2001 Policy Evaluation Law requires each government ministry or agency to conduct an in-house evaluation of its policies and programmes according to specific criteria and procedures. This development was triggered by the government monitoring of its policies and programmes and by the observation that the need for such monitoring was actually more pressing than the need for evaluation of the legality of transactions undertaken by government agencies. However, concrete steps towards such reforms were taken only after the establishment of the 1996 Hashimoto Reform Commission. The Secretariat for this commission studied [US vice president] Al Gore's Government Performance Program, the British programme of evaluation by Public Service Agreements (PSAs), and later the United States' Government Performance and Results Act (GPRA). Laws pertaining to the reorganization of government ministries stipulated that every government agency should self-evaluate the policies and programmes under its jurisdiction in terms of effectiveness, efficiency, and cost-benefit analysis both prior to and following the enactment of programmes.

Some questioned whether this system of self- or in-house evaluation really would be implemented and whether it would be effective. In 2001 lawmakers passed legislation to create a new agency – the Administrative Evaluation Bureau, whose mission it is to monitor the in-house evaluation process conducted by each ministry's evaluation bureau. This agency now has a staff of 160 officials and is located within the Ministry of Public Management, Home Affairs, Posts and Telecommunications (MPMHAPT). In addition to this agency, a commission of academics, accountants and business elites has been established to introduce an external monitoring element that is relatively independent from the bureaucracy. Our analysis of the process surrounding the

Japanese government's study and introduction of policy evaluation reveals that this development came about quite suddenly, and was motivated by ideas imported from abroad rather than by academic knowledge or by available studies of government practices. Although it still is too early to evaluate these reforms, the fact that NPM-type reforms have proven successful at the local government level suggests that great changes in the Japanese public administration system and its procedures can be expected.

6. Evaluating recent reform initiatives

Finally, we should like to compare the 1996–97 Hashimoto Reforms with the two previous large-scale public-sector reforms, that is, the FPARC in the early 1960s and the SPARC in the 1980s. The Hashimoto Reforms differed from previous reforms in several ways. First, the Hashimoto reforms were promoted under coalitional administration and, therefore, were more sensitive to mass media and public opinion expressed during the national elections. In the autumn of 1996, Hashimoto pledged to enact administrative reforms, and won the Lower House election. Second, these reforms increased the powers of the prime minister and the cabinet. It is worth noting that the Ministry of Finance was not a member of the political alliance pushing for administrative reform. The Hashimoto Reforms abolished the Bureau of Bank and replaced it with the Inspection Administration for Banks and other Financial Institutions, which was clearly damaging to the Ministry. Furthermore, some of the Ministry's budget-making authority was transferred to the Cabinet Office.[4] Civil service reform proposals are especially significant. As the relationship between politics and administration changes, the role of bureaucracy has declined: the cabinet now officially controls the promotion of top-ranking bureaucrats, and changes in the civil service examinations and the traditional practice of reemploying civil servants in the private sector have been proposed. Furthermore, the LDP now seeks greater power to control bureaucrats.[5] It typically takes several months to enact basic reforms. However, in late December 2001, the cabinet approved a comprehensive Outline of Civil Service Reform seemingly overnight. The Outline, with its emphasis on increased competition, seems to correspond to the ideas behind NPM personnel administration. There also should be more competition in promotion procedure. Second-job markets for retired bureaucrats should be deregulated in the spirit of free competition. The most controversial issue has been that of the parachuting of upper-level civil servants into the semi-public organizations or into jobs in the private sector. Many claim that this practice could make the business-government relationship less transparent, and increase their dependence on each other. There is a high probability that the less controversial elements of the proposed reform will be enacted; politicians are very much interested in civil service reform, given the weakness of ministry bureaucracies.

It is interesting that administrative reform, despite a slow start, continued even after Hashimoto, Obuchi and Mori cabinets implemented the decentralization reform. Civil service reform began under Koizumi, but the larger political issue of disposal of the non-performing loans in the major banks has received greater attention. In terms of evaluation, what we should have in mind is the establishment of the Policy Evaluation Commission, whose mission is to monitor the in-house monitoring of the policy evaluation that the government organizations are required to do. In the areas of public works, official development assistance (ODA), and scientific research, pre-implementation evaluation is required by law. Each ministry has disclosed some 80 or 90 numerical criteria to be met during the 2002 fiscal year. As to the large-scale policies, a comprehensive evaluation method should be introduced. According to the general law concerning the independent administrative institutions, the Policy Evaluation Commission is given final power to propose the abolishment of the agencies based on achievements. Seeing the disclosed criteria to be used for the evaluation of the agencies every year, numerical criteria of evaluation are accepted by all Japanese agencies. Evaluations of all government organizations will be released at the end of fiscal year 2002 and management improvements of the agencies will be evaluated in several quantitative ways. However, we do not have very specific information to report to our colleagues abroad at this point.

7. Concluding remarks

We have attempted to sketch how NPM-guided public-sector reforms have made their entry in Japan. According to Richard Rose, Japan has adopted foreign ideas, but has always modified them to suit a specific context and time (Rose 1993, pp. 40–44). In other words, the Japanese have invented, imitated others, and preserved the existing system in a deliberate fashion (Westney 1987). It is our view, however, that the past 20 years have been different. During this period, Japanese officials have been conspicuously insensitive to the evolution of public-sector reform theory that was taking place in Europe and America. Because Japanese political actors were at first distracted by the seemingly benign circumstances of the 'bubble economy', then preoccupied with dealing with economic and political fallout once the bubble burst, public-sector reforms did not appear on the political agenda. Government leaders mistakenly assumed that revenue increases in the late 1980s and early 1990s correlated with successful government management (Otake 1999, pp. 381–7). Actually, however, problems were mounting in the public-sector. The revelation of scandals within the higher civil service made the bureaucracy a scapegoat and a target of political attacks. Unethical behaviour and the underlying causes of substandard government performance became the focus of public attention. Following the 1996 general election, however, this intense criticism of the bureaucracy generated a political context in which the reorganization of the central government ministries and civil service reforms could be attempted, despite protests and opposition from within the bureaucracy. Later, the attention of government officials shifted to addressing the problems brought about by the bubble's collapse. Thus, one can say that NPM-guided reforms emerged in Japan 'all of a sudden'.

References

Ito, Mitsutoshi (1997), 'Administrative reform in Japan: Semi-autonomous bureaucracy under the pressure toward a small government', in Michio Muramatsu and Frieder Nashold (eds), *State and Administration in Japan and Germany*, Berlin and New York: de Gruyter, pp. 63–103.

Kumon, Shunpei (1984), 'Japan faces its future: The political-economics of administrative reform', *Journal of Japanese Studies*, 10[1], 143–65.

Kusano, Atsushi (1989), *Kokutetsu Kaikaku* [JNR reform], Tokyo: Chūō Kōronsha.

Mabuchi, Masaru (1994), *Okurasho Tōsei no Seiji Keizaigaku* [The political economy of the Ministry of Finance], Tokyo: Chūō Kōronsha.

Ministry of Transport (1997), *Unyuhakusho Heisei 8 Nendo* [Transport White Paper 1996], Tokyo: Okurasho Insatsukyoku.

Otake, Hideo (1999), 'Developments in the Japanese political economy since the mid-1980s: The second attempt at neo-liberal reform and its aftermath', *Government and Opposition*, 34[3], 372–96.

Ramseyer, J. Mark and Francis McCall Rosenbluth (1993), *Japan's Political Marketplace*, Cambridge, US: Harvard University Press.

Rose, Richard (1993), *Lesson-Drawing in Public Policy*, Chatham, US: Chatham House.

Westney, D. Eleanor (1987), *Imitation and Innovation: The Transfer of Western Organizational Patterns to Meiji Japan*, Cambridge, US: Harvard University Press.

Notes

1. In 1998, Prime Minister Ryutaro Hashimoto was committed to a 'balanced budget' in the period when the Japanese economy needed a Keynesian stimulus. He lost the election in the House of Councillors and had to resign. His successor, Keizo Obuchi, in contrast, presented a huge supplementary budget by issuing national bonds. In the fiscal year 1999, national bonds constituted more than 40 per cent of governmental revenue.
2. We use billion in the American sense, that is, one thousand million.
3. Administrative Reform Commission 1996–97, Final report. Major reforms in central government have been called 'reorganization reforms,' perhaps because the reorganization of the central government ministries attracted greater media and public attention than did other reforms. Prime Minister Ryutaro Hashimoto presided over the Commission's reform deliberations. This was an unusual practice in Japanese reform politics. A typical commission comprises business, labour, media, and academic representatives; recommendations are delivered from the chair of the commission to the prime minister on the final day of their term.
4. The removal of the MOF's authority over banks was actually initiated with the creation of the Financial Supervisory Agency in June 1998 but further organizational reforms related to the reorganization of the financial authorities were carried out as late as January 2001.
5. The most important factor in the party-bureaucracy relationship (and therefore the government approach to administrative reform after 1993) was the LDP's changed stance toward upper-level civil servants. The LDP once maintained strong ties with bureaucrats, but when it became an opposition party under the Hosokawa and Hata administrations, the LDP discovered that these civil servants were not always friends. In our observation, this fact has been the underlining framework in which the various reform ideas have been implemented against both the implicit and the explicit resistance of the ministry bureaucracies. If we use the argument of J. Mark Ramseyer and Frances McCall Rosenbluth, the end of the LDP's predominance in Japanese politics forced the party to find other ways to control bureaucrats because it became impossible to do so by promotions and salary increases (Ramseyer and Rosenbluth 1993, pp. 99–120).

10. Evaluating public-sector reforms in Latin America

Geraldo Tadeu Moreira Monteiro

1. Introduction

The task of assessing public-sector reforms in Latin America is governed by an apparent paradox: on the one hand, perhaps no other geopolitical and cultural space has pushed the State Reform breviary so far, but on the other hand, Latin American outcomes seem simultaneously the most impressive and least effective. These outcomes are quite impressive if set against Latin America's historical and sociological background of authoritarianism and state inefficiency, but very deceptive when compared to the 'great expectations' that reform leaders have had for them.

In order to properly evaluate the achievements of the public-sector reform movement in that context, we must set them against the century-old process of state formation. From colonial times Latin Americans have been subjected to a kind of state–society relationship based primarily on five features: bureaucratism, centralism, formalism, fiscalism and authoritarianism.[1] Even though these characteristics do not necessarily prevent modernization,[2] they constitute a serious hindrance to any movement or change. Paradoxical as it may seem, any single step towards state reform, when understood in light of this background, appear to be a great victory.

For reasons that will be considered later in this chapter, public-sector reform came to impose big changes to the Latin American state system. Globalization, worldwide depression in the 1980s, fiscal crises, current account deficits and drastic shortages in capital flows to those countries strongly contributed to the state reform movement of the 1990s. Everywhere, government's role as provider of social welfare and income security, as director of economic and social development and as service provider came under criticism. Ideas of downsizing government, marketizing, modernizing and maintaining (see Pollitt and Bouckaert 2001, p.179) became widespread and constituted the core of New Public Management's ideology (see Wollmann [ed.] 2001, pp.12–13).

The new context put considerable stress upon the traditional Weberian bureaucratic organization, producing two main outcomes: restraint and restructuring (Schields and Evans 1998, pp.36 ff). These trends drove public organizations to search for devolution, high performance, risk-taking, results-centring, client-focusing and for a learning, multi-skilled and increasingly 'outcontracted' workforce. All these changes have been appropriately called 'marketization of the state' (Pierre 1998).

Managerialism as an ideology became the dominant way of thinking about the public-sector, first in the United States and United Kingdom (Pollitt 1993) and then in other countries – although it assumed mixed forms (Pollitt 1998) in any institutional setting (see Wollmann 2001). Its basic assumptions[3] widely provided the underpinnings of multi-lateral banks' adjustment policies in most developing countries.

These harsh circumstances forced Latin American elites to adopt a 'pure neo-liberal' approach that paved the way for the opening of national markets, once protected against competition by a deliberate import substitution policy.[4] Needless to say, all of these changes had serious consequences in terms of the conditions of governance; they particularly affected the institutional framework of those countries. Latin American economies began the critical task of restructuring their large and inefficient state machineries (Roett and Crandall 1999, pp.274–7). Thanks to this new international environment traditional political forces saw their legitimacy rapidly decrease, opening the gateway to the 'tenets of rationality' that for some time had been kept within tight limits in the Latin American public-sector.

The public-sector in Latin America can be divided roughly into two main areas in terms of efficiency standards: a tiny group of central agencies (mainly financial-budgetary departments) and public enterprises in which rational methods of selection, management and control have been well established (usually called 'islands of efficiency'); and a large, loose and fairly decentralized group of subsidiary agencies (dealing mainly with public health, education and social policies) in which rational methods of management are deliberately avoided or checked to make room for clientelism, patrimonialism or corruption. If we wish to properly understand the role evaluation actually has played or has the potential to play, we need to consider its place within a context of a complex and contradictory public-sector wherein a new 'Rationalitäts-streit' is under way.

As we shall see in the last part of this article, evaluation experiences in Latin American countries are quite new and still are circumscribed by central governments. Only a few Latin American countries have put into place evaluation systems in any institutional way. Everywhere else there are local systems to measure organizational or individual performances, or even the advancement of a series of evaluation procedures to control budget execution. Additionally, there is a myriad of small, localized, ground-floor endeavours that are attributable more to voluntarism than to institutional support. Even in those countries where implementation of evaluation processes has progressed (that is, Brazil and Chile), there are only a few areas that are continuously subject to evaluation.

Before beginning a thorough discussion of the subject, I must say a word about our views on public-sector reforms and of evaluation. I begin with Hellmut Wollmann's statement that 'public-sector reform policies are, by definition, directed, in their immediate intention, at remoulding the political and administrative structures' (2001, p.24). I am not interested in the so-called substantive policies (employment policy, monetary policy, etc.), but only those addressing the process of policy-making itself. There is a good deal of evaluation – either internal or external – of substantive policies,[5] the most remarkable case being the Brazilian Ministry of Education's integrated and multi-level system of evaluating education, both public and private.[6]

The case for evaluation led me to dismiss the 'positivistic standpoint'[7] as being too narrow to fully apprehend the political and ideological character of evaluation. Indeed, it appears to be a wider-ranging matter, since it deals not only with objective goals and technical measures, but also with much deeper questions of values and ideologies. 'Here evaluation shifts to the larger social system of which the action context is a part; it focuses on the instrumental impact of the larger policy goals on the societal system as a whole, and an evaluation of the normative principles and values underlying this societal order' (Fisher 1995, p.19).

This paper has two major aims: to give an overview of the public-sector reforms in Latin America, especially in Brazil, and to set the state of affairs of evaluation procedures either in or outside the public-sector. To accomplish these goals I will begin by situating public-sector reforms within the political and cultural patterns of the relationship between state and society in Latin America. Later I will try to describe the broad outline of the public-sector reforms that came to be implemented in that region and the efforts made to put systematic evaluation procedures into place. In conclusion I will discuss the role evaluation might play in Latin American political context.

2. Latin American political trajectories: Basic trends for an analysis

Latin American countries have been literally invented by European colonizers and have been judiciously called *l'Extrême Occident* (the Far West [Rouquié 1987, p.20]) in light of their cultural and institutional linkages with Iberian countries. With Europeans came capitalism, Christianity and the state. The onslaught on the New World's resources took the form of large land concentration, Indian and Black slavery, the cultural and physical annihilation of native cultures, great regional disparities (due to the external markets drive of colonial economies) and the growing use of repressive means to maintain order and to collect taxes. In these countries, the colonial bureaucrat was the first and most visible expression of overseas power, of a distant, repressive and abstract state (Stein and Stein 1970, pp.55 ff). Since Spain and Portugal lacked the means to occupy the wide territories of the Americas, colonization was delegated to private entrepreneurs (*capitães* in Portuguese and *encomenderos* in Spanish) who claimed their right of exploitation from the same source as their right to command (Véliz 1984, p.36). The intermingling of private and public domains in Latin America dates back to the colonial period and persisted – even after the 19th-century political emancipation – in defining the practice of Latin American regimes even when they were formally democratic.

Because of their elitist bias, the Latin American states prime centralized government through formal procedures, establish prior control mechanisms over administrative activities and take an authoritarian standpoint towards the public, without treating them like 'citizens' entitled to basic rights.[8] The general 'public-sector culture' in Latin America is akin to the Franco-German model[9] even if it appears to be a distorted image of it. This paradigm can be described as 'insulated' from the public at large, although it is very responsive to the elites' views and expectations. If Latin America's political development is characterized by a good deal of instability, this also is due to the notorious social and political inequalities that split those societies into visibly opposite camps: a tiny circle of people that constitute the political, economic and cultural elite; and the mass of 'common people' that includes the middle classes, the working class and peasants. The entire political trajectory of Latin American societies has been highly dependent upon the state of the social struggles, which produce a pattern of upheaval and repression that accounts for the constant advances and setbacks that characterize the region's history.

However adverse these conditions, Latin America has undergone several waves of industrial development that have originated new middle-class political reform movements. The 19th century liberal-emancipatory revolutions established new independent republican[10] states according to classical liberal standards. In spite of those waves of modernization (especially in Argentina, Brazil and Mexico), a legal-rational-institutional framework associated (or dissociated) with a repressive, elitist and patrimonialist apparatus endured.

The 20th-century industrialization and urbanization gave rise to new urban middle classes and a trend towards rationalization of the state. These political movements espoused a populist and nationalist ideology in which an idealized 'people' was to play the key role in the national destiny (Ianni 1975). Still, those movements were the outcomes of strictly controlled top-down policies designed to preserve the bases of elite power. In the 1960s, Octavio Ianni stated that the public administration 'developed along with the survival of elements of the preexistent economic and social order, whose patrimonial techniques of administration (*coronelismo*, nepotism, favouritism, etc.) still persist to a large degree, even in highly urbanized communities' (Schmitter 1971, p.34).

Despite these ambiguities, the continuous growth of the number of personnel in the ministries and in public-owned enterprises contributed to the fixing of a kind of bureaucratic ethos, as noted by Schmitter:

> 'vast numbers of working committees, consultative councils, advisory boards, executive groups, and mixed commissions were created and often had considerable decisional autonomy delegated to them. The expert's role in policy-making became more important, as did the need for accurate, detailed information for predicting the outcome and measuring the consequences of new government programs' (1971, p.223).

The inherent instability of populist arrangements led Latin American political systems to persistent crises that ended for the most part with the establishment of military regimes in the late 1960s. These 'bureaucratic-military states' (O'Donnell 1970) pushed for two distinct, but complementary, outcomes: growing internationalization of economies and increasing statization and control. Since the former strategy required a certain amount of rationalization, the military promoted some limited macroeconomic and institutional reforms. Bureaucratization and control were the price that political and economic elites had to pay to ensure the maintenance of their power. In sum, it was military regimes that most strongly advocated this secular process of statization of the economic and social life.

Until the 1980s modernization was a force that could fully promote the rationalization of state administration. During that decade things got bad in Latin America. Accompanying deep economic recession were an external debt crisis and the financial shortage of the state (see Bresser Pereira 1996, pp.75–148). The inflation rate in Brazil rose from 70 per cent (in 1979) to 1863.5 per cent (in 1989); investment dropped by 50 per cent; external debt rose from US $49 900 billion (in 1979) to US $102 555 billion (in 1988), necessitating heavy payments of more than US $17 billion (in 1988). All of those factors led to an acute social and political crisis that motivated political and institutional changes. From Argentina in 1982 to Paraguay in 1992, all Latin American countries made transitions to democratic regimes, whereby the rule of law has been more consistently pursued and an active mobilization of citizenship through non-government organizations has been observed (see Lua Nova, no. 49, 2000).

New democratic and pluralistic discourses have emerged in recent years in Latin American countries, even though they still remain in the minority. This movement is making its way outside the traditional structures of political participation – political parties and unions – preferring those more flexible and shop floor frames, the NGOs. Since the 1990s an ever-increasing network of NGOs has become more and more influential in Latin American politics, and has formed the groundwork for democracy in these countries.

Paradoxically, most of the state apparatus has managed to avoid this general democratic trend. If, on the one hand, democratic transitions have meant constitutional reforms of democratic mechanisms (free elections, separation of powers, civilian rule, free partisan system, etc.),[11] on the other hand, public administration has remained untouched – on the grounds that it was just another victim of authoritarianism and consequently, the end of this regime would naturally bring about changes in public organizations.

Nonetheless, in the face of the fiscal crisis and virtual immobility of Latin American states, a group of public officials, experts and politicians became aware of the urgent need to reform Public Administration (see Kliksberg 1994).[12] Public debate was dominated by these central themes: the role of the state in the economy and society, the relationship between state and civil society and the real capacity of the state to carry out its new tasks. These concerns have been translated into proposals for decentralization, 'debureaucratization', transparency, new mechanisms of permanent participation or, in a word, a move towards political systems more conducive to citizen participation.

3. Reforming the public sector in Latin America.

The beginnings of the public-sector reform trend in Latin America were determined by the economic turmoil in the aftermath of the Mexican peso crisis in 1982. The causes of this crisis lay in the incapability of the region to adjust its economies to the consequences of the second oil crisis in 1979. In the 1980s, Latin America faced the twofold challenge of coping simultaneously with a deep economic crisis and the uncertainties of the transition to democracy. At the very time that those countries were striving to build up democratic institutions amidst a wave of social struggles (thus liberating major expectations), a severe international economic context imposed emergency exits, opening the door to all kinds of miraculous stabilization formulae that, for their part, generated ever growing frustration.

However, the external crisis, which sharply decreased investment flow to the major Latin American economies, was only one face of the most profound crisis, that of the import substitution model of industrialization. Because this industrial policy requires the intervention of a strong state apparatus capable of strictly regulating and even promoting economic activity, and since the costs of intervention have to be matched either by internal or by external financial resources – that is, extracted from the population's savings through tax levying or obtained from abroad through international loans – this crucial period actually uncovered the Latin American fiscal crisis. Both import substitution and the interventionist state came under severe criticism – they were deemed 'exhausted' and increasingly unable to keep up with the rapid liberalization of the international economy.

Public-sector reform in Latin America followed an identifiable pattern that was implemented in two stages. A 'first wave' of reforms concerned the opening and deregulation of the economy and the privatization of public enterprises. The major outcome of these reforms was a decisive shift in the historical development of the Latin American state, which, for the very first time, was removed from economic and social life. Most of these macroeconomic reforms were undertaken between 1989 and 1996. The second wave of reforms related to the institutional adjustment of the public sector, which led to legal reforms allowing the redirection of state action. It meant developing checks and balances among state powers, strengthening citizen participation, promoting decentralization and introducing managerialism in Public Administration.[13] The second wave of reforms, which took place mostly after 1995, is now considered a kind of 'never-ending story' because of the remarkable distance between the rhetoric and the practice of state reform in Latin America (analogy taken from Pollitt 1998). We will be referring to them as institutional reforms.[14]

In the mid-1980s, the first wave of structural adjustments in Latin America witnessed attempts to reduce inflation with the application of heterodox plans. The dramatic economic situation of Latin America provided the ground for economists to see those countries as a kind of laboratory for their macroeconomic theories. Many different attempts have been made: Brazilians, for instance, saw four of these 'salvation plans' (in 1986, 1987, 1988 and 1991) while Argentines, Mexicans, Venezuelans and Peruvians all had some kind of macroeconomic stabilization plans. All of these plans failed, in as much as they were not based on a view of structural reforms, but merely of reducing inflation rates. (Bresser Pereira 1996, pp.239 ff). These policies must be understood in their proper context: that of the complex transition to democracy after decades of military rule. The very architecture of macroeconomic plans reflected the contradictions of that moment when new demands had to be met by old, exhausted parties and leaders, who were led by traditional antagonisms. This ambiguity accounts for the limited reach of the plans at that time: 'many so-called economic reforms of the first round were actually thinly disguised attempts to use economic "reform" to bolster failed political regimes' (Roett and Crandall 1999, p.275). The experience of transition revealed the difficulties of dismantling the populist states in that region.

Hence, the macroeconomic reforms had to wait for the consolidation of democracy and the rise to power of leaders (such as Carlos Menem in Argentina, Fernando Henrique Cardoso in Brazil and Ernesto Zedillo in Mexico) committed to the idea of restructuring the large and inefficient state. In the 1990s, the flag of institutional innovation was seized by political coalitions led by a new generation of politicians with a strong technical and even academic background.[15] The public-sector reforms in Latin America began with the opening of major economies to international finance and trade. This meant deregulation and privatization.

In 1990, Brazilian president Collor de Mello, a populist leader who was nevertheless prone to accept uncritically the basics of globalization, undertook a series of measures that abruptly opened the Brazilian economy to foreign investors: he started a programme of privatization of large and inefficient public enterprises, dramatically reduced taxes and government controls over the stock and financial markets and established the first programme of quality and productivity. According to official data, between 1990 and 2002 the Brazilian government sold 115 enterprises, which represented a gross of US $105.3 billion,[16] comprising federal and state enterprises in 12 different sectors. Electricity (31%), telecommunications (31 per cent), the iron and steel industry (8 per cent) and oil and gas (7 per cent) were the target sectors of a major reform effort that has been being sustained by different governments throughout the decade.[17]

The 1990s saw the rebirth of inflation after the breakdown of the Collor stabilization plan. The increase in corruption around President Collor de Mello led to mass movements advocating his impeachment. The President's resignation brought Itamar Franco to power for a brief period of 14 months. The bold *Plano Real*, prepared and put into practice by the Minister of Economy, Fernando Henrique Cardoso, did manage to stop the inflationary spiral and restored Brazil back to economic stability. In the following year, Cardoso was elected president. The newly created Ministry of Administration and State Reform, under the leadership of Luiz Carlos Bresser Pereira, reunited a staff of experts that would establish a new epoch in this 'rationality fight'.

As important as those macroeconomic reforms have been, the transition to institutional reforms was not a simple task. The large, authoritarian and highly privatized states in Latin America presented enormous resistance to any endeavour towards change. In fact, 'public-sector reforms were not only words – they did happen – but they did not include public management' (Bresser Pereira, 2001, p.151). Bureaucratic inertia limited administrative reform to a series of scattered projects having merely local impact, thus diluting the reformist movement.

Latin American reformers have sought particularly to put forward measures of decentralization. Brazil's 1988 Constitution adopted a fairly decentralized model whereby municipalities were granted more than 50 per cent of public revenues, which meant that their income more than doubled. However, since these municipalities were for the most part poor and badly equipped, the federal government had to go on providing their services. Other countries have embraced the movement towards decentralization, but initiatives have often been either erratic or short-lived.[18] Although one might expect that citizen participation would follow decentralization, Latin American experience points to the fragility of grassroots organizations, which frequently are non-existent or subordinated to local caudillos. Nuria Cunnill Grau, examining the state of the art of social control in Latin America, made this point: 'if the state is fragile, social control will also be so' (In Bresser Pereira & Cunnill Grau, 2000, p.322).

Although Brazil and Chile can be said to be the only countries in Latin America to have decisively taken the road to managerial reform,[19] only the former has conceived of a rational and well-defined plan to restructure the public-sector: the 1995 *Plano Diretor da Reforma do Estado* (PDRE; Guidelines to State Reform). Founded on a consistent theory of development of the Brazilian State and of the role it must play in society at the end of the 20th century (see Bresser Pereira 1996), the PDRE states that the state should be viewed as a four-stage structure in which a strategic nucleus is responsible for policy formulation, a public sector for activities under exclusive competence of state (such as security or monetary policy), a competitive sector in which the state and the private sector can compete (such as education, health or culture) and finally a productive sector (public enterprises that furnish economic goods and services) that should not necessarily be state-owned. For the first sector, the PDRE proposed the development of a public career along bureaucratic lines; the second sector would be turned into 'executive agencies' with greater autonomy after a managerial-like model (Bresser Pereira 1999, pp.234 ff); it argued in favour of a new kind of public ownership for the third sector – the 'social organization model', similar to that of the quangos, according to which the scientific and social services directly delivered by the state become public non-state entities (see Barreto 1999); for the fourth sector it simply proposed privatization, but accompanied by the establishment of regulatory agencies.

In fact, in 1998 the government succeeded in passing a constitutional amendment (EC no. 19/98) whereby the principle of 'efficiency', along with other reformist dispositions (such as functional progression only by merit or the need for schools of government), has been inscribed in the Brazilian Constitution. Since then, numbers of regulatory agencies have been created and implemented: *Agência Nacional do Petróleo* (ANP; National Oil and Gas Agency), *Agência Nacional de Energia Elétrica* (ANEEL; National Electricity Agency), *Agência Nacional de Telecomunicações* (ANATEL; National Telecommunications Agency), *Agência Nacional de Vigilância Sanitária* (ANVS; National Health Supervision Agency), *Agência Nacional de Saúde Complementar* (ANS; National Health Agency) and *Agência Nacional de Águas*

(ANA; National Water Resources Agency). Some foundations have applied to become 'executive agencies' but it is still too early to evaluate results, as is true of 'social organizations', which were only lately made into executive agencies. It becomes clear that only by the second half of the 1990s had Latin American countries put into operation enough modernization initiatives to sustain claims against which to evaluate their results.

4. Taking stock of evaluation in Latin American

The settling of systems of evaluation in Latin America has come to the political agenda as a consequence of the adoption of rational development plans or state modernization plans by central governments.[20] In contrast to other countries in which values like 'transparency' or 'accountability' were the main focus, Latin American modernizers used evaluation as a tool to impose reform. Evaluation is always the competence of a highly technical department directly linked to the top offices (often the presidency itself). The generation of goals, objectives, indexes and indicators typically follows a top-down logic according to which managers have to adopt (and adapt themselves to) externally-defined standards: a kind of 'do or die' scenario.

Latin American evaluation dates back only to the mid-1990s, which makes it difficult to assess its results in any consistent time series. Although I have found references to evaluation in at least twelve countries in the region, just four of them (Brazil, Colombia, Costa Rica and Chile) can be said to have conceived of nationwide systems for evaluating public policies. Other countries (Argentina, Bolivia and Mexico) have set up more limited systems to assess organizational or individual performance. A third group (Nicaragua, Paraguay and Uruguay) has adopted only a more sophisticated version of budgetary evaluation, which implies a kind of accountant control of budget execution.

All of these systems of evaluation, however, are strictly internal (in-house) and mostly based in central executive bodies. Relative isolation and the top-down strategy embraced by state modernizers to overcome the resistance of an old and deeply anchored bureaucratic culture tend to remove evaluators from the reality of the state machinery. This institutional emplacement of evaluation units allows us to anticipate problems with implementation and, indeed, the few reports available point to limited success in the achievement of the expected objectives, even though there is no overall evaluation of results of those initiatives.

This review of the evaluation programmes in Latin America will be made according to a pattern that divides countries into three groups: those that tried to develop state-wide evaluation systems; those that set up only limited evaluation systems, though they were supposed to integrate broader modernization plans; and those that put only budgetary evaluation systems in place. For each group of countries I shall discern major actors and institutions involved with evaluation as well as whether the evaluation is internal or external. Employing available information, I shall discuss the real state of these initiatives – that is to say, the extent of their implementation.

Beginning with countries that have set up national systems of evaluation (Brazil, Colombia, Costa Rica and Chile), it is important to spot their similarities and differences. Brazil, Colombia and Costa Rica have developed these systems as tools for modernizing their states; in contrast, Honduras's system was created for the betterment of public management. All of them, however, designed their systems of evaluation to serve as a tool for the rationalization of public management and for democratization.

In Costa Rica's case, even if the *Sistema Nacional de Evaluación* (SINE; National System of Evaluation) created in 1994 is allegedly 'a tool to define priorities, allocate resources, monitor the execution of strategic programmes and projects and fundamentally to evaluate its results', this evaluation is based upon 'priorities and goals established by the National Development Plan' (Sibaja et al., 2002, p.4). From this plan derives a 'Matrix of Institutional Performance' which defines strategic actions, the programmes to be evaluated, and the criteria and indicators by which actual organizational performance is to be compared. The workings of SINE are ultimately based on a kind of a yearly performance contract (the *Compromisos de Resultados* [Engagement for Results]) signed between the president of the Republic and the top officials of each institution involved. SINE is operated by a Central Coordination Unit, a department of the Ministry of Development and Planning (Mideplan), which makes it an internal evaluation system. Linked to this central unit are the 'institutional knots', which are in fact the servants who are responsible for evaluation in each organization.[21]

The same holds true for Colombia, where in 1992 the National Department of Planning was assigned the duty of designing and organizing systems of performance and results evaluation (Decree no. 2.167). In 1994, the federal government created the *Sistema Nacional de Evaluación de Gestión y Resultados* (Sinergia) whose aim is to determine efficiency and efficacy of public administration.[22] In the next year,

Sinergia would be made part of a broader 'Plan for Betterment of Public Management', which was intended to set standards, goals and engagements for public managers. The pursuit of those objectives called for monitoring and evaluation. During that year, the newly constituted 'Efficiency Unit' developed and tested the methodology of 'indicative plans' and promoted the first systematic evaluation of results in the Colombian administration. The system since has been being continuously reworked so as to 'generate a change in Colombian administrative culture' (Bozzi 2001, p.100) and to 'diffuse a new management results-oriented culture' (Doc. 38). In 2001, a new development plan, 'Change to Build Peace', emphasized the importance of proceeding with the systematic evaluation of public administration,[23] but there is no available information on the actual state of its implementation.

In Chile, another path was chosen. Instead of a unique, unified evaluation system, Chileans have opted for an integrated system with which to implement the *Programa de Mejoramiento de la Gestión Pública* (Programme for the Betterment of Public Management). It is the joint responsibility of the Ministry of Economy and the Ministry of Planning and Cooperation to run the *Programa de Evaluación de Proyectos Gubernamentales* (Programme of Evaluation of Governmental Projects): which is a branch of the former Programme. An 'Assessor Committee' and a 'Technical Committee' – made up of representatives of the ministries involved and the Secretary General of Presidency – direct the Programme. From its beginnings in 1997 until 1999 (the year of its last available report), the Programme has achieved the evaluation of a record 311 central government programmes and 115 organizations and services.[24] Chile provides us with the only example in Latin America of systematic and state-promoted evaluation performed by private consultants, universities and international consultants[25] who make a joint diagnosis and issue, after a period of three months, a technical report on the programme's performance in comparison with stated government standards. As observed by Neirotti (2001), the Chilean model of evaluation comprises not only that of central government, but of many other initiatives on various government levels.

A fourth exemplary case of the development of an overall system of evaluation is the Brazilian *Plano Plurianual* (PPA),[26] a multi-year development plan, corresponding to a constitutional mandate, that sets the guidelines for the allocation of public resources over a four-year term. In 2000, the current federal government passed Law no. 9.989, which instituted the PPA and provided a legal basis (Art. 6) for the establishment of an evaluation system. An annual report must be sent to the

National Congress in order to subsidize resource allocation during the formulation and discussion of the Law on Budgetary Directives for the subsequent year.[27] The point to be highlighted here is this looping whereby the evaluation feeds the public system back into the process of resource allocation.

To establish a system of monitoring and evaluation it was necessary first to define and execute a new management model in federal public administration. Between 1999 and 2000 more than 1700 civil servants were trained in programme management techniques. In 2000, a new Managerial Information System was developed to ensure linkages between top officials and all those responsible (managers) for the implementation of the plan. Only after these measures had had some impact could a proper evaluation system be put into operation.

The process of evaluation was entirely conducted by the technical staff of the Ministry of Planning, Budget and Management, which gave it a mostly cost-benefit-like bias. Divided into three steps, evaluation began with a self-evaluation by the programme manager of practical and financial execution in relation to its expected results. In the second phase, programme performance was to be set against the 'President's Strategic Directives' and 'Sector Strategic Directives'; this assessment was made by the technical staff of the planning area of the ministry. The final step was an overall analysis by the ministry of the programmes' performance in comparison to the 'Plan's Strategic Directives'. To take into account the client's needs, the ministry took a national poll of the consumers of the goods and services delivered by those federal programmes in order to learn their 'degree of satisfaction'.[28]

As we can see from this summary, the Brazilian system of evaluation establishes unique objective, even quantitative, standards by which to assess programme performance and to subside new resource allocation. Moreover, this system does not create a permanent structure devoted to gathering current information, to training people to take part in evaluation, to developing new techniques to assess performance and citizen satisfaction or to diffusing an evaluation culture inside the organization. This highly centralized model falls short of autonomy and seems likely to become more an endorsement than an evaluation. In any event, despite their shortcomings, these systems are the most important attempts in Latin America to build a permanent instrument to improve public management and, in some way, to increase state transparency.

The second group of countries comprises those who have managed to bring into being only limited systems of performance measurement

(Argentina, Bolivia and Mexico).[29] These systems have focused either on social policies and programmes or on performance evaluation. Although the institution and implementation of these systems have permitted the introduction of rational management techniques and the feeding back of decisions, their impact does not extend to the rest of the public administration. The main problem with these systems is that they are not coupled with other procedures regulating resource allocation or career progression. Hence, not only does the commitment of public organizations to these systems become rather tenuous, but their eventual findings also are likely to be duly forgotten.

The Bolivian system of evaluation provides us with a typical case. The *Sistema Nacional de Administración de Personal* (SAP; National System of Personnel Management), turned uniquely to personnel management, established a 'sub-system of performance evaluation' whose attribute is to measure productivity in order to provide standards for the entitlement of new financial advantages.[30] However, this system has not yet been implemented.[31]

Argentina, on the other hand, developed an entire evaluation system to assess social programmes, the *Sistema de Información, Monitoreo y Evaluación de Programas Sociales* (SIEMPRO; System of Information, Monitoring and Evaluation of Social Programmes), which was instituted in 1995 and which relies on the Ministry of Social Development and Environment (See Neirotti, 2001 and www.siempro.gov.ar). Since 1997 it has been producing systematic polls (*Encuesta de Desarrollo Social* 1997 [Inquest into Social Development] and *Encuesta sobre las Condiciones de Vida* [Inquest into Living Conditions], 2001) that generated the 'Poverty Maps' intended to guide new resource allocation. It has also developed a system of monitoring social programmes and has made six localized evaluations of such programmes. It relies on 18 provincial units to accomplish its tasks. However, its reach has not extended to most federal social programmes (Neirotti, 2001).

In Mexico there is no federal unified system of systematic evaluation of public administration. In some areas, such as education, there has been a growing trend to set up evaluation systems like the *Centro Nacional de Evaluación para la Educación Superior* (CENEVAL; National Centre for the Evaluation of Higher Education). However, programmes of evaluation of public management performance have been observed at state levels (such as in the states of Campeche, Chihuahua, Coahuila, Durango, México and Nuevo León). Even if it is true that in 1994 the Mexican government had already entrusted her National Secretary of Economy and Public Credit with the task of control and evaluation related to the execution of the National Development Plan,[32] successive governments appear to have lost interest in this initiative.[33]

Finally, let us consider a third group of countries (Nicaragua, Paraguay and Uruguay), which have put little more than a sophisticated system of budgetary control into place. The main problem with these systems is that they are strictly tied to the process of budget execution without any concern about impacts.

Among these countries, the Nicaraguan case looks most typical of these highly technical programmes. In 1995, the coordination unit of the Programme for Public-sector Modernization and Reform began designing, developing and implementing the *Sistema Integrado de Gestión Financiera, Administrativa y Auditoria* (SIGFA; Integrated System of Financial, Administrative and Auditing Management),[34] which aims at converting the 'public accounting, as a processing and integrating information subsystem about government transactions with economic and financial effects, into an effective tool for decision for public managers'.[35] In later years, the system was further developed through the installation of seven subsystems, which were intended to enhance control over budget execution. Between March 1996 and February 1997, a *Sistema de Evaluación de los Servicios* (SES; System of Evaluation of Services), coupled with other systems, was put into operation.[36] The SES was in fact a wing of the Programme for Public-Sector Modernization and Reform and was designed to compel organizations to change. The Nicaraguan evaluation system appears to be no more than an accounting and auditing system with tighter controls.

The other countries have seen much the same developments. Paraguay has only recently been engaged in some sort of budget evaluation,[37] as has Uruguay, which included requirements of evaluation in the *Ley del Presupuesto Nacional* 1995–99 (Law of National Budget).[38] Although these countries had started the process of state reform some ten years earlier, measures towards administrative reform – to say nothing of evaluation – had to wait until the second half of the 1990s.

As we can conclude from this summary of the present Latin American experience, the setting up of evaluation practices and their systematic development is still in its infancy. For most countries, not only is the experience too recent to produce consistent results, but it also has been erratic. However, in spite of the evident progress towards the implementation of evaluation procedures, evaluation remains confined either to the analysis of social programmes or to the measurement of their outcomes in strictly budgetary terms, without addressing their social impacts. Another failure lies in the absence of process evaluations. Even if in some countries (Chile and Brazil) there has been a huge effort to implement management by programme, no systematic evaluation of these (or other) initiatives is available.[39]

To sum up, evaluation in Latin America (although it has boomed recently) is still a dependent variable of the movement of state modernization, which in turn is considered the weakest link of public-sector reform. This kind of 'negative cascade effect' can account for the very limited role evaluation presently plays in that context. Despite rhetoric about 'accountability' and 'transparency', the establishment of evaluation systems in the region has not been valued in itself, but only as a tool. As long as they lack autonomy, evaluation procedures cannot play an active role as a mechanism to inform decisions with valuable information from the public. This is another chapter in the ambiguous relationship between public administration and citizenship in Latin America.

5. Conclusion

To take stock of evaluation in Latin America in this chapter I had to consider two complimentary dimensions: the technical and the political. It is true that the evaluation literature bears out that doing evaluation involves complicated political arrangements (Weiss 1975), but in Latin America it raises sensitive questions about the role of the state in the reproduction of secular power inequalities. As we have seen, 'evaluation in Latin America is a technicality that acquires full political sense' (Monteiro 2001). That is why both its technical and political significance must be analysed.

Using the language of technicality, I propose to assess the region's experience using the following criteria: institutionalization of the function of evaluation and its development into systems; use of evaluation as an input for decisions; use of evaluation for better budget management; correlation between evaluation capabilities in public and private sectors; purposes of evaluation (for example, to make public administration more efficient, to better public management or to enhance transparency).

With regard to the first factor, we saw that only four countries instituted and systematized the function of evaluation. In any case, problems with the autonomy of the function have been detected that ultimately tarnish their achievements. In terms of the second and third factors, it became clear that the use of evaluation as an input for decision-making – even if restricted to budget allocations – is not mandatory. Furthermore, there are no serial evaluations available to allow us to assess either the relation between budget performance and reallocations or innovations in terms of management.

The fourth criterion points to the poor capabilities of both sectors in Latin America to perform consistent and continuous evaluations. In the public sector, I found very few departments uniquely devoted to evaluation; most lacked full institutional insertion or were politically isolated. The private sector (private consultants, universities and private research institutes) has not yet developed expert groups and specialized centres to cope with the growing demand.

Finally, the purpose of evaluation has been understood to be that of making public management more efficient, although many official texts contain rhetoric about transparency and accountability. The sheer efficiency bias has to do with the nature of the actors involved in promoting evaluation: by and large the technical staff of the ministries of planning.

The importance of the operational considerations expressed above accounts for the state of evaluation in Latin America; the crux of the matter lies in the political realm. Evaluation in this region is currently one of many battlefields. It is just an instance of the much broader 'Rationalitätsstreit' that opposes the tenets of modernization: efficiency, efficacy and accountability; the traditional political leadership is more interested in the maintenance of those loose administrative links, personal ties and bureaucratic isolation. If there are, across the state machinery, many actors searching to promote nepotism, clientelism and corruption, there are also 'rationality fighters' who maintain personal and professional links with private interests (the 'bureaucratic rings', as Cardoso (1976) once said) that contribute to the same result: 'intransparency'. The point is not to depict a battle between Good and Evil, but to understand that the actual role evaluation can play in this political dynamic is that of an instrument of citizenship. Evaluation, if it is not used only as a tool for implementing state's own goals, but as an autonomous assessment of public policies in terms of societal legitimacy, can provide citizens with a valued tool for enhancing democracy and accountability. The 'enlightened' technicians that are currently responsible for evaluation in Latin American countries will never close the gap without leaving their ivory towers and developing closer links with civil society. What is to be sought is the constitution of an evaluation community, which would provide evaluation with consistency and autonomy, because it would comprise in-house evaluators, private consultants, universities and non-governmental organizations reunited to evaluate government not on its own terms, but on society's terms.

The historical failure of the state in Latin America lies in its incapability to act in the interest of the majority, or to reduce social inequalities. It is evident that evaluation alone will not be able to manage such a gigantic undertaking, but as long as it is done with the citizens in mind it will contribute to social betterment. Evaluation has the potential to change the relationship between state and society in Latin America.

References

Amaral Vieira, R.A. (1975), *Intervencionismo e Autoritarismo no Brasil*, São Paulo: Difel.

Barreto, Maria Inês (1999), 'As organizações sociais na reforma do Estado brasileiro', in Luiz Carlos Bresser Pereira and Núria Cunill Grau (eds), *O Público não-estatal na Reforma do Estado*, Rio de Janeiro: Fundação Getúlio Vargas, pp.107–50.

Boeninger, Edgardo (1997), 'Latin America's multiple challenges', in L. Diamond et al., *Consolidating the Third Wave Democracies: Regional Challenges*, Baltimore: John Hopkins University Press, pp. 26–63.

Botero, Dario Restrepo (2000), 'El mito de sísifo o veinte años de pujanza descentralizadora en Colombia', *Revista del CLAD. Reforma y Democracia*, 17[June], 77–128.

Bozzi, Sonia Ospina (2001), 'Evaluación de la gestión pública: conceptos y aplicaciones en el caso latinoamericano', *Revista del CLAD. Reforma y Democracia* 19[February], 89–122

Bresser Pereira, Luiz Carlos (1996), *Crise Econômica e Reforma do Estado no Brasil. Para uma nova interpretação da América Latina*, São Paulo: Editora 34.

Bresser Pereira, Luiz Carlos (2001), 'New Public Management Reform: now on the Latin America reform agenda, and yet...', in *Revista Internacional de Estudos Políticos*, Special issue[September], 143–65.

Bresser Pereira, Luiz Carlos and Núria Cunill Grau (eds) (1999), *O Público não-estatal na Reforma do Estado*, Rio de Janeiro: Fundação Getúlio Vargas.

Bresser Pereira, Luiz Carlos and Núria Cunill Grau (eds) (2000), *La Responsabilización en la Nueva Gestión Pública Latinoamericana*, Buenos Aires and Caracas: EUDEBA/CLAD.

Bresser Pereira, Luiz Carlos and Peter Spink (eds) (1998), *Reforma do Estado e Administração Pública Gerencial*, Rio de Janeiro: Fundação Getúlio Vargas.

Briceño-León, Roberto (2002), 'Introduction: Latin America – a challenge for Sociology', *Current Sociology*, 50[1], 9–18.

Burki, Shahid Javed and Sebastian Edwards (1996), *Dismantling the Populist State: the Unfinished Revolution in Latin America and the Caribbean*, Washington, DC: World Bank Latin American and Caribbean Studies.

Burki, Shahid Javed and Perry, Guillermo E. (eds) (2000), *Decentralization and Accountability of the Public Sector*. Washington, DC: The World Bank.

Camp, Roderic Ai (1996), *Democracy in Latin America. Patterns and Cycles*, Wilmington, US: Jaguar Books.

Cardoso, Fernando Henrique (1976), *Autoritarismo e Democratização*, Rio de Janeiro: Zahar Editores, 1976.

Debate. Estado, Sociedad y Administración Pública. Caracas: CLAD, n° 7, April, 2002, http://www.clad.org.ve/estuconclu.html.

Eichegreen, Barry (1999), 'The Baring crisis in a Mexican mirror', *International Political Science Review*, 20[3], 249–70.

Estevez, Alejandro and Fabián Calle (n.d.), 'El Institucionalismo ingenuo: las Reformas del Estado de "segunda generación"', www.espaciospublicos.com.ar.

Faoro, Raymundo (1976), *Os Donos do Poder. Formação do Patronato Político Brasileiro*, Porto Alegre: Editora Globo.

Fisher, Frank (1995), *Evaluating Public Policy*, Chicago: Nelson Hall.

Ianni, Octavio (1971), *Estado e Planejamento Econômico no Brasil (1930–1970)*, Rio de Janeiro: Civilização Brasileira.

Ianni, Octavio (1975), *A Formação do Estado Populista na América Latina*, Rio de Janeiro: Civilização Brasileira.

Karl, Terry Lynn (1996), 'Dilemmas of democratization in Latin America', in Roderic Ai Camp, *Democracy in Latin America: Patterns and Cycles*, Wilmington, US: Jaguar Books, pp. 21–46.

Kliksberg, Bernardo (ed.) (1994), *El Rediseño Del Estado. Una perspectiva internacional*, Mexico City: Instituto Nacional de Administración Pública/Fondo de Cultura Económica.

Lua Nova. N° 49 (2000), *Dossiê América Latina*, São Paulo: CEDEC.

Ministerio para las Administraciones Públicas (1988), *Administración y Función Pública en Iberoamérica*, Actas del II Seminario de Antiguos Alumnos Iberoamericanos del INAP, Madrid: Instituto Nacional de Administración Pública.

Monteiro, Geraldo Tadeu Moreira (2001), 'Evaluation as a political arena: an inquiry into the use of rational methods within imperfect legal rational states', Annals of the VI Congress of CLAD, www.clad.org.ve/anales6/monteiro.

Montricher, Nicole de (1998), 'Public sector values and administrative reforms', in Guy B. Peters, and Donald J. Savoie (eds), *Taking Stock: Assessing Public Sector Reforms*, Montreal: McGill-Queen's University Press, Canadian Center for Public Management, pp. 108–36.

Neirotti, Nerio (2001), *La Función de Evaluación de Programas Sociales en Chile,* Brasil y Argentina, Annals of the VI Congress of CLAD, www.clad.org.ve/anales6/neirotti.

Palazzo, José Luis, Domingo Sesín and Victor Lembeye (1992), *La Trasfor-mación del Estado. Tendencias Actuales, Innovaciones en el Derecho Itali-ano y Europeo*, Buenos Aires: Ediciones De Palma.

Parry, J. H. (1966), *The Spanish Seaborne Empire*, London: Hutchinson.

Peters, Guy B. and Savoie, Donald J. (eds) (1995), *Governance in a Changing Environment*, Montreal: McGill-Queen's University Press, Canadian Center for Public Management.

Peters, Guy B. and Savoie, Donald J. (eds) (1998), *Taking Stock: Assessing Public Sector Reforms*, Montreal: McGill-Queen's University Press, Cana-dian Center for Public Management.

Pierre, Jon (1998) 'The marketisation of the state: Citizens, consumers and the emergence of the public market', in Guy B. Peters, and Donald J. Savoie (eds.), *Taking Stock: Assessing Public Sector Reforms*, Montreal: McGill-Queen's University Press, Canadian Center for Public Management, pp. 55–81.

Pollitt, Christopher (1993), *Managerialism and the Public Services*, London: Oxford University Press.

Pollitt, Christopher (1998), 'Managerialism revisited', in Guy B. Peters, and Donald J. Savoie (eds.), *Taking Stock: Assessing Public Sector Reforms*, Montreal: McGill-Queen's University Press, Canadian Center for Public Management, pp. 45–77.

Pollitt, Christopher and Bouckaert, Geert (2001), 'Evaluating public sector reforms: an international perspective', *Revista Internacional de Estudos Políticos*, special issue[September], 167–92.

Roett, Riordan and Russell Crandall (1999), 'The global economic crisis, contagion and institutions: New realities in Latin America and Asia', *International Political Science Review*, 20[3], 271–83.

Rojas, Fernando (1999), 'The political context of decentralization in Latin America' in: Burki & Perry, pp. 9–31.

Rouquié, Alain (1987), *Amérique Latine: Introduction à l'Extrême-Occident*, Paris: Seuil.

Schields, John and B. Mitchell Evans (1998), *Shrinking the State. Globaliza-tion and Public Administrative Reform*, Halifax, Canada: Fernwood Pub-lishing.

Schmitter, Philippe C. (1971), *Interest Conflict and Political Change in Brazil*, Stanford, US: Stanford University Press.

Schneider, Ben Ross (2001), 'La política de la reforma administrativa: Dilem-mas insolubles y soluciones improbables', *Revista del CLAD. Reforma y Democracia*, 20[July], 7–34.

Sibaja, Asdrubal Fonseca et al. (2002), El Sistema Nacional de Evaluación: un instrumento para la toma de decisiones del Gobierno de Costa Rica. Paper presented to the XVth CLAD's Awards (Control and Evaluation of Gov-ernmental Performance), Caracas, 2001, 27 pp.

Spink, Peter; Echebarria, Francisco Lungo y Koldo; Stark, Carlos (2001), *Nueva Gestión Pública y Regulación en América Latina. Balances y desa-fíos*. Caracas: CLAD.

Stein, Stanley J. and Barbara H Stein (1970), *The Colonial Heritage in Latin America: Essays on Economic Dependence in Perspective*, London: Oxford University Press.

United Nations, Department of Economic and Social Affairs (2001), *World Public Sector Reform Report. Globalization and the State 2001*, New York: United Nations.

Véliz, Claudio (1984), *La Tradición Centralista de América Latina*, Barcelona: Ariel.

Weiss, Carol (1975), 'Evaluation research in the political context', in Elmer L. Struening and Marcia Guttentag, *Handbook of Evaluation Research*, vol. 1, London: Sage, pp.13–26.

Wollmann, Hellmut (ed.) (2001), Evaluating public sector reforms: an international and comparative perspective, *Revista Internacional de Estudos Políticos*, special edition [September].

World Bank (2000), *Development in Latin America and the Caribbean 1999. Decentralization and Accountability of the Public Sector*, Washington, DC: World Bank.

World Bank (2001), *Instituciones para los Mercados: Informe sobre el Desarrollo Mundial, 2002, Panorama General*, Washington, DC: World Bank.

World Bank (n.d.), *Privatization and Deregulation in Mexico*, Operations Evaluation Department, www.worldbank.org.

World Bank (n.d.), *Privatizing Argentina's Public Enterprises*, Operations Evaluation Department, www.worldbank.org.

Notes

1. Bureaucratism is one of the most salient features: it is essentially the ethos of an unbound civil service. Centralism is a notorious and highly persistent feature of BPA (Brazilian Public Administration). From colonial times to the present, the Brazilian state has always been highly centralized. The centralization is particularly important in tributary matters, for 80 per cent of total fiscal charges go to the Federal Government – to the detriment of federal states and municipalities. Formalism is a feature that we owe to the Portuguese administration, whose exploitation of its colonies created a complex network of officials who exercized rigid control over economic activity. Every act of production might be recorded in official books and duly reported to the Central Office. Still today BPA praises aprioristic control and written reports, and uses an abundance of official seals to validate documents. Fiscalism and authoritarianism go hand in hand. The need to control the economic production by private (and unreliable) entrepreneurs led the Portuguese administration to increase the number of fiscal agents as well as mechanisms of confiscation. This model was based upon repressive means that coerced people to comply with government exigencies. That is why authoritarianism has always been the other side of the same coin. Authoritarianism has endured even under formally democratic regimes, and even after more than a decade of democratic consolidation, it hides in the daily practices of police forces.

2. Let me offer these words from Guy Peters: 'attempting to say in advance which reforms of public administration will work and which will not is an extremely hazardous occupation. Far too many 'logical', 'necessary' and 'appropriate reforms have failed miserably, and an equal number of unlikely reform adventures have produced greater benefits than those anticipated...' (Peters and Savoie 1998, p. 78)

3. The assumptions are that management is an activity distinct from politics; that managers should be allowed to manage; that management is a dynamic force; and that in managerial matters, no difference exists between public and private sectors (Pollitt 1998, p.47).

4. An overview of the conditions and processes of getting rid of the old import substitution policy can be found in Burki and Edwards 1996.

5. SIARE's (*Sistema Integrado de Analisis en Reforma del Estado [Integrated System of Analysis of State Reform]*) database features 660 evaluation initiatives not integrated in an overall system.

6. The oldest and best-known initiative is the evaluation of post-graduation courses by the Ministry of Education through an autonomous foundation (Capes). Since 1982, a team of experts has established a permanent evaluation system covering all master and doctoral courses in Brazil, which are assessed by academic experts according to strict and clearly stated measures of performance. Courses that do not meet minimum requirements are not entitled to grant diplomas. Currently, more than 1500 courses are evaluated according to a well-developed and peer-reviewed methodology of data collection. The most important outcome of this twenty-year-old system of evaluation is the noticeable improvement in the quality of Brazilian post-graduate education even in relation to that of developed countries. Other extensive evaluations in Brazil have also promoted by the Ministry of Education. The *Exame Nacional de Cursos* (ENC; National Examination of Undergraduate Courses), which verifies and evaluates graduates according to national standards set by a group of leading specialists. The *Exame Nacional do Ensino Médio* (ENEM; National Examination of High Schools) consists mainly of an examination to measure the performance of high-school graduates. The *Sistema de Avaliação do Ensino Básico* (SAEB; Evaluation System of Primary School) establishes valid measures and procedures to assess performance at the primary levels. These point evaluations really have managed to constitute a 'system' in its truest sense. They do not simply compare performance against a set of accepted standards; they have effective means to reward or to punish those who do not meet the system's requirements.

7. Evaluation has been defined as 'the *systematic assessment* of the *operation* and/or the *outcomes* of a programme or policy, compared to a set of *explicit* or *implicit standards*, as a means of contributing to the *improvement* of the programme or policy' (Weiss 1998, p.4). This classical definition makes explicit the necessary terms of an evaluation of programmes and policies: a) systematic assessment b) of operation or outcome according to c) a set of standards. Moreover, it manifests the pragmatic character of evaluation as a means of improving programs and policies.

8. On the bureaucratic, complex and oversized administration in the Spanish Indies, see Parry 1966, pp.204 ff; on the Brazilian case, see 'General traits of colonial organization' in Faoro 1976, vol. 1, pp. 171–202.

9. In this model, 'public sector transcends society [where] the dominant culture prefers to see the role of the public sector organizations as one of promoting action rather than regulating it. Therefore, it is the administrative body that defines the public in-

terest of the community and, for this reason, it is subject to a specific legal code.' See Montricher 1998, p. 112.

10. The sole exception, the emancipation of Brazil was led by Prince D. Pedro I, son of the King of Portugal. A constitutional monarchy was established in 1824 and lasted until 1889, when a positivistic military movement installed a federalist republican state.

11. The path the transition to democracy took in Latin American countries has circum-scribed changes to the constitutional domain, leaving other critical areas out of reach. This is the case of the political system, income distribution, social policies as well as the administrative apparatus. Under such conditions the Brazilian State turned out to be an imperfect rational legal state. Although it now disposes of a new institutional framework espousing rational-legal values and procedures, it tolerates many non rational practices within the state machinery. This kind of contradiction is typical of Brazilian political process insofar as it allows compromise between opposing elites, consequently avoiding any form of open dissension.

12. This movement culminated in the creation of the *Centro Latino Americano de Administración para el Desarrollo* (CLAD) that aims at joining all the people that share its ideas about state reform.

13. This is not a regional development, but a global trend. See *World development report 1997: The state in a changing world*. Washington, DC: Oxford University Press 1997.

14. We must be very cautious when dealing with this subject because of the number of initiatives recorded in public data banks (see www.clad.org.ve/siare). In a detailed 1998 survey of the attempts at modernization in Latin America, Peter Spink found 196 proposals. Most of them, however, remained at the level of formulation or even mere rhetoric (pp. 2–3). As Bresser Pereira said: 'for lack of reforms the Latin American states for sure will not perish...'(2001, p.149).

15. This is especially the case of Mexican president Ernesto Zedillo and Brazilian presi-dent Fernando Henrique Cardoso. Even if we think of both Argentine president Car-los Menem and Peruvian president Alberto Fujimori as counter-examples, we must consider the configuration of their staffs, composed mostly of civil servants with highly technical backgrounds or of leading academics. The launch of public-sector reforms at that time should be attributed to this new political and administrative coa-lition.

16. Data were obtained by the *Banco Nacional de Desenvolvimento Economico e Social* (BNDES), the largest development bank in Brazil, which is responsible for the im-plementation and evaluation of the Privatization Programme. Data available at www.bndes.gov.br/privatizacao/historico.

17. The same path was taken by Argentine president Menem, who, emboldened by deep public discontent, introduced a reform plan that was more ambitious even than the formula proposed by the World Bank. It called for the privatization of all public en-terprises, particularly in three major sectors: telecommunications, railways and hy-drocarbons. Thanks to the World Bank's generosity (that granted the Argentine gov-ernment up to US \$1.5 billion), this restructuring of public sector in Argentina re-sulted in the almost complete privatization of major state-owned companies (espe-cially ENTEL, YPF, GdE and the suburban railways company) and a dramatic drop in employment rates. (In Argentina, from 1991 to 1996, unemployment had risen from 6.5 to 18.6 per cent, according to official data [see Burki & Edwards 1996,

p.11]). The Mexican case, although always cited as an exemplar of public-sector reform, is yet another that fits the pattern created by the World Bank. As in other Latin American countries, privatization began with the 1991 sale of the state monopoly, Telmex (*Teléfonos de México*) and the 1990 deregulation of the trucking industry. Mexico, however, before becoming the champion of World Bank's reform strategy, had been a typical Latin American state: large, centralist, bureaucratic, corrupt and inefficient. The first to face crisis (in 1982), Mexico was also the first to adopt a new conception of the public sector. It adopted in 1985 a stabilization plan with a strong fiscal adjustment; in 1987, it initiated a series of important economic reforms including the liberalization of the economy and the privatization of the public enterprises (see Bresser Pereira 1996, p.57). A general agreement (the 1987 *Pacto de Solidaridad Social* [Social Solidarity Pact]) between major socio-economic actors aimed to end the inflationary escalation. In 1991, the Mexican economy began to recover thanks to increasing confidence in the government and also to the North American Free Trade Agreement (NAFTA), which increased Mexico's access to the huge American market.

18. According to a World Bank survey, the cases of Nicaragua (1990), Colombia (1986–93), Venezuela, Bolivia and Peru show clearly that centralism is a very well-established characteristic of these regimes – almost an invincible obstacle to the decentralization movement (see Rojas 1999).

19. The case of Chile is quite different from those of other countries: public-sector reform did not happen in a transitional period, but under Pinochet's dictatorship when Chilean officials privatized most public enterprises. After redemocratization, Chile began to implement managerial reform with the launching of a programme of performance measurement based on budgetary indicators. The core of the 1993 programme was strategic planning and control by national budget outcomes; it has been gradually extended as other public bodies join it (see Bresser Pereira, 2001, pp.155–57). In contrast to the Brazilian example, Chile took a gradualist, piecemeal path to modernization.

20. 'Taken its own political strengths and weaknesses the administrative reform is conveyed as if it was a parasite living in a politically stronger body. The body can be a global reform project, either in economy or in politics or even in both simultaneously' (Schneider 2001, p.15).

21. For detailed and relatively up-to-date information about the implementation of SINE see 'Informe SINE 2000 – El desempeño del Gobierno en su accionar estratégico. Evaluación de los Compromisos de Resultados 2000'.

22. Information about the history and workings of Sinergia has been extracted from SIARE's databases (SIARE: Sistema Integrado y Analítico de Información sobre Reforme del Estado, Gestión y Políticas Públicas). See Documents 21, 23, 38, 75 and 78.

23. By May 2002, the 1999 and 2000 evaluation reports were issued by the coordination unit of Sinergia. Unfortunately there are no year 2000 results for most sectors, which may point to problems of implementation. See the home page of the Departamiento Nacional de Planeación (www.dnp.gov.co).

24. Information extracted from www.modernizacion.cl/indicadores/compromisos. Analysis of data from 18 ministries showed that many programmes (48 per cent) had attained more than 50 per cent of their stated goals.

25. To be fair, since 1996 the Brazilian Ministry of Education has made extensive use of private consultants to evaluate undergraduate and graduate courses. However, this is not evaluation of the government itself, but of private universities (or public foundations). More information can be obtained at www.inep.gov.br.

26. The adoption of multi-year plans dates back to 1991, but no information about the development of this plan is available. The government elected in 1994 presented a 1995 plan called *Brasil em Ação* (Brazil in Action), which was implemented between 1996 and 1999. There was no systematic evaluation of this plan, but the government home page (www.abrasil.gov.br) states that 25 of 47 programmes had fully attained their goals. The re-elected government proposed the 2000 *Avança Brasil* (Go Brazil) plan to evaluate 360 federal programmes during the 2001–2003 period. In fact, the evaluation covered 346 of 389 programmes.

27. According to the Brazilian Constitution (Art.165), the federal budget must be elaborated in three stages: 1) The *Plano Plurianual* (PPA; Multi-year Plan), which 'establishes (...) the directives, objectives and goals of public administration'; 2) The *Lei de Diretrizes Orçamentárias* (LDO; Law of Budgetary Directives), which 'comprehends the goals and priorities of public administration (...) for the subsequent fiscal year...'; and 3) The *Lei Orçamentária* (LO; Annual Budgetary Law), which sets fiscal budgets for the organs of federal constituted powers, public enterprises, social security and public investments. The annual budget is sent to the National Congress as a proposal of law, and must observe the directives of the PPA and the LDO (Art.165, par.5 and 9).

28. Decree 3.507/2000 instituted a permanent system of evaluation of user satisfaction. The first poll had some unexpected results, particularly that 71.2 per cent of users are 'very satisfied' with government services in the areas of health, education and social security. There is no information about the sample. It is a surprising result because other, independent polls do not rate government services so highly.

29. It must be stressed that the setting of such partial systems does not mean that these countries have not been able to proceed, but that they have taken another approach: a step-by-step strategy. See Bozzi (2001) and Neirotti 2001.

30. The National System of Personnel Management, created 16 March 2001 by Supreme Decree no. 26.115, establishes four sub-systems: personnel allocation, training, personnel mobility and registration and performance evaluation.

31. SNAP's home page (www.bolivia.gov.co/snap) gives no information about its implementation.

32. Concerning the 1989–94 National Development Plan, the Secretary has made evaluations upon 15 different lines and developed clear standards with which to measure the efficiency and efficacy of many public enterprises. In any event, the latest information available dates from 1994 (see www.clad.org.ve/siare).

33. The Economic Programme for 2002, developed by the National Secretary of Economy and Public Credit and submitted to the National Congress, still proposes the 'implementation of an evaluation system' as if it were an innovation (see www.shcp.gob.mx/docs/pe2002/pef/temas/expo_motivos/capituloV).

34. From 1996 to 1999 this programme strengthened controls over budget execution and changed the very structure of organizations responsible for the budget.

35. An introduction to the programme may be found at www.clad.org.ve/siare.

36. The System of Evaluation of Services was created at the same time as two other integrated systems: The System of Civil Service (intended to develop a professional

public service) and the Integrated System of Financial, Administrative and Auditing Management.
37. A new financial administration law (no. 1.535/99) passed 31 December 1999 has established the Integrated System of Financial Administration (SIAF) and provided grounds for the implementation of the 'evaluation of budget [which] consists of measuring the actual outcomes of each one of the programmes' (www.paraguaygobierno.gov.py/).
38. Uruguayan Law charged the Executive Committee for State Reform with the implementation of administrative reform. Among its stated objectives is a 'System of Evaluation by Results of Public Management', which, despite the grand name, is designed to 'better and to evaluate management of items of the budget in accordance with a programme of planning'. This shows the accounting nature of this evaluation system.
39. In Brazil, the Ministry of Planning, Budget and Management, through the *Escola Nacional de Administração Pública* (ENAP; National School of Public Administration), provides annual grants to the most innovative public management programmes. Despite its importance, the grant obviously is not a substitute for evaluation.

11. Learning from evaluation practice: The case of public-sector reforms

Jean-Claude Thoenig

1. Introduction: A pragmatic perspective

The diffusion of evaluation across polities and policy domains owes much to the intrinsic merits of evaluation as well as to the political will and the intellectual capacity of those who govern public affairs. Nevertheless, empirical evidence suggests that these factors do not suffice. Appropriation and learning processes among policy makers show that knowledge as such competes with routine and that improvements made today may be cancelled tomorrow.

This chapter underscores the content and the legitimacy of a pragmatic approach to evaluation. In order to be called upon or undertaken by political and administrative actors, the need for evaluation should be modest. Despite a world in which strong inertia or vested interests make the use of evaluation quite problematic and restrictive, practice suggests that progress is possible on an incremental basis. Such a pragmatic approach may be perceived as a less than perfect solution or as a disappointment. A science-driven model provides the core of ideal evaluation. Knowledge should be produced by independent sources. Decisions would be made according to a causal-analytical approach. In contrast, a pragmatic approach considers that soft- or quasi-evaluation, descriptive inputs, knowledge produced by the policy makers themselves or even attitudes sympathetic to the actors' situation should not be discarded, at least in certain circumstances.

Public-sector reforms present an interesting scenario for at least three reasons. The first is theoretical. There is a lively debate in the social sciences concerning the feasibility of administrative reforms. 'New Institutionalism' perspectives question the value and the efficiency of changes based upon rational-choice criteria (March and Olsen

1984). Policies are not the outcomes of the rational calculation of expected utility and prior consequences. Appropriateness, not consequences, informs the logic of policy-making acts (Brunsson and Olson 1997). Preferences are endogenous. Therefore efficiency and legitimacy do not coincide in political orders. Policy evaluation has not much future in such a context, for it postulates that political actors are driven by a logic of consequences: policy makers are free to reform, and political orders are able to change public life (Olsen 2001).

The second set of reasons deals with public-sector reform as a policy domain, one with few stakeholders and not very visible outcomes. Public administration reform belongs to the class of constitutive policies. Governmental authorities mobilize a very low degree of public coercion. Constitutive policies allocate costs and benefits that are perceived as rather diffuse (not concentrated) and mid-term (not short-term) by the population. To some extent, they are of concern only to a narrow circle: politicians, public servants and their trade unions. Evaluation, therefore, should receive less attention than other sectors of public life, and in any case, it would be difficult to handle analytically.

Public-sector reforms offer a third set of reasons for study. Despite what has been underscored above, a form of evaluation is at work: pragmatic evaluation. While public-sector-reforms may be used as symbols of the will of a new government or as means of ideological electoral platforms, initiatives of 'modernization' taken in the 1980s and 1990s – marketization of public goods and services, adoption of so-called New Public Management approaches, and decentralization of organizations and tasks – have reshaped the public-sector, especially at the state level. Such a trend raises one interesting question, which is how far the rationalization of the outcomes can be processed in an institutional setting that is so dependent on political rationales. Power games, electoral competition, and getting very short returns on initiatives play a predominant role (see Christensen, Lægreid and Wise, Chapter 4 in this volume). Specifically, the issues that shall be addressed are the content and the function of evaluation. Do public-sector-reforms really consider and use evaluation? Is there room for identifying real outcomes as well as for a governmental monitoring that is mid-term-oriented and organizationally centred? What practices has experience brought to light? Does evaluation have a future?

We shall argue that at first sight, evaluation – at least defined in an orthodox way – remains a rather marginal factor. Nevertheless, very diverse and sometimes imaginative appropriations are made piecemeal of what is academically defined as evaluation. The fate of evaluation is basically linked to a wider organizational learning approach. In other words, while straight evaluation is rather lacking, some forms of tinkering – such as quasi-evaluation or soft evaluation – are at work. In such an approach, the cognitive appropriation of evaluation is what matters. It requires an endogenous process, by which reform outcomes are linked to the monitoring of organisational. Empirical observations shall be used which were collected from a secondary analysis of public reforms in countries belonging to the OECD (for an alternative international comparison, see Pollitt and Bouckaert, Chapter 2 in this volume).

2. The long road to evaluation

In the 1970s and 1980s, it was hardly imaginable that administrative and public-sector management reforms would be developed and implemented blindly, thoughtlessly and impulsively, solely by order of the hierarchical authorities. This being the case, a widespread demand existed on the part of practitioners, for there were significant deficiencies in the monitoring of the changes introduced in the public-sector. There was every reason to believe that evaluation would play a major role in meeting these expectations, at least in part, since it provides relatively rigorous tools and a largely rational approach – at least on paper – to producing information and advice on a specific public policy (Levine, Solomon, Hellstern and Wollmann 1981; Rossi and Freeman 1982). A market of evaluation should have grown, fuelled by consulting companies and legitimized by social scientists. Effectiveness, optimism and democratic governance were the names of the game. In a way, evaluation was to conquer public management.

However, a careful examination of the facts at the beginning of the twenty-first century shows a rather unanticipated evolution which looks like a grey picture. In many countries evaluation has been used, but only in a relatively limited and sporadic way that has thus far proved disappointing. Consultants do not make a real living selling their methods. Academic experts question the values evaluation should induce. Practitioners express mixed feelings. In their opinion, orthodoxy as defined by evaluation experts is not compatible with real life in policy-making activities. Methodological ambitions are hardly implementable. For instance, the high public servants in charge of national public-sector reforms, who participated in the 1999 OECD Public Management Committee symposium concerning 'the government of the future', did not express extremely enthusiastic expectations (OECD 1999). As was mentioned by an Italian representative, 'the priority is more to take initiatives and keep the momentum than to measure outcomes... we have to unfreeze the administrative body more than to keep track of where we have already gone.'

What is more, there is reason to believe that the reluctance to use evaluation more extensively is not necessarily or primarily due to ignorance, cynicism or unwillingness. It sometimes happens that governments publicly affirm the need for evaluation, but fail to practise what they preach. There are numerous examples of this tendency. White papers, bills or official statements made by the central government or by leaders of the parliament, stress the importance of evaluating specific problems and reforms of administrative and staff policy. But no subsequent initiatives have been launched to assess the reforms carried out thus far. Conversely – and more surprisingly – one encounters some scepticism about evaluation, particularly among well-informed and experienced practitioners of public management reform, some of whom speak of an allergy to evaluation that seems to prevail in their own governments. Such an attitude may derive from a variety of causes, such as the reluctance of policy makers to feel challenged by experts who are not 'hands-on,' the arrogance of evaluators in defining the goals and the content of reforms, the fact that evaluations may take too much time, the idea that reforms are also a political tool, or that some seasoned high public servants may feel a threat to their old-fashioned expertise. In any case the demand from policy makers seems to remain rather flat. This is particularly the case at the national level, whereas the sub-national levels of government and administration seem to be a little bit more enthusiastic as clients. Experience suggests that demand can be a problem: ministers, wanting to hear only the good news and not what has gone wrong, fear they may be embarrassed by the information generated by evaluators; the public and the media may use it as an opportunity to 'beat up' on governments (Kessler, Lascoumes, Setbon and Thoenig 1998). However, this paradox is more apparent than real, and it would be wrong to throw out the baby with the bath water.

Admittedly, from a quantitative standpoint, there is no reason to conclude that there is an irresistible trend towards a generalized use of evaluation. In a number of countries, public management reform may seem to be lagging behind or to be out of step with other government policy fields – such as research and development, health care, social welfare, education or social assistance. At the same time, practice has shown that evaluation does occur and is used to provide governments with information. We can briefly review a number of examples of public management reforms that, during the 1990s, were coupled with genuine evaluation work or practices. All things considered, although the results are limited, they are far from negligible.

In 1995, the Finnish government launched a concerted and detailed programme aimed at identifying and assessing the results produced by a series of major reforms implemented since the mid-1980s. This programme included groups of senior civil servants that were involved in the reforms, and teams of domestic and foreign experts (Pollitt et al. 1997).

In the United Kingdom, the national Best Value pilot programme was launched in 1997 by the 'New' Labour administration. Its purpose was to modernize key public services at the local level. Evaluation and evaluators played a more significant role in the management of such a policy than in previous Conservative governments.

As early as the late 1980s, France coupled its administrative modernization policy with a series of ongoing evaluations. The Conseil Scientifique de l'Evaluation, established by the Prime Minister Michel Rocard, supervised two projects which followed up, explicitly or implicitly, organizational reforms linked to policy changes in sectors such as education and social affairs. Ministries such as the Ministère de l'Equipement undertook an intensive and participatory evaluation effort, with particular regard to the management of the objectives and resources assigned to their field agencies (Trosa 1992). The French example suggests that rather qualitative approaches have been favoured. Very few evaluation activities have tried to measure the impact of reorganizations against the costs and productivity of the State machinery – an environment in which the neutrality (if not the tacit support) of public servant trade unions remains highly valued by the ruling élites (for Germany, see Wollmann, Chapter 7 in this volume).

In 1995, the New Zealand State Service Commission and Treasury commissioned a highly respected US academic to make an independent assessment of the changes produced by the wide-ranging reorganization of the public sector in structural, organizational, strategic, financial, budgetary, and management control terms (Schick 1996). Later this same country produced a 'state of the State' report. In 1998 and 1999, a central agency was given responsibility for the systematic collection of data on the overall performance of the public system and the individual performance of each of its agencies (see Halligan, Chapter 5 in this volume).

Initiatives for signalling public management reforms ahead of time are interesting approaches which are adopted in several countries. Such is the case in Canada, where a structured and lasting approach is being carried out. Annual reports set out what are considered the key management issues and the priorities to be addressed in the coming year. The Clerk of the Privy Council Office, who reports to the Prime Minister, publishes a document that offers a vision for management reform. Task forces have been set up which are responsible for monitoring the programme review of the reform and for investigating subjects, such as service provision to citizens or management of intersectoral and interagency issues. The aim is to promote horizontal coordination with a view to improving the consistency of initiatives and their impact on the implementation of programmes in the various fields of government responsibility. This top-down approach is supplemented with a bottom-up approach, for each department is encouraged to gather information on the results and progress achieved in its own sector. This is aimed at adapting evaluation to the various levels within the public system. It simultaneously covers the two facets of internal efficiency and external effectiveness, and includes both structures and processes.

A fuller picture would be given if the list were not confined to formal or traditional evaluation initiatives, since some countries have practices that might be described as 'quasi-evaluations', through which policy makers and their staff gather information and conduct reviews and assessments of various aspects of their reforms both before and after they make decisions. This sort of informal, ad hoc approach is found in varying degrees in many countries.

The United Kingdom has conducted reviews of various reform programmes, such as 'Next Steps', the 'Citizen's Charter' or 'Market Testing and Contracting Out'. In the late 1990s, Ireland's Committee for Public Management Research wrote up a partial review of the plans of the customer service section of departments and offices in a discussion paper.

A specific kind of administrative reorganization – the delivery of public goods and services by non-administrative bodies, such as private firms or not-for-profit entities – remains to a large extent a black box. Contracting out, privatization of public agencies and deregulation are, in theory, expected to lower transaction costs and raise the quality level. While some studies and reports have been done on very narrow domains, a wider and more mid-term focused evaluation of deregulation remains an open question. Even in countries whose governments have been driven by a neo-liberal approach, not much is available that could provide a comprehensive view of the outcomes. What exactly has changed after five or six years: who benefits and who does not benefit? The question remains open whether such shyness is linked to technical parameters or to the fear ruling authorities may experience about unforeseeable results that could be politically damaging.

What are the reasons for the emergence of different modes of evaluation across the OECD democracies? Two general observations may be made at this stage. The first is that, to some extent, the pace and rate of evaluation is influenced by the national context – more precisely, by institutional factors. Characteristics of state or administrative culture may matter: roman-law-inspired states are rather averse to evaluation, whereas common-law-oriented countries are quite supportive of it. The examples given above do suggest that evaluation is used more frequently in countries where reforms are more comprehensively framed, or where references to neo-liberal mechanisms are openly expressed. The PUMA initiatives, launched by OECD during the 1990s, were rather clearly expressing the perspective and experience of experts from Anglo-Saxon and Scandinavian countries.

The most significant institutional differences are those in values, in norms and expectations that define publicness, and in the functions or roles public authorities perform in a society or economy. For instance, are public organizations narrowly defined as goods and services providers, or are they also accountable for providing cohesion and maintaining integration among scattered social fabrics? The former approach is relatively functional and agnostic, and belongs to the Anglo-Saxon tradition. Evaluation is a common tool of governmental control in daily life. How much taxpayer money has been saved thanks to the reallocation of field agents across the country? The latter approach to public administration is common among continental European countries and policy makers, whether socialist or centre-right oriented. This approach covariates with a parsimonious use of evaluation. Governments want to know what impact the goods and services have on society. Does, for instance, the reallocation of field agencies increase or decrease inequities between town and country?

The second observation suggests that it is not sufficient to have qualified internal or external experts, reliable tools and ample information at hand if awareness of the importance of evaluation is to spread throughout the system and be incorporated into the management of reforms. Evaluation may be practised even if the public system is not permeated by an evaluation culture. What is important is not the availability of top-flight experts and sophisticated systems, for individual civil servants are free to decide whether or not to carry out an evaluation – sometimes even without realizing consciously what they are doing. In other words, barriers to evaluation are pragmatic rather than technical or ideological.

3. Pragmatic evaluation

What are the reasons that lead to different modes of evaluation? Under what conditions might evaluation practices be used to develop and implement public-sector reforms? The answer suggested by experience is obvious: when they are adopted and used by policy makers. But this cannot be done by applying a ready-to-use magic formula or by following a single procedural model of best practice. The examination of a number of practices teaches some persuasive lessons.

Observation of evaluation practices makes it possible to refute the truisms or stereotypes that encourage scepticism or fatalism about the possibility of successful evaluation. By nature public organizations are not self-evaluating (Wildavsky 1979). They do not continuously monitor their own activities in order to assess whether they meet their policy goals. Their objectives are uncertain: different internal audiences require different evaluations, and policies are self-perpetuating. On another level, the problem is laid at the door of policy makers, whose way of thinking is presented as generally incompatible with an interest in the practice of evaluation. And there are other supposedly sound arguments that the problem lies in the very nature of the reforms undertaken. For example, it is argued that because they are ideologically motivated, comprehensive authoritarian policies – such as those transferring whole sectors of goods and services to the market – do not encourage government to focus on projected or actual costs and benefits. However, to conclude that nothing can be expected of evaluation seems just as extreme as to state that it is the inevitable wave of the future.

Usefulness for action

The first lesson is that a pragmatic approach to evaluation practices is needed. In other words, they must in each case be focused on specific needs and ad hoc opportunities for action. The needs of policy makers should be pushed to the fore in deciding what to evaluate. This common-sense remark is not abstract in its implications. The decision to evaluate a programme is rarely made unilaterally by decision-makers or by administrators in a kind of ivory tower. Needs often are not clearly formulated beforehand by policy makers. Initiatives are motivated by routines, imitation processes (such as benchmarking), and short-term or marginal reasons. When needs are explicitly addressed, it is by and large the senior officials involved in the reform who take the initiative to use evaluation practices. The will or the interest of the top legitimizes monitoring activities. The role that the budget department or the ministry of finance can play in this regard should also be underscored. Evaluation functions as a substitute for control. In some countries, the willingness of senior officials and advisers to use evaluation practices is no coincidence, in that their university and professional training has made them aware of the contributions of the social sciences and modern management. In this respect, they differ from staff with strictly legal and administrative training.

There is little likelihood that evaluation will be adopted for its own sake, for it is simply a means to an end. It will only be credible and acceptable if it meets three conditions. The first is that evaluation must be sponsored by individuals and groups that have practical experience with evaluation as well as direct access to policy makers, or may even have a policy-making role in the reform. The second requirement is that evaluation must be based on a concrete need or problem that policy makers face and from which they will derive value added at their level. Abstract reasons based on matters of principle – for instance, evaluation as an ideal in itself – are hollow discourse. Third, evaluation must be well-timed in relation to reform – neither too early nor too late in the process.

These windows of opportunity often prove to be essential, especially when the practice of evaluation is still uncommon in a particular country, but also in public systems where it is already more widespread. Poor timing can kill a reform initiative. If evaluation is out of step with the governmental agenda, it will ultimately have no impact and merely be forgotten. Such has been the case in France between 1992 and 1997, the successive prime ministers showing a high degree of aversion to public-sector reforms as well as to the modernization of public management. By the same token, this also means that evaluation systems must continually adapt to changing needs and that policy makers must have easy access, if not close control.

Providing information
According to some academics, evaluation and policy analysis should be considered distinct enterprises (Geva-May and Pal 1999). In their view, evaluation is a phase of policy analysis that is primarily research-oriented, whereas policy analysis plays a political role. Evaluators adopting advocacy techniques to promote recommendations run two risks. First, they jeopardize the intrinsic humility of evaluation. Evalua-

tion faces a lack of sufficient context data; therefore it is misleading and lacking in credibility. Experience calls into question the relevance of such distinctions.

If the use of evaluation is action-oriented, this means that evaluation focuses on delivering usable knowledge. Evaluation is much more likely to gain acceptance and be of use if its potential to inform is stressed, and its prescriptive aspects deemphasized. In this regard, the theoretical distinction between evaluation and quasi-evaluation, although it satisfies methodological purists, is artificial and detrimental.

A usable evaluation is one that first and foremost is aimed at making available information based on empirical data, as the examination of the practical experiences of public-service reform repeatedly has shown. The reason for this is clear, and it lies in the very nature of the decision-making process. Specifically, two significant facts can be distinguished.

Public decision-makers are much like corporate executives (Mintzberg 1980). They give priority to practical or qualitative information obtained by speaking to individuals they feel close to or trust. This is a far cry from the theoretical model that assumes that problem-solvers take the time to analyse the problem by exhaustively reviewing all available information on the specific empirical situation and the quantitative merits of the alternatives. This implies that evaluation will be more credible if it is adapted to the reality of the decision-making process. Political and governmental action is not comprehensive and all-embracing; specific public-sector reform choices do not derive from strategic master plans. Be that as it may, policy makers engaged in action do not stop thinking. Analysis – or evaluation – is one of many inputs they use. They rely heavily on ordinary knowledge, learning and interactive problem-solving. Consequently, analysis must compete with these other inputs (Lindblom and Cohen 1979) and is not automatically given priority. Very few public-sector reforms are the products of linear and deductive reasoning.

These two facts point to a concept of evaluation as an activity that is relatively limited in scope, focuses on clearly defined problems, employs language policy makers can understand, readily uses the data available even if they are not perfect, and aims at describing a state of affairs rather than analysing it. Evaluators are responsive to varying conditions and they use data not necessarily as a competing argument, but as a means of getting policy makers' attention, by providing explanatory information and assistance rather than judgement.

This attempt to give evaluation greater credibility assumes that evaluators do not lightly make snap judgements and assessments. This is particularly true when they must evaluate ongoing reforms. They run the risk not only of substituting their own judgement for that of policy makers – a technocratic deviation – but of failing to give an objective account of the situation, in particular by focusing on mistakes, dysfunctions or deficiencies, without balancing them fairly against achievements, progress and successes. This amounts to a pessimistic bias.

This selective short-sightedness of ongoing evaluation as to the real impact of a policy is encountered in a number of reform initiatives. During the second half of the 1990s, the Canadian government was extremely cautious about auditors' reports, which tend to emphasize the shortcomings of a reform – in terms of value for money as well as external effectiveness – and give the impression that little progress is being made and a great deal remains to be done. In such cases evaluation is of no practical help to governments and, because of its overall assessment function, selects information that makes it difficult to design the next stages of reform. Evaluation thereby becomes, in a sense, self-defeating.

Should evaluations make judgements? The debate remains rather open inside the professional community and the reform entrepreneurs. Some practitioners prefer that evaluations refrain from making judgements, and instead remain either exploratory or informational; they are nevertheless aware that judgements often are implied even if not explicit. But an equal number of practitioners expects evaluators to make judgements: not to do so would reduce the value of learning from evaluation – especially when ministers want to get a clear view on a situation. Learning implies judgements, as far as human action is concerned. Information as such simply does not make sense.

Internal evaluation
A rather widely diffused practice is internal evaluation, which includes self-review. Policy makers responsible for public-service reforms are likely to use evaluation and find it that much easier if evaluation practices are developed within the public system itself, especially at the various levels that initiate, design and implement the reform. Such a preference is strongly expressed by high public servants, which suggests some degree of mistrust towards outsiders – especially academics – that may be fuelled by corporatism. Although some politicians are more cautious and may express doubts about the neutrality and the skills of administrative bodies to monitor the activities of the state machinery, once they are in power they may change their minds and rely upon their own staff.

A number of countries have commissioned private or academic experts to conduct evaluations. These kinds of evaluations tend to be less useful to governments and are strongly perceived as such by many high public servants. They remain somewhat theoretical, in as much as their approach focuses on aspects or themes that do not match the specific concerns of governments, the actual agenda of the reform, the pace of policy implementation and the capabilities of policy makers. Their overall evaluation may be perceived as critical or passive, for it is an ex post assessment made a number of months – or even years – after the actual events, and therefore provides few guidelines and directions for the next stages in the field. The limitations and frustrations are seen more clearly when – as in Finland, for example – internal evaluations are carried out concurrently by groups or networks of civil servants that are directly involved in implementing the reforms. The value added for action is comparatively greater in this case. In all fairness, it must be pointed out that an external evaluation can be a favourable solution in exceptional cases, as when a government finds it politically expedient to have so-called independent experts advocating the necessity for changes in the administrative machinery or even 'forcing' the government to accept a public-sector reform agenda that it will then put into practice. This was the case with Greece's 1994–96 reform of the management of European structural funds; the prime minister asked the commission to launch an evaluation of the Greek administration, and promised not to reject any outside expertise that Brussels might appoint.

It is necessary to define just what is meant by 'internal' evaluation. Some countries have administrative bodies, such as the audit board and the court of accounts, or ad hoc bodies, such as administrative reform task forces and public policy evaluation units. This is – or has been – the case in France, the Netherlands and the United Kingdom. But the fact that technical and human resources are available within the public system does not necessarily guarantee that the evaluation of public-sector reforms will be assigned to them or that their work will have a significant impact in practice. It has been suggested that evaluation should foster the development of separate balancing centres of authority within the public system. This approach is, at present, unrealistic. Ownership of evaluation is not the same as ownership of public-management reform policies. Internal professional corps do little to make evaluation more useful to policy making. There would still be the same barriers mentioned above, since the evaluator can easily take on the role of judge, who pronounces a favourable or unfavourable verdict without being held accountable for it.

The operational implications of these observations are clear. In many ways public-management reforms differ from other policies. Health or education policies may concern more visible or tangible social issues than do public-sector reforms. People see less directly the benefit of new accounting methods or flatter organization charts. Public-sector reforms are considered highly symbolic manifestations of governments' discretionary action. Accordingly, if evaluation is to be useful, there is basically one group who would be responsible for evaluation: the policy makers themselves. Evaluators must take their needs and wishes into account and tailor their approaches to specific contexts.

Another lesson learned from experience is that the trend towards internal evaluation reflects the determination of those responsible for reform to maintain an ongoing review of individual agencies and of the public-sector as a whole. Internal evaluation is a way to keep administrative reform on the governmental agenda and to send a message to the agencies and their staff, making them aware of the attention of decision-makers. Otherwise, without fulfilling a function of symbolic pressure, evaluation will become a mere bureaucratic ritual and the reports of experts will simply be ignored.

An incremental and opportunistic approach

Public evaluation should be adopted and diffused incrementally. Anyone can carry out an evaluation, and a quasi-evaluation can be a perfectly good way to start. There is no surer way of stifling evaluation at the outset than to confine it to the ghetto of methodology. Moreover, the practice is not the exclusive prerogative of top policy makers and their staff. There are ways of disseminating evaluation throughout agencies and down the chain of command, provided that the evaluation is linked to a problem that is relevant to those who are carrying it out.

Broad-based evaluation is seen in cases in which the reform is aimed at the internal structures and processes of the public system, and is implemented either through a participatory and decentralized approach or through the ongoing government monitoring of a reform programme. Examples of this kind of evaluation may be found in a specific sector or ministry – for example, in the Ministère de l'Equipement in France – or throughout the public system, as is the case in the Canadian federal government. The incremental approach also means that the information obtained, and its uses for reform, make sense to all concerned – from policy makers down to rank-and-file staff – and are perceived neither as a threat nor a constraint, but as a resource and an opportunity.

Undue importance should not be attached to differences in types of approaches or methods. No methods or mixes of approaches are intrinsically better than others. However, provided that utility remains the basic criterion, i.e. technical considerations are based on how the evaluation will be used, the following observations may be made.

From a technical standpoint, evaluation should consider the empirical data that are available – or can be obtained rapidly and at low cost – even if they are not perfect or absolutely reliable. It is better to start delivering something than to dream about the perfection of numbers. Credibility is at stake. Evaluators are aware of one general fact of life: public systems, especially in Roman-law-based countries, have relatively little data on performance and effectiveness. Such a deficit cannot be overcome overnight. Evaluation should aim less at providing an overall understanding of a vast range of parameters than at producing indicators on a few well-defined aspects that can be considered reasonably useful proxies.

Ex post evaluations – evaluations made once a specific reform policy has been completed – are used relatively rarely, for they do not really meet the needs of government and are expensive and time-consuming. Nevertheless, they may inform our perspective about the reasons certain outcomes and impacts were generated and the relative value of the tools and processes that were mobilized.

Ex ante evaluations – or evaluations made while reform programmes are elaborated by the policy makers – are closer to informal or quasi-evaluations. They may predict the outcomes of various options that could be adopted. They actually are a secondary source of information, for reasons linked to time pressures and the political visions of policy makers.

Ongoing evaluations are better used as a managerial tool, although they require relatively intensive and well-informed monitoring. This said, they are ill-suited to unilateral 'top-down' or 'one-shot' policies, particularly when a reform consists of a transfer to the market sector.

Policies aimed at ensuring the year-to-year continuity of reforms of the internal processes and structures of government departments leave greater leeway for the use of more formal and technically diverse evaluations. Last, but not least, evaluation practices can be developed far more easily if there are existing systems of information on costs and performance, although they do not stand in the way of developing quasi-evaluation.

Performance management as a learning process
On paper, one can evaluate many aspects of public-sector activity, such as productivity and the quality of services, the ratio of expenditure to goods produced and services provided, and the extent to which social, economic or other problems are solved and the goals of reform are achieved. In practice, in most countries evaluation tends to emphasize internal concerns, that is, the performance management of staff and departments. This has been the case in Ireland, Norway, Canada and New Zealand.

This general approach – which is more managerial than strategic, and oriented towards value-for-money and efficiency rather than effectiveness – is intended to close the information loop and keep policy makers informed about what is working and what is not. It is also designed to provide information that will be used by decision-makers to improve future reforms.

This realistic managerial approach meets decision-makers' needs. It also predominates because it is generally difficult – and even arbitrary – to evaluate reforms in terms of their overall external effectiveness. This is why the aims and objectives of public-sector-management reform are rarely set in a clear and operationally measurable way when a policy is defined or launched.

It cannot always be assumed that indicators and data on performance will be available. There are sometimes no structured information systems that measure time spent, departments' outcomes, costs, and the intrinsic quality of services. It is difficult to say objectively what has been done, or is being done, by a given organization at a given time, to say nothing of comparing different organizations and agencies. At times, the attempt to gather information clashes with existing systems that are not designed for performance management, but for checking compliance or monitoring budgets. Consequently, there is a risk that data collection will require extra time and money. The good will of agencies responsible for monitoring is a far from negligible factor. But to argue that it is pointless to undertake evaluation because adequate management data are lacking is to enter into a circular argument about cause and effect.

The advantage of stressing quasi-evaluation aimed at providing performance proxies rather than at assessing external impacts and overall performance is that it makes it possible to avoid the data collection/policy evaluation dilemma through a gradual learning process that fosters an information culture among policy makers and agencies without calling on outside statisticians, computer specialists and accountants. In this way, evaluation has a pump-priming effect. One possible starting point could be to carry out ad hoc reviews using available data, while realizing the relative value of the instruments being used and the analysis made. This process later could be organized on a much larger scale. For example, a central agency could systematically gather performance data on the system as a whole and on its constituent agencies (as is done in New Zealand), or an administrative modernization office might consider performance data on key public-management issues to be addressed in the coming year in its annual report (as is done by the Clerk of the Canadian Privy Council Office).

Above all, performance evaluation must not be viewed as a comprehensive, centralized system run solely by specialists. Good practices naturally lead to performance evaluation as a living management tool. In other words, culture and people are its core components, and production of information is merely an outcome or a means to an end. The goal is to raise people's awareness – to disseminate a new kind of focus on performance, cost, quality and the relevance of the services provided – and also to give agencies and staff the capacity to evaluate themselves. The goal of a structured approach to performance at all levels of the public system is achieved by enabling each level to produce the information it needs for its own day-to-day decision-making and to conduct a self-review that will have an impact on the quality of its everyday work. 'Learning-by-doing' evaluative performance review lends credibility to evaluation based on factual data.

A response that works particularly well, as suggested by the experience of Ireland, Canada and France, consists of a decentralized and participatory approach to evaluation. A performance culture can only be achieved if agencies are encouraged to collect and share information on good practices, to promote these practices, and to encourage other agencies to do the same and to adopt them in turn. The sharing of all types of practices is a major vehicle for reform. It involves participants and makes it possible to draw lessons as to whether these practices work in different situations and structures. The lessons will have been learned when actors have acquired the capacity to see how a technical innovation is relevant to a problem they face, and can provide new useful solutions for their day-to-day work.

Central policy makers and units whose main mission is public-management reform play an important role in this regard. They have a two-fold responsibility that consists, firstly, of ensuring the accountability of basic units through vertical reporting, as well as horizontal communication between departments. The centre should monitor the 'big picture' performance of the public-sector. Secondly, they must help agencies and bureaus to learn how to take initiatives, give them greater visibility, and even provide incentives and support – for example, through training schemes, training seminars or voluntary experiments. In practical terms, this obviously means that the centre must have the necessary professional skills at its disposal. It also means that it must be careful to strike the right balance between uniformity and diversity, combining a mix of approaches that fits the needs of each national context. Being responsive to local units (their inventiveness and diversity) goes hand in hand with developing overall coordination. The use of informal evaluations that are designed to be part of 'business as usual' often makes it possible to introduce adjustments and changes without attracting the attention of internal or external interest groups that might be tempted to see a formal evaluation as an opportunity to resist reform.

In summary, the examination of good practices suggests that evaluation can increase efficiency (the degree to which goals are reached, relative to available resources). It also makes it possible to generate other forms of value added that are far from negligible. It gives visibility to a judgement or a measurement in terms of adequacy (the degree to which the goals assigned are reached). It supports the administrative memory of action solutions. It provides skill variety for decision-makers at all levels. It supports an attitude of wisdom (acting with knowledge while questioning what one knows), helps create competition for status based on managerial skill. It may, to some extent, impress users and outside observers.

One among a few interesting experiences is provided by the national Best Value pilot programme in England. Forty local authorities and two police forces were selected and piloted between 1998 and 2000. Their commitment is to undertake fundamental reviews of all their services. The rationale for activities is challenged, and the performance of services is compared with the best on offer throughout the private and public sectors. The competitiveness of alternative modes of service delivery is tested. Users, key stakeholders and the wider public are consulted. In such a case, academics and researchers might be appointed to fulfil two tasks: to identify the real improvements in the efficiency, effectiveness and quality of service delivery; and to act as change agents, consultants and trainers. Combining summative analysis of impacts and outputs with formative approaches (in which local public services are given advice and understanding about the content and the process) bridges the gap between policy evaluation and policy for-mulation (Martin and Sanderson 1999).

4. The next step: Analysis for learning

The reform of the public sector is now becoming an ongoing task of governments. The days when it sufficed to decree a reorganization of government once in a generation and then resume day-to-day routines are likely gone forever. At the same time, the pressures for change are becoming increasingly global and constraining, which has put countries that have been relatively reluctant to adopt reforms in a difficult posi-tion. Two factors should be underscored in particular.

The first is the extension of forms of partnership in the governance of public affairs. The best example of this is the European Union, a public entity that exercises responsibilities – particularly the allocation of financial resources among programmes or projects (such as structural funds) – that once were borne by individual countries. The development of these partnerships and of the principle of subsidiarity between Brus-sels and the national administrations has involved a remarkable exten-sion of the use of evaluation procedures.

The second factor concerns financial constraints. There is every rea-son to believe that these constraints are going to increase in the public-sector for some time to come. The European Union is again a case in point. The Maastricht and Amsterdam Treaties establish a macro-budgetary regulation mechanism that will have a considerable impact. National systems, including subnational authorities, will thus be forced not only to limit expenditures, but also to contain their revenues drasti-cally. These trends will reinforce a centralized approach that will rely on control by budget agencies. Whether they like it or not, both national ministries and local authorities will find it necessary to step up their efforts to rationalize, beginning with their internal efficiency (costs, productivity, and quality).

These developments suggest that, although further privatization of public services remains operationally possible, efforts will be focused mainly on internal reforms of the public sector, such as eliminating duplication and simplifying institutional units in various fields. It will be increasingly difficult and costly for a country to remain outside this generalized trend of reform. In other words, at least in OECD countries, the current disparity between a few pioneering countries and other more cautious countries can be expected to narrow. The competitiveness of public systems, which so far has been to some extent a rhetorical aspect of reform policies, is likely to become a very real imperative that will be felt even in the day-to-day life of individual government departments. At the same time, it will become easier to compare the performance of departments and various levels of government, at both the domestic and international levels. Although relative to other fields such as health and R&D, the reform of government departments is still a policy in which comparability (and thus the reference to good practices and benchmarking) has been rare (as has evaluation), the situation is likely to change rapidly. It will become more difficult to refuse to carry out some public-sector reforms by arguing that they are based on ideological or political considerations. Reform is becoming a functional imperative in itself.

Consequently, the overall situation appears to be shifting towards a relative extension of evaluation practices: the need for more ongoing fine-tuning, comparability, large-scale partnerships and macro-budgetary regulation will all play a role. There is no reason to believe that, regarding the good practices identified above, there is a substantial change in the profile of evaluation itself. It will remain oriented more towards internal efficiency than towards external effectiveness, more internalised than externalized, informal (but more systematic), and will be accompanied by cultural and behavioural changes while being increasingly linked to solving the concrete problems of policy makers. Evaluation is and will remain a valuable tool for anyone willing to take advantage of it.

The lesson to be learned from the experience of evaluation in the late twentieth century is one of realism and of modesty. One might have thought that the pressure for democratic accountability would have led to greater transparency collectively shared by citizens regarding the impact of public reforms on society or that the use of more 'scientific' guidance methods would have made it possible to implement rigorous comprehensive data systems more rapidly. However, there are also reassuring aspects. The guidance of reforms remains broadly under the realistic control of governments, and the use of scientific methods has not made policy makers any less accountable. In this regard, evaluation has not gone the way of the planning programming budgeting system (PPBS), which was a good idea in itself, but proved unusable because it was alien to policy-making practices and it arrogantly ignored the judgement of public officials (Wildavsky 1970). On the contrary, evaluation teaches an optimistic lesson through its emphasis on the principle of usable knowledge. In this regard, it is both its focus on describing the specific circumstances of policy action and its ability to foresee cause and effect that make evaluation a realistic tool for action.

Reforms of public-sector management which are lasting and relevant could be described as having satisfied four main criteria. First, they are aimed at genuinely changing the bottom line of the day-to-day behaviour of government employees and transforming the way organizations really operate. Second, they have the discretion to model the processes, structures and strategies that actually bring these changes about. Third, they can make these changes lasting. And finally, they can limit the unwanted effects these changes may have on the efficient and equitable provision of goods and services to society.

The focus on empirical information and operational consequences of reform actions that modern evaluation provides may offer safeguards against misdirected efforts, especially in an era in which an unsuccessful reform may well prove to be as unsatisfactory and harmful as the refusal to undertake a reform at all. The optimistic lesson for the future is that more and more countries have entered a process of cumulative learning about reform actions. The quest for efficiency, effectiveness, transparency and democratic accountability no longer stops after a single reform step. Learning is an ongoing and organic process, to which evaluation can offer critical insights, rather than being treated as a one-off exercise. To some extent the analytical aspect of government has improved recently – even if external, independent evaluations have lessened. At the same time it takes a certain maturity, sophistication and mindset to make good use of evaluative information as a learning tool that can help governments and the public to form well-based views and make informed decisions.

Setting up learning bureaucracies has become a major requirement. While theoretical models have been designed, the practice remains a challenge, even for those countries that are usually viewed as the most innovative. Prescriptions about public-policy management cannot disregard findings generated by field research. Two lessons have to be considered seriously. Rational-choice-based designs often fail, as shown by the 'New Institutionalism' inspired studies of public-sector reforms. Learning processes in political orders are slow to emerge, given the fact that adaptative behaviours are straitjacketed by experiential logics. A 'hot-stove effect' governs the selection of policy alternatives, that is, policy makers reproduce former successes but discard new and more efficient alternatives that have never been tried (Denrell and March 2001).

Opportunities to use an orthodox evaluation approach emerge when rather dramatic changes occur (Duran and Thoenig 1996). The cognitive frames or lenses that political and administrative authorities use to set up their acts and to decode their policy environment become fuzzy. Their implicit action theories no longer enable them to manage public problems as they were accustomed to do. They consider their tool kits to be outdated or non-adapted. Most issues they are in charge of are perceived as increasingly complicated or multi-dimensional. Solutions get uncertain. The limits of the territories which are under their jurisdiction are bypassed. Finally, their legitimacy is eroded.

In such circumstances, when public institutions become more accountable for the outputs and for the outcomes of their policies, they have the opportunity to establish themselves again as relevant actors in the government and the governance of public affairs. Evaluation makes more sense to them. Giving serious attention to the consequences of their acts may reinforce a level of legitimacy their position of authority no longer ensures.

References

Brunsson, N. and J.P. Olsen (1997), *The Reforming Organization*, Bergen, Norway: Fagbokforlaget.

Denrell, J. and J.G. March (2001), 'Adaption as information restriction: The hot stove effect', *Organization Science*, 12[5], 523–38.

Duran, P. and J.C. Thoenig (1996), 'L'Etat et la gestion publique territoriale', *Revue Française de Science Politique*, 46[4], 580–623.

Geva-May, I. and L.A. Pal (1999), 'Good fences make good neighbours: Policy evaluation and policy analysis – Exploring the differences', *Evaluation*, 5[3], 259–77.

Kessler, M.C., P. Lascoumes, M. Setbon and J.C. Thoenig (eds) (1998), *L'évaluation des politiques publiques*, Paris: L'Harmattan.

Levine, R.A., M.S. Solomon, G.M. Hellstern and H. Wollmann (eds) (1981), *Evaluation Research and International Perspectives*, London: Sage.

Lindblom, C. and D. Cohen (1979), *Usable Knowledge: Social Science and Social Problem Solving*, New Haven, US: Yale University Press.

March, J.G. and J.P. Olsen (1984), 'The new institutionalism: Organizational factors in political life', *American Political Science Review*, 78[5], 734–49.

Martin, S. and I. Sanderson (1999), 'Evaluating public policy experiments: Measuring outcomes, monitoring processes or managing pilots?', *Evaluation*, 5[3], 245–58.

Mintzberg, H. (1980), *The Nature of Managerial Work*, London: Prentice Hall.

OECD-PUMA (1999), *Government of the Future: Getting from Here to There*, Paris: OECD.

Olsen, J.P. (2001), 'Garbage cans, new institutionalism, and the study of politics', *American Political Science Review*, 95[1], 191–98.

Pollitt, C. et al. (1997), *Trajectories and Options: An International Perspective on the Implementation of Finnish Public Management Reforms*, Helsinki: Ministry of Finance. See also *Public Management Reforms: Five Country Studies*, Ministry of Finance, Helsinki, 1997.

Rossi, P.H. and H.E. Freeman (1982), *Evaluation: A Systematic Approach*, London: Sage.

Schick, A. (1996), *The Spirit of Reform: Managing the New Zealand State Sector in a Time of Change*, Wellington, New Zealand: State Service Commission.

Trosa, S. (1992), 'La modernisation est-elle évaluable?', *Politiques et Management Public*, 10[4], 65–84.

Wildavsky, A. (1969), 'Rescuing policy analysis from PPBS', *Public Administration Review*, 29[2], 189–202.

Wildavsky, A. (1979), *Speaking Truth to Power: The Art and Craft of Policy Analysis*, Toronto: Little Brown.

12. Evaluation in public-sector reform. Trends, potentials and limits in international perspective

Hellmut Wollmann

In this concluding chapter an attempt will be made, in a comparative perspective, to identify some salient patterns and trends in the 'twinned' development of public-sector reforms and evaluation thereof. For this purpose, cursory accounts on the development in some of the countries under inspection in this volume will be given before some summarizing remarks are made.

1. Analytical framework

Empirically the following cursory accounts will draw on the preceding chapters of this book as well as on other related sources (particularly the country reports in Pollitt and Bouckaert 2000, pp. 129 ff.). Conceptually they will be guided by an analytical scheme in which, drawing on the 'neo-institutionalist' debate[1] and on the institutional transformation literature[2], the following factors are hypothesized to have particular (explanatory) relevance:[3]

1. *Starting conditions.* Probably more than in other areas of institution building and institutional choice, the institutional choice in public-sector reforms is influenced by the very starting conditions, that is, the current format and profile of the public sector (in its various dimensions) from which the modernization process is bound to take off (see also Pollitt and Bouckaert 2000, pp. 62 ff.). The leverage of the starting conditions on the modernization course is readily apparent, since in the perception of the relevant actors they define the country's modernization deficit or reform need as measured against the imperatives of the dominant modernization discourse – or, conversely, the starting conditions may, in the interpretation of the ac-

tors, signal no need or a minimal need for modernization and may suggest even a modernization 'lead' over their respective country on some crucial scores (Wollmann 1996, pp. 15 ff.);

2. *Socio-economic and 'external' factors* (budgetary crises, 'external' influences [for instance, of the European Union or World Bank]);

3. *Institutional and cultural traditions* (such as legacies or path-dependencies[4]). Public-sector modernization decisions are likely to be strongly influenced also by the institutional and cultural traditions and givens of the country's institutional world. The impact of these factors is probably the stronger, the more firmly (to the point of eliciting a path-dependency) such institutional and cultural givens are empirically and normatively rooted in the country's history and tradition. The different strands of the *Rechtsstaat* (in Continental European countries) and of the 'civil culture public interest' traditions (in the Anglo-Saxon world) are exemplary (see Pollitt and Bouckaert 2000, pp. 52 ff, Wollmann 2000b, pp. 4 ff.);

4. *Institutional (polity) setting* (unitary/centralized versus federal/decentralized, majoritarian versus consociational/consensual, multi-actor versus single-actor[5] countries);

5. *Actor constellations, intentions, interests, 'will and skill'*. As the decisions on public-sector modernization are prepared and taken in discourse and decision-making arenas made up of the relevant political, administrative and socio-economic actors (as well as of academics and consultants), the actors' constellations, intentions, interests and 'will and skill' are likely to have significant influence on the institutional choice finally embarked upon;

6. *(National as well as international) discourses and discourse coalitions*[6], including the increasing interpenetration of national and international discourse arenas and networks with ensuing exchange, learning and adaptation processes.[7]

For an (explanatory) account of the specific profile of evaluation in and on public-sector reforms in the different countries, the distinction should be recalled particularly between *internal* evaluation in terms of (self-) evaluative tools and procedures within the operating administrative units, on the one hand, and *external* evaluation, particularly of the social science-guided evaluation *research* type, on the other hand. In explaining the former, the emergence and state of public-sector reforms appears to be a strong predictor. With regard to the latter, the existence of institutional actors (such as parliament, court of audit) that advocate external evaluation and the degree of 'maturity' of the country's evaluation culture[8] probably have a strong impact. As a caveat it must be mentioned, however, that the following sketches – including the tentative 'causal interpretation' – are liable, due to brevity and selectivity, to be imperfect and patchy.

2. Some selected country profiles – as cases in point

Great Britain

Since the early 1980s Great Britain has been a frontrunner and pacesetter in what, under the now familiar label of New Public Management (see Hood 1991), has become the main current in the international debate on and practice of public-sector modernization guided by neoliberal and managerialist beliefs. The decisive shift is explained by a constellation of factors. When elected to office in 1979, the new Conservative government under Margaret Thatcher was determined to initiate large-scale neo-liberal and managerial reforms. The country's 'starting conditions' (among other things, over-centralized government and the quasi-monopoly of public personnel in the delivery of services) called for major changes. Great Britain's unitary ('Westminster') system provided the institutional levers to effect and enforce such changes from central to local levels nationwide.

The Financial Management Initiative of 1982, the Next Steps Initiative of 1988 (which led to the creation of some 140 executive agencies), and the 1991 Compulsory Competitive Tendering (*CCT*) and Citizen Charters were crucial steps. The Financial Management Initiative of 1982 embraced the whole of central government with its philosophy of decentralized management, decentralized budgets, more targets and more professionalism (see Pollitt and Bouckaert 2000: 273, Gray and Jenkins 1992: 64 ff). The National Audit Office and Audit Commission were created with a mandate that stressed the '3 Es' (economy, efficiency and effectiveness).

From the outset the introduction and employment of performance measurement systems was advocated as a central management and evaluation tool (for details and references see Pollitt and Bouckaert 2000, pp. 273 ff.). The setting of performance goals and indicators (by contracts or legal prescriptions) and their monitoring, measuring and reporting (via 'internal' evaluation) has been applied to the agencies as well as to the local authorities. The annual publication of national 'league tables' for schools and hospitals, which receives considerable media attention, was just another expression of the 'performance indicator culture' that has emerged in the UK (see also Jann and Reichard, Chapter 3 of this volume).

The performance indicator (PI) movement has still gained more momentum under the New Labour Government. In repealing CCT and replacing it with its Best Value (BV) regime, statutorily introduced in the Local Government Act 1999, the Blair government turned to using an expanding set of performance indicators to put the local authorities and their service-related activities particularly under rigorous top-down surveillance (see Wilson and Game 2002: 337 ff.). A crucial role came to be played by the Audit Commission, which was established in 1982 in order to monitor the financial and managerial competence of local government (and a number of specified quangos, including the health service). In the Local Government Act 2000 the responsibility of the Audit Commission was extended to ascertain whether local authorities are providing 'value for money'. The 2001 White Paper (DTLR 2001) took the BV regime a conspicuous step further by stipulating an elaborate evaluative scheme, revolving around the Audit Commission, in which local authorities were to be classified as 'high performers', 'strivers', 'coasters' or 'poor performers' whereby, as a remarkably centralist and interventionist feature (see Wilson and Game 2002: 338), the 'good performers' are to be rewarded by central government by getting more money and 'more freedoms', while the 'poor performers' can be sanctioned to the point, in the last resort, of placing the failing council into the hands of Government-appointed administrators. The first round of such stringent top-down performance measurements and assessments was recently carried out by the Audit Commission on the local authorities in the counties. The report (assessing all counties under the aforementioned four categories) was published in early December 2002, arousing considerable public attention and controversy (particularly from those county authorities that came out with a poor rating).

By contrast, fully-fledged external evaluations had seldom been undertaken during the Conservative era.[9] Under the New Labour government external evaluation has been on the rise. In line with the new emphasis on 'evidence-based decision-making' (Sanderson 2000, p. 433), a Centre for Management and Policy Studies has been created in the Cabinet Office; the Centre is intended to provide a 'window in the heart of government' for research and evaluation evidence (Cabinet Office 2000). Mention should be made, for instance, of the evaluation conducted by a team of independent consultants (see DETR 2001) on an extensive pilot programme that preceded the introduction of the full BV regime (see Wilson and Game 2002: 338).

New Zealand

New Zealand, also a frontrunner in the new modernization wave, has generated the 'purest' theoretical formulation of the New Public Management doctrine (see Halligan, Chapter 5 in this volume) and also has gone further by simultaneously realizing the privatization, agencification and marketization elements of NPM (see Pollitt and Bouckaert, Chapter 2 in this volume). A similar constellation as that in the UK (overcentralist government, quasi-monopoly of public personnel in the delivery of services, and a majoritarian Westminster government setting) has probably had some bearing on the sudden shift in 1984, except for the fact that it was effected by a Labour government, which in the face of a pressing economic crisis turned (almost overnight) from its traditional social-democratic to a neo-liberal persuasion. This policy change was conceived and engineered by a small (and almost secret) circle of Labour Party leaders, business leaders, neo-liberal university economists and like-minded Treasury officials (see Halligan 2001, p. 85). The pronounced management orientation of the reform was evidenced by the emphasis placed on guiding the newly created agencies by performance and reporting requirements – that is, by variants of internal evaluation. In fact, this performance orientation has even been characterized by an 'obsessive concern with outputs and accountability' (Halligan, Chapter 5 in this volume).

Notwithstanding this heavy stress on performance management, New Zealand has also initiated major evaluative reviews, first by mandating the Steering Group for Review of State Sector Reforms in 1991 and then by commissioning Allan Schick, an internationally renowned expert, to conduct a comprehensive review in 1994[10] (see Halligan, Chapter 5 in this volume).

Australia

Australia's 1983 Financial Management Improvement Programme reforms included strong elements of management and programme budgeting as well as mandatory evaluation to 'close the loop' for a new system of results-oriented management (see Halligan, Chapter 5 in this volume and Pollitt and Bouckaert 2000, pp. 202 ff). Australia's modernization approach did without the theoretical NPM-related stringency that was characteristic of New Zealand's path. The constellation of factors that triggered Austrialia's modernization move was quite different from that of New Zealand. The main motive of the new Labour government's push for large-scale public-sector reforms was the *politi-*

cal concern 'to re-establish ministerial control and greater responsiveness to government policies and priorities' (see Halligan, Chapter 5 in this volume and Pollitt and Bouckaert 2000, p. 202). Vis-à-vis the federal structure of the country (as a crucial starting condition), agencification – being one of the pivotal concepts of NPM – was understandably of little relevance.

Reflecting the specific orientation of Australia's reform drive, due to the absence of agencies, the introduction of indicator-based performance management and measurement systems was given less importance, whereas the employment of evaluation has been writ large. First, this applies to the employment of policy and programme evaluation at large. In fact, the frequency and volume of policy evaluations has lead the (Australian) State Services Committee to gibe that the Australian approach can be 'characterized as evaluating everything that moves' and as a 'picture of evaluation overkill' (State Services Committee 1999, quoted from Halligan, Chapter 5 in this volume). Both the country's court of audit and its parliament have proven to be advocates of widespread evaluation.[11]

Regarding the evaluating of public-sector reforms, Australia has probably gone further than any other country. In 1991, after a decade of intensive reforms, the first (and probably the most extensive yet) evaluation was undertaken by the Task Force on Management Improvement, a quasi-independent group of public servants (see Halligan, Chapter 5 in this volume). In addition, for instance, a prominent business leader was commissioned to do further (more sectoral) reviews. Small wonder that Australia has been ranked, in an internationally comparative assessment of the 'evaluative culture' at large in 21 countries, among the 'top five' (see Furubo and Sandahl 2002a, p. 11).[12]

USA

In the USA, a significant move towards reforming the federal government was undertaken under the (Democrat) Jimmy Carter by the Civil Service Reform Act of 1978, which introduced performance appraisal and merit pay. In 1992 the Bill Clinton administration launched a major reform project. The centrepiece of the programme, entrusted to vice-president Al Gore, was the National Performance Review (NPR), which produced a report, subtitled 'Creating a Government that Works Better and Costs Less'. Borrowing directly from the title of Osborne and Gaebler's bestseller, 'reinventing government' (known as REGO) became the trademark and battle-cry of reform (see Pollitt and Bouckaert 2000, p. 282; Rockman 2001, p. 8). For one thing, the 'better and less government' shibboleth fell well in line with the country's long-standing managerialist tradition (which reaches back to the progressive movement of the late 19th century) as well as with American anti-bureaucratic and anti-big government beliefs.[13] Moreover, the politically shrewd Clinton/Gore reform policy, in calling for 'less government and less government spending', embraced a traditionally Republican position and was meant to bring the Clinton administration political gains (see Rockman 2001, p. 8 ff.). Furthermore, the new administration was faced with a huge federal deficit inherited from the Reagan and Bush administrations.

Conceptually the NPR aimed at turning the agencies of federal government into performance-based organizations (PBOs) or more flexible decentralized management structures that would focus on results (see Rist and Paliokas 2002, p. 230). The US Congress ratified elements of the NPR by passing the Government Performance and Results Act (GPRA) of 1993, which required executive agencies to periodically report on their achievements with regard to their agency and programmatic goals. For the first time, Congress created a legislative structure whereby data on government performance would be fed systematically into the budget process, thus linking performance results with funding decisions (see Rist and Pakiolas 2002, p. 230).

The reform legislation significantly revolved around the idea of institutionalizing and stepping up agency-based (internal) evaluation procedures. At the same time, the (internal) evaluation function has strong advocates and watchdogs both in the General Accounting Office (GAO), which reports to the US Congress, and in the Office of Management and Budget (OMB), which reports to the president. Since the Civil Service Reform Act (CSRA) of 1978, which was enacted under the Carter administration, within each agency the Office of Inspector General (OIG) has had the responsibility of auditing operations to advance efficiency and effectiveness, and it may execute special audits and evaluation studies (see Christensen, Lægreid and Wise, Chapter 4 in this volume). Furthermore, the Government Performance and Results Act of 1993 requires performance auditing in federal agencies. Since 1998 outputs have had to be quantified and measured by indicators in the entire federal administration. Moreover, in 2001, under the Bush administration, OMB put the Executive Branch Management Scorecard System into effect. This 'can be seen as a form of oversight and ranks agency performance on five areas of management against stated criteria of success' (Christensen, Lægreid and Wise, Chapter 4 in this volume).

In sum, the federal government (internally) produces a large volume of evidence about programme performance.

Regarding external evaluation, it must be noted that this rise of management-oriented and result-based internal evaluative procedures has been accompanied, since the 1980s, by a decline in external evaluation (see Rist and Pakiolas 2002, pp. 230 ff.), in which the US federal government has been a 'world leader' since the 1960s. However, it should be borne in mind that, in line with a legislative tradition which goes back to the upsurge of evaluation in the mid-1960s, evaluation requirements are still included in legislation on administrative reforms such as in the Civil Service Reform Act of 1978. So, while making allowances for reservations (such as by Rist and Pakiolas 2002), one may still speak, particularly in comparative terms, of a 'flourishing culture of evaluation' (Pollitt and Bouckaert 2000, p. 284).[14]

Finally, it should be added that this account on the USA addresses only the federal level. In order to get a more complete and more adequate picture, developments at the state and local government levels would have to be included. 'In fact, state and local government can be seen as leaders and initiators of the movement to reinvent government' (Christensen, Lægreid and Wise, Chapter 4 in this volume, referring to Brudney et al. 1999).

Sweden
Since the early 1980s, when it faced a mounting budgetary crisis and, consequently, a challenge to its traditional welfare state model, Sweden has embarked upon a 'double track' reform trajectory. On the one hand, the Swedish government turned in 1985 to further decentralization of public functions to the counties and municipalities in what, based on the country's traditional multi-function local government model, already has represented an unusually decentralized government system (see Premfors 1998). On the other hand, a series of strong financial management reforms were implemented between 1988 to 1993, including result-oriented budgeting and accrual accounting. Result-oriented management was officially adopted for all state organisations from 1988 (see Pollitt and Bouckaert 2000, pp. 264 ff.). The reason for this 'mixed' strategy, combining 'traditional' reforms with NPM-inspired components, may be seen in the particularities of Sweden's 'starting conditions': on the one hand, the existence of the country's politically and functionally strong local government levels invited further decentralization as means to further pare down the (already comparatively spare) central agencies. On the other hand, some 300 agencies, which

operate as single-purpose bodies with a high degree of autonomy from central government guidance, lend themselves to result-based operation and, hence, performance management (see Furubo and Sandahl 2002b, p. 119).

In its evaluation profile Sweden is characterized, first, by widespread adoption and practice of result-oriented steering, monitoring and reporting tools in the agencies as well as in the local authorities. In addition to purely economic information, the annual reports of the agencies contain primarily information about what has actually been produced, and what this output has cost, and not normally evaluation. Many agencies are often given special assignments by the government to evaluate certain matters and to report back the results in their annual report (see Furubo and Sandahl 2002b, p. 120).

Second, a number of strong public authorities play a significant role in the (external) evaluation of government activities. The National Audit Board (RRV) conducts about 20 audits of agency and ministry-level performance per year (see Christensen, Lægreid and Wise, Chapter 4 in this volume). The Performance Audit Department within RRV investigates and promotes efficiency and effectiveness in government activities. Another important player is the Swedish Financial Management Authority (*ekonomistyrningsverket* [ESV])[15] which, among other things, makes comparisons among national organizations, and between Sweden and other countries, and benchmarks performance.

Third, the typical 'commission system' bears mentioning (see Vedung 1992). Including representatives of political parties and stakeholders, such as trade unions, businesses, and academics, these commissions are appointed for the preparation of practically all legislative projects and drafts. They are seen as a conduit of evaluative knowledge (see Furubo and Sandahl 2002b, pp. 116 f.). The parliament can establish commissions to evaluate specific aspects of public management reform. Finally, there is evidence of a growing interest in the academic research community in conducting social science-based evaluations of public management reforms (see Vedung 1997).

In sum, the variants of internal and external evaluation add up to a extensive and dense evaluation network and potential. These are embedded in an evaluation culture and tradition which dates back to the 1960s (when Sweden was among the few European frontrunners)[16]and earlier.[17]

Netherlands

In the early 1980s, under Prime Minister Lubbers, the Netherlands government initiated an administrative reform package, in which the decentralization of executive functions to lower levels of government was writ large. In the 1980s, new autonomous public bodies (ZBO) were created. Some were long-established (such as the state universities), but almost half of them were established after 1980 (see Pollitt and Bouckaert 2000, p. 247). In the 1990s, the decentralization drive was accelerated by the setting up of departmental agencies as the Dutch variant of agencification. Between 1991 and 1998 more than 20 agencies were established (see Pollitt and Bouckaert 2000, p. 247) with the intention of increasing the efficiency within the central government by means of result-oriented management. The (time-honoured) inspectorates within the ministries have become increasingly involved in evaluation, quality assessments and impact studies, in addition to their traditional legality control. Moreover, in each ministry a central financial and economic affairs department has been set up in order to stimulate and coordinate evaluation activities within the ministry (see Leeuw, Chapter 6 in this volume). As a management concept and tool the 'new steering model' was formulated and put in practice (see Kickert and In't Veld 1995).

The evaluation system got a decisive push in 1990 when the court of audit published a government-wide study of evaluation practices in the executive branch of the central government. This triggered activities of government and parliament in which systematic and periodic evaluation research was envisaged as a crucial instrument for reviewing the effectiveness and efficiency of policy programmes. In practical terms it was concluded that the evaluation function needed to be installed in the existing departmental frameworks and structures in order to optimize the linkage to existing policy and budgeting processes (Bemelmans-Videc 2002, p. 98). There has been a trend towards developing and refining performance indicators for a widening range of public services. Autonomous public bodies (ZBOs) as well as agencies are obligated to present data on costs and benefits annually (see Leeuw, Chapter 6 in this volume).

The National Court of Audit (*Algemene Rekenkamer*) has an important advocate and actor in external evaluation. Over the years it has repeatedly carried out government-wide investigations as well as performance audits and occasional meta-analyses of evaluations ('meta-evaluation'; see Leeuw, Chapter 6 in this volume).

Germany

Germany has been a latecomer to the international NPM-inspired modernization movement. The reason for this time lag can be seen in the country's specific 'starting conditions'. First, the traditional federal-decentralized constitutional fabric, characterized by a politically and functionally strong local government level, as well as the traditional principle of subsidiarity (leaving the delivery of social services largely to non-public welfare organizations), has made key NPM concepts (such as agencification and outsourcing) appear less pertinent and less necessary. Furthermore, in the *Rechtsstaat* tradition the salience of legal regulation and judicial review of public administration have been institutional, cultural and normative impediments to an easy access and adoption of private-sector-derived managerialism. Last but not least, Germany's multi-level administrative system has had a good record of administrative reforms over time, including the reform push of the 1960s and 1970s (see Wollmann 2000a, pp. 920 ff. and in Chapter 7 of this volume). The dramatic shift and overture to NPM-inspired concepts in the early 1990s was triggered largely by the mounting budgetary problems arising from the financial costs of German unification and from the need to meet the Maastricht parameters.

Since the early 1990s local governments have taken the conceptual and practical lead under the guidance of the so called 'New Steering Model' which, drawing on NPM managerialism and, in part, on pertinent Dutch experience, was formulated and propagated by a municipality-financed consulting institute (KGSt). A growing number of municipalities and counties have introduced budgeting, cost-to-achievement accounting, and in some cases accrual accounting and controlling – with a focus on (internal) performance management tools. It is only recently that outsourcing has gained momentum.

Somewhat later the *Länder* have entered the reform trail, exhibiting the typical variances among them. In some *Länder* traditional schemes of decentralisation and of reorganizing the regional (meso-)level have been adopted. In most *Länder* variants of internal performance management have been addressed. Finally, in late 1999, the federal government turned to administrative reforms, revolving also largely around performance management concepts.

Concerning the speed and direction of public-sector reforms, two features of Germany's politico-administrative system should be considered. First, at each of the three government levels the actors operate quite independently on administrative reform issues – vertically as well as horizontally – which fosters the traditional 'incrementalist' reform style. Second, administrative reforms have been an 'executive' issue, while the parliaments have shown little interest – perhaps regarding and respecting administrative reforms as an executive prerogative.

Following and mirroring the adoption of managerialist concepts and components, variants of management-oriented and output-based internal monitoring and (information feedback-related) controlling procedures have been extensively introduced. Furthermore, intermunicipal benchmarking, through inter-municipal cooperation, has been put in place.

External evaluation so far has hardly been undertaken at any level. This may be explained by the short time that has passed since the introduction of the NPM-inspired reform measures. But it also reflects that neither the federal and *Länder* courts of audit nor their parliaments have so far shown interest in initiating and conducting evaluation of the public-sector reforms underway. The scant attention that the evaluation of public-sector reforms has so far elicited in Germany contrasts with the observation that the evaluation of 'substantive' policies has played a significant role in Germany since the 'first wave' of the 1960s (see Wagner and Wollmann 1986; Derlien 1990). Germany has continued to have policy evaluation at a fairly high and stable level (see Wollmann 1989), especially since the early 1990s, because of EU structuring funding in East Germany and of ensuing evaluation (see Derlien 2002, pp. 84 ff.).[18]

Mention should finally be made, however, of the (applied) social science and public policy research that academic (mostly university-based) research groups and institutions have conducted on public-sector reforms measures – with a focus on the local government level and on the institution-building dimension of reforms (in the implementation research stance) rather than on outputs (see Wollmann, Chapter 7 in this volume).

Italy

Italy is another example of a Continental European latecomer to NPM-inspired public-sector reforms. Throughout the 1990s, in several legislative waves, a host of reform laws and decrees were passed in an attempt to reform Italy's political and administrative arenas (including privatization, organizational and personnel reforms, and introduction of management tools) in an intentionally radical manner (see Lippi, Chapter 8 in this volume). Well into the 1990s, public-sector reforms had been largely impeded by the Italian legalist tradition, with its body of administrative laws and its priority of legal review over economic efficiency (see Stame 2002). Moreover, reforms were blocked by party competition. In the early 1990s, the politico-economic context changed dramatically. The corruption scandals which broke after 1992 led to crisis for the country's political elites. The mounting budgetary problems were aggravated by the perceived need to meet the Maastricht parameters as a precondition of becoming a founding member of the European monetary union. Thus, there was mounting pressure for stringent public-sector reforms. Since the early 1990s, NPM-guided reforms have been on Italy's political agenda.

The first major modernization push came in 1993 with the newly formed (post-scandal) government of 'technocrats' under Prime Minister Ciampi and under Minister of Public Function Sabino Cassese, a reformist law professor. A 1993 decree, with explicit NPM references,[19] introduced performance management (*controllo di gestione*) and prescribed the formation of evaluation units (*nuclei di valutazione*) in each public agency. In 1997 and 1998, a set of legislative acts, the 'Bassanini laws', were passed by the centre-left Ulivo (Olive tree) coalition (under Franco Bassanini, again a reformist law professor, heading the Ministry of Public Function). These laws pushed for the streamlining of the administration and for the realization of administrative federalism (see Stame 2002). So far the modernization of political and administrative structures appears to have advanced furthest at the local government level (see Lippi, Chapter 8 in this volume).

Following the legislative introduction in 1993, the prescribed performance control (*controllo di gestione*) has been realized and put in place by various public agencies,[20] with performance indicators varying widely for each sector. Many local authorities have changed their operations by adopting management tools, such as result-oriented management control (see Lippi, Chapter 8 in this volume). Although the court of audit (*Corte di Conti*) was instructed, by legislation, to take up performance auditing, it has largely retained its traditional judiciary orientation and profile.

Policy evaluation at large saw a real upsurge in Italy during the 1990s, particularly resulting from the spree of external evaluation conducted on the European Structural Funds (Italy is a prime beneficiary of European funding; see Stame 2002). In the field of public-sector reforms, however, external evaluation so far has seldom been undertaken.[21] 'Neither the scientific community nor the institutions have sought to evaluate public-sector reform policy' (Lippi, Chapter 8 in this volume).

Japan

While Japan is another latecomer to NPM-guided public-sector reforms the country saw some noticeable changes during the major public-sector reforms of the 1980s (see Chapter 9 in this volume). In reaction to the oil price shocks of the 1970s, in 1981 the (Second) Provisional Administrative Reform Commission (SPARC)[22] was set up; SPARC put forth a number of reform recommendations, particularly the controversial privatization of the Japan National Railways. Subsequently a series of Administrative Reform Commissions (ARCs) was established in order to monitor the reform process. In early 1993, the reform movement picked up momentum. In 1995, the Decentralization Promotion Act emphasized decentralization by strengthening local governments.

Following the national elections of 1996 and the formation of a new government under Ryutaro Hashimoto, public-sector reform policy shifted conspicuously into high gear. A reform commission was set up which, unusually enough, was chaired by the prime minister himself. The commission's recommendations related to a broad spectrum of reforms, including strengthening the cabinet (vis-à-vis the previous 'autonomy' of the ministerial bureaucracy), reorganizing the central government, reforming the civil service and policy evaluation system as well as pronouncedly NPM-inspired components, such as agencification and performance management – with explicit borrowing and 'importing' from US and UK experience (see Muramatsu and Matsunami, Chapter 9 in this volume).[23] Various factors led to the dramatic shift in public-sector reforms under the Hashimoto commission. First of all, it was a reaction to the mounting budgetary crisis which followed the burst of the bubble economy (see Chapter 9 in this volume). Second, mounting criticism of the inflexibility and reform-resistant inertia of the government's bureaucracy (almost forming a 'government within the government') finally came to a point. As a major consequence, some 60 Independent Administrative Institutions (IAIs) were created to operate under a 'sunset' – that is, a pre-set 'termination' – formula and to monitor and report on their performance on the basis of performance criteria.

The Basic Law on the Administrative Reform of the Central Government of 1998[24] was intended to reorganize central ministries and agencies – particularly by institutionalizing and employing evaluation – by the year 2001. Conceptually and especially instrumentally, two stages of evaluation are stipulated. First, inside each ministry and agency the establishment of an evaluation unit was prescribed; furthermore, it was mandated that every government agency should self-evaluate the policies and programmes under its jurisdiction in terms of effectiveness, efficiency and cost-benefit analyses both prior to and following the enactment of the programmes. Second, within the Ministry of General Affairs – which was to play a crucial role in the development of a evaluation system – a 'Committee on Policy Evaluation and Evaluation of Independent Administrative Institutes' was designed to fulfil a government-wide, interorganizational coordinating and 'meta-evaluating' function (see Yamaya 2002, p. 344).

While the already existing Management and Coordination Agency continues to monitor the efficiency and economy of government, the Board of Audit (that is, the court of audit) is still largely concerned with checking the budgetary correctness of government activities. Although Japan has recently moved conspicuously towards institutionalizing internal evaluation (implementation still is in an incipient stage; see Yamaya 2002, p. 344), external evaluation is still lacking. 'Contractual research' still has a mostly prospective (ex ante) consultancy character – the lion's share is carried out by the commercial consulting sector and research firms (so-called 'think tanks'; see Wollmann 2002a, p. 11577 with references). This also reflects the reserve and distance Japan's university-based social science has traditionally exhibited with regard to applied, or evaluative, research (see Wollmann 1983; Watanuki 1991).

In sum, notwithstanding the rapid moves which Japan has recently made towards evaluation in public-sector reforms, she has much room for development.[25]

Brazil

A caveat should be made when considering Brazil as a Latin American case in point. On the one hand, it shows the most interesting (and politically and geographically, the most relevant) case in the region. On the other hand, being more advanced than the other Latin American countries (with the exception of Chile) in terms of the matters under discussion here, Brazil is not typical or representative (for more comprehensive overviews, see Monteiro, Chapter 10 in this volume and Bresser Pereira 2001).

Since colonial times Latin Americans have been subject to a kind of state–society relationship heavily based on bureaucratization, centralism, formalism, fiscalism and authoritarianism (see Monteiro, Chapter 10 in this volume). Leaving aside the historical peculiarities of administrative development in Latin America which lie in the colonial past, reference should be made to the military regimes of the 1960s that brought forth 'bureaucratic-military states' whose policies were characterized by an internationalization of the economy and by centralization, 'statization' (*'étatization'*) and authoritarian control of the public sector. Since the 1980s Brazil's development has, like that of other Latin American countries, been marked by two features: to wit, the return of the country to democracy and a deepening budgetary crisis (triggered by the peso crisis in Mexico). Reflecting the reintroduction of democracy, Brazil's 1988 constitution aimed at a far-reaching decentralization of the country by devolving political and administrative responsibilities to the regional and local levels (see Bresser Pereira 2001, p. 152). At the same time, in reaction to the 'first generation' reform concepts and demands of the World Bank, the country undertook the deregulation and privatization of public enterprises (see Monteiro, Chapter 10 in this volume). NPM-specific modernization concepts were not considered at that point, apparently also due to the influence of the World Bank which, at that time, embraced a 'sequencing' strategy according to which developing countries should first complete civil service and (Weberian, as it were) bureaucratic reforms before engaging in NPM-inspired management reforms (see Bresser Pereira 2001, p. 147 with references).

Since 1995 Brazil has seen a second wave of public-sector reforms in which NPM components have been adopted. Key concepts were laid down in the *Plano Diretor da Reforma do Estado* (Guidelines to State Reform) under the Cardoso presidency. The main elements were a broad spectrum of goals, including institutional adjustments of the public sector, checks and balances among state powers, strengthening of citizen participation, decentralization and introduction of NPM components: control by contracted outcomes, managed competition and social control (Bresser Pereira 2001, p. 158). These concepts were turned into constitutional language by the constitutional amendment of 1998.[26]

Under the programmatic heading 'Entrepreneurial Management' evaluation has made its entry to Brazil's administrative system (Bresser Pereira 2001, p. 161). The process of evaluation has come to be directed by the technical staff of the Ministry of Planning, Budget and Management – the key player in the evolving evaluation system. Divided into three steps, evaluation begins with self-evaluation (conducted by the program managers themselves) of expected or 'contracted' results. Then it goes on to a second phase, in which programme performance is to be set against the President's Strategic Directives and to Sector-Strategic Directives. The final step is an overall analysis by the Ministry on the programme's performance. In this institutional and instrumental design, evaluation has been observed to be a tool with which the central government imposes and enforces institutional re-forms. 'The generation of goals, objectives, indexes and indicators typically follows a top-down logic according to which managers have to adopt (and adapt themselves to) externally-defined standards' (Monteiro, Chapter 10 in this volume). Hence these evaluation tools have been used largely in internal (in-house) evaluation; external evaluation seldom has been commissioned or conducted.

3. Public-sector reforms in comparative perspective: convergence or divergence?

In taking up the much-debated question as to whether the trajectories of public-sector modernization pursued in the various countries show convergence or divergence, the empirical evidence is somewhat ambivalent (see also Wollmann 2003). On the one hand, the sample of countries considered in this volume (and beyond) suggests that NPM-inspired public-sector modernization and 'twinned' evaluation are on a 'victorious march' throughout the OECD world. This suggests convergence.[27] On the other hand, significant differences between the countries exist with respect to the timing, packaging and mix of reform concepts and components – whether NPM-related or 'traditional' – hinting at divergence.[28]

The divergence hypothesis becomes even more compelling when it is assumed that a country's trajectory of institutional development is greatly shaped by factors which are deeply rooted – even in a 'path-dependent' manner – in the tradition and history of the country. Without further unfolding and substantiating this argument, it should suffice to single out two factors that plausibly make a difference in shaping the divergence of trajectories between countries and cultural groups (see, for example, Wollmann 2000b, 2000c with references).

One set of factors is evident in the juxtaposition of the *Rechtsstaat* and public interest tradition. The Continental European countries are still based on the *Rechtsstaat* tradition, in which the activitities of public administration are for the most part regulated by legal provisions and subject to juridical review. This puts a structural limit to the relevance of management tools, such as contracting and outsourcing. By contrast, in the Anglo-Saxon countries public administration is seen as being guided by 'public interest' principles and as being rooted in the Common Law tradition in which – unlike the Roman Law tradition of the Continental European countries – no divide between state and society or between public and private law is recognized. Hence, the concepts of contractualism, marketization and managerialism have a much easier cognitive and normative entry and acceptance (see Pollitt and Bouckaert 2000, pp. 52 ff, Wollmann 2000b, pp. 4 ff).

Another pivotal factor is the type of local government, particularly in its political and administrative functions in the country's government system. In countries that have a politically and functionally strong local government system (such as Germany and the Scandinavian countries), the multi-function local government model is likely to be maintained, if not strengthened, thus limiting extensive use of (NPM-inspired) outsourcing of public functions. By contrast, in countries with politically and functionally weak local governments (such as the UK or New Zealand), the outsourcing and 'quangoization' of public functions may be widespread.

Referring to the ideal-type exaggeration in which Johan Olsen has juxtaposed the 'Supermarket State' and the 'Sovereign State' models of government (1988), two scenarios can be depicted. First, one might discern a type of public-sector trajectory in which the main function of the (programmatically 'lean') public sector is simply to facilitate public services, and the delivery of the services should essentially rely on marketization, outsourcing and on 'one-function' agencies – marginalizing the traditional democratically-elected and politically accountable local self-government. Some of these (ideal-type) features of Olsen's 'Supermarket State' can be identified, in real terms, in Anglo-Saxon countries.

By contrast, another pattern may be seen (again with some ideal-type exaggeration) in a public-sector trajectory in which, despite its absorption of significant neo-liberal and NPM impulses to increase the cost-efficiency, the state's main function continues to be legal regulation and application; and in which the bulk of public tasks continue to be carried out by (a still Weberian) public administration, primarily on the decentralized level of multi-function local self-government. These (ideal-type) features of Olsen's 'Sovereign State' can be said to characterize the politico-administrative system of Germany and, perhaps of Sweden (and the other Scandinavian countries) – with an even stronger emphasis on decentralized multi-functional local government (see Wollmann 2003).

4. Evaluation in public-sector reform in international perspective

The introduction, institutionalization and employment of the evaluation function (in the broad sense) has, on the one hand, shown significant commonalities among the countries. On the other hand, considerable differences in the timing, the profile and packaging of the evaluative variants and approaches are apparent.

Internal evaluation in public-sector reforms – setting off a 'third wave' of evaluation

Perhaps the most striking and salient common trend can be seen in the new conceptual focus, strategic emphasis and institutional gravity of the goal-oriented, performance-related and result-based conduct of the administrative activities and operations. During the 'planning phase' of the 1960s and 1970s, it is true, the evaluation function was conceptually guided by the idea of a 'policy cycle' (goal setting, implementation, evaluation) in which it played a crucial role in the policy-making process. But evaluation was functionally and operationally aimed at identifying the goal attainment of public policies rather than at a permanent monitoring and feedback reporting as an integral part of the 'public management package' (see Furubo and Sandahl 2002a, pp. 20 ff.). It is the strategic importance of performance management and of the permanent monitoring and feedback reporting as a primarily internal and self-evaluative operation that gives a new dimension, quality and gravity to NPM-inspired evaluation: the 'third wave' in the development of evaluation.

Reflecting this intrinsic 'twinning' with performance *management and performance indicators (PI)*, approaches to internal evaluation have progressed furthest in countries that have been front runners in public management. This applies to the Anglo-Saxon countries, but also to the Netherlands (with a traditional pronounced auditing tradition) and to a lesser degree to Sweden as well (where the time-honoured state agencies lend themselves to performance-orientation). In countries with a pronounced Continental European *Rechtsstaat* and legal regulation tradition that have been latecomers to adopting NPM, it may be this very *Rechtsstaat* tradition (and the significant role the application of law still plays in the day-to-day activities of public administration) that puts an institutional, cultural and normative limit to performance management, and hence to concomitant forms of internal evaluation.

External evaluation in public-sector reforms – still lagging behind, but gaining momentum

The development and state of *external* evaluation on public-sector reforms (that is, of evaluation initiated or conducted by institutions outside the operating unit) exhibits considerable cross-country variation that appears to be influenced by different sets of actors and factors.

External evaluation of public-sector reforms in terms of methodologically rigorous (social science-based) evaluation research is still more or less a rarity throughout all countries, particularly with a comprehensive mandate.

Yet evaluative efforts which are directed, in a 'meta-evaluation' stance, at externally assessing (and comparing) the performance reports of public agencies based on internal evaluation (monitoring) procedures are increasingly being undertaken, particularly by institutions of the auditing type and provenance. The performance assessment which has recently been put in place in the U.K. under the Best Value regime (revolving around the Audit Commission which reviews the performance of the local authorities on the basis of manifold indicators and criteria) is the most conceptually and instrumentally most advanced (and, it should be recalled, most centralist) example yet of a combined application of external and internal evaluation. In addition, the Best Value evaluation machinery has been given teeth by allowing central government to 'reward' or 'punish' the local authorities according to their high or low performance quality. Another telling example is offered by Japan where central agencies have recently been created which operate under a 'sunset' formula according to which they will be continued or terminated depending on the results of internal as well as external evaluation.

Institutions within the executive

Whereas on the 'demand side', the operating administrative units (agencies, divisions and sections with sectoral ministries) often show little interest in inviting and allowing external evaluation and outside evaluators to 'penetrate' their internal operations, executive government actors with cross-cutting (coordination, planning, budgetary, planning, etc.) interests are more readily disposed and eager to initiate and conduct evaluation of the activities of sectoral ministries and agencies, including their administrative reform measures. In some countries (such as Australia and New Zealand) the Minister of Finance has been charged with promoting evaluation, including 'meta-evaluating' of the (internal) evaluative activities of sectoral ministries; in others a ministry or agency explicitly put in charge of engineering the administrative reform (such as the Ministry of Planning and Budget in Brazil or a newly created unit within the Ministry of General Affairs in Japan) performs this function.

Parliament

The United States Congress has traditionally promoted the (external) evaluation of policies, as a crucial instrument of its scrutinizing function, by passing new legislation along with evaluation requirements. But in some parliamentary (Westminster) systems, particularly Australia's, parliament has taken an active part in external evaluation. In other countries, such as in Germany, parliaments have, in the past, called for the evaluation of 'substantive' policies (environmental protection, economic promotion, etc. policies), but so far have paid little attention to the evaluation of administrative reform measures, probably because they traditionally have regarded administrative reforms as an executive prerogative.

Court of audit

In most countries the court of audit has moved in the direction of policy evaluation, including administrative reform measures In the USA, the General Accounting Office (GAO) is designed to support Congress, but in 'parliamentary' countries that have moved towards the GAO model, such as Sweden or the Netherlands, the courts of audit have been explicitly assigned, or have assumed, an advocacy role in initiating, conducting or monitoring ('meta-evaluating') evaluation of public-sector reforms. In some countries, such as Japan, the function of the court of audit has only recently been redefined accordingly. In other countries, such as Germany and Italy, the courts of audit have largely retained their traditional focus on scrutinizing the budgetary compliance and bookkeeping of administrative activities, and have refrained from reviewing performance and policies.

International actors and discourses

In most countries the incipient moves towards external evaluation came with the advent of the NPM modernization discourse, which in turn was strongly influenced by the ongoing international debate and practice. In some countries, the introduction of policy evaluation and of evaluation of public-sector reforms was clearly promoted by international or supra-national organizations (such as the European Union structural funds in the case of Italy, see Stame 2002, and Lippi, Chapter 8 in this volume) and transnational conceptual borrowing and learning (as in the case of Japan, see Muramatsu and Matsunami, Chapter 9 in this volume).

Scientific/research community
On the supply side, the extent of external evaluation was also influenced by the degree to which researchers, whether university-based or commercial, have embarked upon forming an active and assertive evaluation research community advocating the need for methodologically sound and intellectually independent policy evaluation. The recent expansion and activities of national as well as international evaluation societies express the growing interest and readiness of reseachers and analysts worldwide to engage in professional evaluation and 'contractual research' (see Wollmann 2002a).

It needs to be pointed out, however, that, particularly with regard to external evaluation, there is still a glaring discrepancy between the claim of transparancy of political and administrative processes and activities and the still low profile of (external) evaluation of public-sector reforms (see also Pollitt and Bouckaert, Chapter 2 in this volume).

References

Barzelay, M. (1997), 'Central audit institutions and performance auditing: A comparative analysis of organizational strategies in the OECD', in *Governance*, vol. 10, no.3, pp. 235–60.

Bemelmans-Videc, M. L. (2002), 'Evaluation in The Netherlands 1990–2000: Consolidation and expansion', in Jan-Eric Furubo, Ray C. Rist and Rolf Sandahl (eds), *International Atlas of Evaluation*, New Brunswick and London: Transaction, pp. 115–28.

Bresser Pereira, Luiz Carlos (2001), 'New Public Management Reform: now on the Latin America reform agenda, and yet...', in *Revista Internacional de Estudos Políticos*, Special issue [September], 143–65.

Cabinet Office (2000), *Adding it Up: Improving Analysis and Modelling in Central Government*, London: Central Office of Information.

Christensen,Tom and Per Lægreid (2001), 'A transformative perspective on administrative reforms', in Tom Christensen and Per Lægreid (eds), *New Public Management*, Aldershot: Ashgate, pp. 13–39.

Department of the Environment, Transport and the Regions (DETR) (2001), *Improving Local Public Services: Final Evaluation of the Best Value Pilot Programme*, London: DETR.

Department of Transport, Local Government and the Regions (DTLR) (2001), *Strong Local Leadership – Quality Public Services,*(London: DTLR.

Derlien, Hans-Ulrich (1990), 'Genesis and structure of evaluation efforts', in Ray Rist (ed.), *Program Evaluation and the Management of Government*, New Brunswick and London: Transaction, pp. 147–76.

Derlien, Hans-Ulrich (2002), Policy evaluation in Germany: Institutional continuation and sectoral activation', in Jan-Eric Furubo, Ray C. Rist and Rolf Sandahl (eds), *International Atlas of Evaluation*, New Brunswick and London: Transaction, pp. 74–91.

Derlien, Hans-Ulrich and Ray C. Rist (2002), 'Policy evaluation in international comparison', in Jan-Eric Furubo, Ray C. Rist and Rolf Sandahl (eds), *International Atlas of Evaluation*, New Brunswick and London: Transaction, pp. 439–55.

Dolowitz, D. and D. Marsh (1996), 'Who learns from whom? A review of policy transfer literature', *Political Studies*, 343–55.

Furubo, Jan-Eric, Ray C. Rist and Rolf Sandahl (eds) (2002), *International Atlas of Evaluation*, New Brunswick and London: Transaction.

Furubo, Jan-Eric and Rolf Sandahl (2002a), 'A diffusion-perspective on global developments in evaluation', in Jan-Eric Furubo, Ray C. Rist and Rolf Sandahl (eds), *International Atlas of Evaluation*, New Brunswick and London: Transaction, pp. 1–26.

Furubo, Jan-Eric and Rolf Sandahl (2002b), 'Coordinated pluralism – the Swedish case', in Jan-Eric Furubo, Ray C. Rist and Rolf Sandahl (eds), *International Atlas of Evaluation*, New Brunswick and London: Transaction, pp. 115–27.

Gray, Andrew and Bill Jenkins (1992), 'Implementing evaluation: Lessons from the UK', in J. Mayne et al. (eds), *Advancing Public Policy Evaluation*, Amsterdam: Elsevier, pp. 59–68.

Hall, Peter A. (1993), 'Policy paradigms, social learning and the state. The case of economic policy making in Britain', *Comparative Politics*, 275–90.

Halligan, John (2001), 'The process of reform in the era of public sector transformation: Directive and retrospective', in Tom Christensen and Per Lægreid (eds), *New Public Management: The Transformation of Ideas and Practice*, Ashgate: Aldershot, pp. 73–89.

Hood, Christopher (1991), 'A public management for all seasons?', *Public Administration*, 69[1], 3–19.

Karl, T. L. and P. C. Schmitter (1991), 'Modes of transition in Latin America, Southern and Eastern Europe', *International Social Science Journal*, 43, 269–84.

Kickert, Walter and R. In't Veld (1995), 'National government, governance, and administration', in Walter Kickert and F. van Vught (eds), *Public Policy and Administration Science in the Netherlands*, London: Harvester Wheatsheaf, pp. 45–62.

Levine, Robert A. (1981), 'Program evaluation and policy analysis in western nations', in Robert A. Levine, Marian A. Solomon, Gerd-Michael Hellstern and Hellmut Wollmann (eds), *Evaluation Research and Practice*, Beverly Hills and London: Sage, pp. 12–27.

Lippi, A. (2000), 'One theory, many practices. Institutional allomorphism in Italian reorganization of local government', in S. Gherardi and B. Jacobsson (eds), 'Managerialism as the Latin of our times: Reforming Italian public sector organisations', *Scandinavian Journal of Management*, 4.

Olsen, J. P. (1988), 'Administrative reform and theories of organization', in C. Campbell and Guy Peters (eds), *Organizing Governance: Governing Organizations*, Pittsburgh, US: University of Pittsburgh Press, pp. 233–54.

Osborne, D. and T. Gaebler (1992), *Reinventing Government: How the Entrepreneurial Spirit is Transforming the Public Sector*, Reading, US: Addison Wesley.

Peters, Guy 1995, 'Political institutions: old and new', in: Goddin, Robert and Hans-Dieter Klingemann (eds.), *A New Handbook on Political Science*, Oxford: Oxford University Press, pp. 205–20.

Pollitt, Christopher (1995), 'Justification by works or by faith? Evaluating the New Public Management', *Evaluation*, 1[2 (October)], 133–54.

Pollitt, Christopher and Geert Bouckaert (2000), *Public Management Reform. A Comparative Analysis*, Oxford: Oxford University Press.

Premfors, R. (1998), 'Reshaping the democratic state: Swedish experiences in a comparative perspective', *Public Administration*, 76[1], 141–59.

Rebora, G. (1999), *La valutazione dei risultati nelle amministrazioni pubbliche*, Milan: Guerini e associati.

Rist, Ray C. and Kathleen L. Paliokas (2002), 'The rise and fall (and rise again?) of the evaluation function in the US government', in Jan-Eric Furubo, Ray C. Rist and Rolf Sandahl (eds), *International Atlas of Evaluation*, New Brunswick and London: Transaction, pp. 225–45.

Rockman, Bert (2001), 'Politics by other means: Administrative reform in the United States', *International Review of Public Administration*, 6[2], 1–13.

Rose, Richard (1993), *Lesson-Drawing in Public Policy*, Chatham, US: Chatham House.

Sabatier, Paul (1987), 'Knowledge, policy-oriented learning and policy change. An advocacy coalition approach', in *Knowledge: Creation, Diffusion, Utilization*, pp. 649–92.

Sandahl, Rolf (1992), 'Evaluation at the Swedish national audit bureau', in J. Mayne et al. (eds), *Advancing Public Policy Evaluation*, Amsterdam: Elsevier, pp. 115–22.

Sanderson, Ian (2000), 'Evaluation in Complex Policy Systems', in: *Evaluation*, vol. 6, no. 4, pp. 433–54.

Schmidt, Vivien A. (2000), 'Values and discourse in the politics of adjustment', in Fritz W. Scharpf and Vivien Schmidt (eds), *Welfare and Work in the Open Economy*, vol. 1, Oxford, UK: Oxford University Press, pp. 229 ff.

Stame, Nicoletta (2002), 'Evaluation in Italy: an inverted sequence from performance management to program evaluation?', in Jan-Eric Furubo, Ray C. Rist and Rolf Sandahl (eds), *International Atlas of Evaluation*, New Brunswick and London: Transaction, pp. 273–90.

Stillman, Richard J. (1998), *Creating the American State*, Tuscaloosa and London: University of Alabama Press.

Vedung, Evert (1992), 'Five observations on evaluation in Sweden', in J. Mayne, M. L. Bemelmans-Videc, J. Hudson and R. Conner (eds), *Advancing Public Policy Evaluation*, Amsterdam: North-Holland, pp. 71–87.

Vedung, Evert (1997), *Public Policy and Program Evaluation*, New Brunswick: Transaction.

Wagner, Peter and Hellmut Wollmann (1986), 'Fluctuations in the development of evaluation research: Do "regime shifts" matter?' *International Social Science Journal*, 108, 205–18.

Watanuki, J. (1991), 'The impact of social sciences on the process of development in Japan', in Peter Wagner, Carol Weiss, Björn Wittrock and Hellmut Wollmann (eds), *Social Science and Modern States*, Cambridge: Cambridge University Press, pp. 221–29.

Wilson, D. and Chris Game (2002), '*Local Government in the United Kingdom*', 3rd edition, Houndmills: Palgrave.

Wittrock, Björn; Wagner, Peter; Wollmann, Hellmut (1991), 'Social science and the modern state: policy knowledge and the political institutions in Western Europe and the United States', in: Wagner, Peter; Weiss, Carol; Wittrock, Björn; Wollmann, Hellmut (eds), *Social Science and Modern States*, Cambridge: University Press, pp. 28 –51.

Wollmann, Hellmut (1983), *Development and State of Policy Research in Japan*, Tokyo: National Institute for the Advancement of Research (NIRA).

Wollmann, Hellmut (1989), 'Policy analysis in West Germany's federal government: A case of unfinished governmental and administrative modernisation', *Governance*, 2[3], 233–66.

Wollmann, Hellmut (1996), 'Verwaltungsmodernisierung: Ausgangsbedingungen, Reformanläufe und aktuelle Modernisierungsdiskurse', in Christoph Reichard, and Hellmut Wollmann (eds), *Kommunalverwaltung im Modernisierungsschub?*, Basel: Birkhäuser, pp. 1 ff.

Wollmann, Hellmut (1997), 'Institution building and decentralization in formerly socialist countries, the cases of Poland, Hungary, and East Germany', in: *Government and Policy*, vol. 15, pp. 463–80.

Wollmann, Hellmut (2000a), 'Local government modernization in Germany: Between incrementalism and reform waves', *Public Administration*, 78[4], 915–36.

Wollmann, Hellmut (2000b), 'Comparing institutional development in Britain and Germany: (Persistent) divergence or (progressing) convergence?', in Hellmut Wollmann and Eckhard Schröter (eds), *Comparing Public Sector Reform in Britain and Germany*, Aldershot: Ashgate, pp. 1–26.

Wollmann, Hellmut (2000c), 'The development and present state of local government in England and Germany', in Hellmut Wollmann and Eckhard Schröter (eds). *Comparing Public Sector Reform in Britain and Germany*, Aldershot: Ashgate, pp. 107–31.

Wollmann, Hellmut (2000d), 'Local government systems. From historic divergence towards convergence? Great Britain, France, and Germany as comparative cases in point', *Government and Policy*, 18, 33–55.

Wollmann, H. (2001a), 'Germany's trajectory of public sector modernization: continuities and discontinuities', *Policy & Politics*, 29[2], 151–69.

Wollmann, Hellmut (ed.) (2001b), 'Evaluating public sector reforms', special issue of *Revista Internacional de Estudios Políticos*,127–43.

Wollmann, Hellmut (2002a), 'Contractual research and policy knowledge', *International Encyclopedia of the Social and Behavioral Sciences*, 5, 11574–11578.

Wollmann, Hellmut (2002b), 'Verwaltungspolitik und Evaluierung: Ansätze, Phasen und Beispiele im Ausland und in Deutschland, Evaluation und New Public Management', *Zeitschrift für Evaluation*, 1, 75–101.

Wollmann, Hellmut (2002c), 'Verwaltungspolitische Reformdiskurse und -verläufe im internationalen Vergleich', in Klaus König (ed.), *Deutsche Verwaltung an der Wende zum 21. Jahrhundert*, Baden-Baden: Nomos, pp. 489–525.

Wollmann, Hellmut (2003), 'Policy change in public sector reforms in cross-country perspective. Between convergence and divergence', in: Munshi, S. et al. (eds), *Good Governance in Democratic Societies: Cross-cultural Perspectives*, London, New Dehli etc.: Sage (forthcoming).

Yamaya, Kiyoshi (2002), 'The art of policy evaluation in Japan', in Jan-Eric Furubo, Ray C. Rist and Rolf Sandahl (eds), *International Atlas of Evaluation*, New Brunswick and London: Transaction, pp. 337–55.

Notes

1. For its ('historical', cultural, actor-centred, etc.) variants see, for example, Peters 1995.
2. See, for example, Wollmann 1997 (on institutional transformation of local government structures in post-socialist countries). In this context, mention should be made particularly of the concept of institutional 'legacies' and 'path-dependencies' which was first applied to the (institutional) transition and transformation in Latin America and to the former socialist Central East European countries, see Karl and Schmitter 1991.
3. For similar conceptual schemes see Pollitt and Bouckaert 2000, Chapter 2 in this volume, and Christensen and Lægreid 2001 for an explication of their 'transformative' approach.
4. See Note 2, above.
5. See Schmidt 2000, pp. 232 ff.
6. On the concept of discourse and of discourse analysis, see Wittrock, Wagner and Wollmann 1991, pp. 43 ff; Hall 1993; Schmidt 2000, pp. 229 ff. On the application of discourse analysis on public-sector reform, see Wollmann 1996, pp. 21 ff; and Wollmann 2002c.
7. On the concepts of (policy) learning, see Rose 1993; and Dolowitz and Marsh 1996.

8. On the concept of 'maturity' of evaluation culture and an attempt to grasp it by means of a nine-indicator scale, see Furubo and Sandahl 2002a, pp. 7 ff.
9. See Pollitt and Bouckaert 2000, p. 274: 'Conservative ministers tended to take the line that reform was essential, and self-evidently desirable, and that formal, public evaluation might prove a delay and distraction'.
10. Allan Schick concluded that although the reforms were 'more comprehensive and rigorous than those introduced in other countries, they have been neither complete nor perfect' (quoted in Halligan, Chapter 5 of this volume).
11. See Halligan, Chapter 5 in this volume: '[Parliamentary] committees have produced over 3000 reports covering the past three decades [that] have come to provide an integral component of the evaluation system'.
12. This ranking was made by Furubo and Sandahl by formulating nine indicators and by filling them (qualitatively) on the basis of available information (from the 21 country reports in their volume). See Furubo and Sandahl 2002a, pp. 7 ff.
13. See Dwight Waldo 1980: 'We did not *want* a European-style state, we did not *need* a European style state, and we did not *develop* a European-style state' (quoted from Stillman 1998, p. 172).
14. This is corroborated by the Furubo/Sandahl ranking according to which the USA is still 'number one' on the 'evaluative culture' score (see Furubo and Sandahl 2002a, p. 10).
15. Before 1998, ESV was a part of RRV, but became a governmental agency in its own right in mid-1998.
16. For an early assessment, see Levine 1981: 'Evaluation is ... endemic throughout the Swedish system'.
17. In Furubo/Sandahl's ranking of 21 countries Sweden is among the 'top five'on the evaluative culture scale (see Furubo and Sandahl 2002a, p. 10).
18. It should not come as a surprise that on the Furubo/Sandahl scale on 'evaluative culture' in 21 countries (see previous note), Germany is in the upper third, that is, in seventh place (see Furubo and Sandahl 2002a, p. 10).
19. See Stame 2002, note 5: 'Most of these reforms... are under the direct inspiration, sometimes even wording, of their English prototypes. The famous "efficiency, effectiveness, economy" (3Es) principle became a refrain of public managers'.
20. In research on the implementation of the 1993 decree Rebora found (see Rebora 1999) 'that, in general, Ministries have created a system of internal control through consulting ... local governments have preferred a mix of internal control and consulting' (quoted from Stame 2002).
21. It should be remembered, however, that it was a comprehensive (highly critical) evaluation-type report (named 'Giannini report' after its main author) on the state of public administration, commissioned by Parliament and published in 1979, that broke the ground for radical administrative reforms.
22. SPARC was composed of business, labour and academic representatives as well as former high-ranking civil servants.
23. See Muramatsu and Matsunami, Chapter 9 in this volume: 'The secretariat of this commission studied [US vice-president] Al Gore's Government Performance Programme, the British program of evaluation by Public Service Agreements (PSAs) and later the United States Government Performance and Result Act (GRPA)'.
24. Law No. 103 of 1998. For details see Yamaha 2002, pp. 341 ff.

25. Hence, in Furubo/Sandahl's aforementioned ranking of 21 countries in which, on the basis of 6 indicators, the 'advancedness' ('maturity') of the country's 'evaluative culture' is (tentatively) assessed (see note 18), Japan comes out at the very bottom.

26. 'The constitutional amendment played an important part in public-management reform, because, besides allowing for the reform, it roused a national debate that changed traditional views of public administration' (Bresser Pereira 2001, p. 158). At the same time the responsiblity for the reforms was transferred from the (small) Ministry of Federal Administration and Reform of State to the larger (and more powerful) Ministry of Planning, Budget and Management.

27. See Thoenig, Chapter 11 in this volume: 'At least in OECD countries, the current disparity between a few pioneering countries and other more cautious countries can be expected to narrow'.

28. See Pollitt and Bouckaert 2000, p. 96, and Chapter 2 of this volume; Christensen and Lægreid 2001, pp. 20 ff; Wollmann 2000b (on the British and the German government systems); and Wollmann 2000c (on local government systems in the UK, France and Germany).

Subject Index

Name Index

266   *Evaluation in Public-Sector Reform*

Weiss, C. 70, 78, 111, 198, 203–204, 255
Westney, D.E. 179, 181
Wewer, G. 38, 53, 121, 136
Whitfield, D. 19, 32
Wholey, J. 70, 78
Wik, M.H. 61, 78
Wildavsky, A. 5, 10, 216, 227, 230
Wilenski, P. 92, 103
Williams, D. 29, 35
Wilson, D. 234, 255

Wise, L.R. v, ix, 36, 56, 64–5, 67, 70, 72, 75–6, 78, 79, 210, 237, 238–9
Wollmann, H. 3, v, vi, ix, 1, 2, 7, 10–11, 13, 22, 35, 37, 54, 59, 70, 80, 103, 118–22, 124–8, 131–2, 134–9, 183–4, 203, 211, 213, 229, 231–2, 241–2, 245, 247–8, 252–3, 255, 256, 258
Wright, D.S. 72, 75
Wright, V. 29, 35
Yamaya, K. 245, 256
Zedillo, E. 189, 205

Country Index